Jung's Psychoid Concept Contextualised

Jung's Psychoid Concept Contextualised investigates the body-mind question from a clinical Jungian standpoint and establishes a contextual topography for Jung's psychoid concept, insofar as it relates to a deeply unconscious realm that is neither solely physiological nor psychological. Seen as a somewhat mysterious and little understood element of Jung's work, this concept nonetheless holds a fundamental position in his overall understanding of the mind, since he saw the psychoid unconscious as the foundation of archetypal experience.

Situating the concept within Jung's oeuvre and drawing on interviews with clinicians about their clinical work, this book interrogates the concept of the psychoid in a novel way. Providing an elucidation of Jung's ideas by tracing the historical development of the psychoid concept, Addison sets its evolution in a variety of contexts within the history of ideas, in order to offer differing perspectives from which to frame an understanding. Addison continues this trajectory through to the present day by reviewing subsequent studies undertaken by the post-Jungian community. This contextual background affords an understanding of the psychoid concept from a variety of different perspectives, both cultural and clinical. The book provides an important addition to Jungian theory, demonstrating the usefulness of Jung's psychoid concept in the present day and offering a range of understandings about its clinical and cultural applications.

This book will be of great interest to the international Jungian community, including academics, researchers and postgraduate students engaged in the study of Jungian or analytical psychology. It should also be essential reading for clinicians.

Ann Addison completed her PhD at the University of Essex in July 2016 and currently teaches and works as a Jungian analyst in private practice.

Research in Analytical Psychology and Jungian Studies Series

Series Advisor: Andrew Samuels
Professor of Analytical Psychology, Essex University, UK.

The *Research in Analytical Psychology and Jungian Studies* series features research-focused volumes involving qualitative and quantitative research, historical/archival research, theoretical developments, heuristic research, grounded theory, narrative approaches, collaborative research, practitioner-led research and self-study. The series also includes focused works by clinical practitioners, and provides new research informed explorations of the work of C. G. Jung that will appeal to researchers, academics and scholars alike.

Books in this series:

Shame and the Making of Art
A Depth Psychological Perspective
Deborah E. Cluff

Modern Myths and Medical Consumerism
The Asclepius Complex
Antonio Karim Lanfranchi

The Archetypal Pan in American Culture
Hypermasculinity and Terror
Sukey Fontelieu

Marian Apparitions in Cultural Contexts
Applying Jungian Concepts to Mass Visions of the Virgin Mary
Valeria Céspedes Musso

Jung's Psychoid Concept Contextualised
Ann Addison

For more information about this series please visit: www.routledge.com/Research-in-Analytical-Psychology-and-Jungian-Studies/book-series/JUNGIANSTUDIES.

Jung's Psychoid Concept Contextualised

Ann Addison

LONDON AND NEW YORK

First published 2019
by Routledge
2 Park Square, Milton Park, Abingdon, Oxon OX14 4RN

and by Routledge
711 Third Avenue, New York, NY 10017

Routledge is an imprint of the Taylor & Francis Group, an informa business

© 2019 Ann Addison

The right of Ann Addison to be identified as author of this work has been asserted by her in accordance with sections 77 and 78 of the Copyright, Designs and Patents Act 1988.

All rights reserved. No part of this book may be reprinted or reproduced or utilised in any form or by any electronic, mechanical, or other means, now known or hereafter invented, including photocopying and recording, or in any information storage or retrieval system, without permission in writing from the publishers.

Trademark notice: Product or corporate names may be trademarks or registered trademarks, and are used only for identification and explanation without intent to infringe.

British Library Cataloguing-in-Publication Data
A catalogue record for this book is available from the British Library

Library of Congress Cataloging-in-Publication Data
Names: Addison, Ann, author.
Title: Jung's psychoid concept contextualised / Ann Addison.
Description: Abingdon, Oxon ; New York, NY : Routledge, 2018. |
  Series: Research in analytical psychology and Jungian studies series
Identifiers: LCCN 2018030866 (print) | LCCN 2018031584 (ebook) |
  ISBN 9781315147345 (E-book) | ISBN 9781138550766 (hardback)
Subjects: LCSH: Jung, C. G. (Carl Gustav), 1875–1961. | Jungian psychology. |
  Psychoanalysis.
Classification: LCC BF173.J85 (ebook) | LCC BF173.J85 A335 2018 (print) |
  DDC 150.19/54—dc23
LC record available at https://lccn.loc.gov/2018030866

ISBN: 978-1-138-55076-6 (hbk)
ISBN: 978-1-315-14734-5 (ebk)

Typeset in Sabon
by Apex CoVantage, LLC

Contents

Acknowledgements — viii

1 Introduction — 1
   Setting the scene 1
   Bifurcations 5
   Chapters 10
   Summary 12

PART I
Historical contexts — 13

2 Jung, vitalism and "the psychoid": A historical reconstruction — 15
   Introduction 15
   Etymology 17
   Driesch's concept of Das Psychoid *18*
   Jung and vitalism 20
   Jung's dissertation 21
   A case of hysteria 22
   Freud and Jung and their meeting 23
   Bleuler's concept of Die Psychoide *24*
   Jung's concept of "the psychoid" 27
   Discussion 31
   Conclusion 33

3 Jung's psychoid concept: A hermeneutic understanding — 35
   Introduction 35
   Jung's studies 36

Discussion 50
Conclusion 51

4 Jung's psychoid concept and Bion's proto-mental concept: A comparison 52

Introduction 52
Jung's opus 52
Bion's opus 53
Influences 54
Jung's mature thinking 62
Bion's group work 63
Conclusion 67

5 The post-Jungians and the psychoid concept 69

Introduction 69
Background 69
The biological conception of the psychoid 71
Conclusion 89

6 Interrogation of the psychoid concept: An empirical study 91

Introduction 91
Methodology 91
Trauma Project 92
Implicit theories 94
Present research 96
Discussion 105

PART II
Empirical contexts 109

7 The empirical study: An example of a data analysis by grounded theory 111

Introduction 111
Example 112
Discussion 123
Conclusion 125

8 The results of the empirical study 126

Introduction 126

Session 126
General results 129
Discussion 145
Conclusion 146

9   Conclusion: Drawing together the results   148

Introduction 148
The psychoid concept – a historical understanding 149
The psychoid concept – an empirical understanding 152
The transference field – an empirical understanding 155
Discussion 157
Conclusion 160

Appendix A: Data analysis tables	162
Bibliography	165
Index	179

Acknowledgements

I should like to thank all those who have helped to make this project possible and who have supported me in the process of conceiving it, shaping it, implementing it, writing it up and living through it.

In particular, I am grateful to Professor Karl Figlio, who has encouraged me throughout and who always helped me to see something more, even when I thought I had covered every angle, and to two other members of the Centre for Psychoanalytic Studies at Essex University, Professors Roderick Main and Bob Hinshelwood, who have been unstintingly available to provide guidance and direction. The staff and students in the Centre have proved a stimulating and lively environment for this project, often fuelling new ideas and grounding existing ones with their input and discussion.

Very special thanks go to all those who have made the empirical strand of my research possible, by agreeing to take part in my interviews and small group discussion. For reasons of confidentiality their names are omitted here, but this project could not have been completed without them. Without exception everyone gave most generously of their time and thought, offering serious and thoughtful observations, original viewpoints and an enlivening attitude to the questions posed. Their input has not only supported and enriched my research; it has also significantly grounded and deepened my own clinical work and understanding. For this, I bring a very personal note of gratitude.

Next, Sonu Shamdasani is to be thanked for his scholarly teaching in his *Red Book* seminars, as also are the participants of his seminars for conferring a lively and stimulating learning environment, during the last six years, all of this contributing to the content of one of my chapters at least.

And, finally, my thanks go to my family, including David, Clare, John, Michael and Hannah, for being there, for taking an interest, and for supporting me throughout the long time that I have been engrossed by this work.

Chapter 1

Introduction

Setting the scene

The present book concerns a particular aspect of the clinical situation, being especially occupied with unconscious interactions between patient and analyst of a kind involving psyche and soma in relation. It thus has a bearing on the mind-body question, as experienced in the analytic consulting room, and hence embraces not merely a philosophical or theoretical position but also most especially an empirical one.

There is a very long history in the discipline of philosophy to the issue known as the mind-body problem, one having many contributors, just a relevant few of whom are highlighted below. The primary origins are popularly attributed to René Descartes. In his search for a solid foundation for knowledge, Descartes started from the one premise that he considered to be reliable, that of his own existence, conceived as the certainty of himself as a thinking being (*cogito ergo sum*). He came to the view that his existence as a thinking being was independent of the existence of anything non-mental, that is, of anything in the physical world. The mind as substance is distinct from its objects in the material world. This led him to the Cartesian dualism that the substance that is mind is independent of the physical body.

According to Descartes, the behaviour of physical objects was governed by the rational principles of science, and could be understood in these terms, and the body, its health and its disease, could thus be assigned to a mechanistic model. The mind, distinct from the body, could not be so understood but was seen by Descartes as guided by reason-explanations, in the form of rationales for this wish or that emotion.

The Cartesian approach still leaves open the question of the body-mind interaction, which has been addressed since from various viewpoints. Some twentieth-century philosophers (e.g. Place (1956) and Smart (1959)) argue for a mind-brain identity to deal with this question, and this is cogent in the face of increasing understandings of the brain imparted by neuroscience; and, in the field of psychoanalysis, this has generated a neuropsychoanalytic strand of thinking (e.g. Solms and Turnbull (2011)). Other, earlier approaches to this question came from the monists, such as Spinoza, James and Russell, who opposed the dualist views of Descartes and conceived the universe as comprising a single unifying reality or substance embracing both the mental and the physical. In contemporary analytical psychology, Atmanspacher and Fach (2013) subscribe to a monistic approach, ascribing a dual-aspect monism to the ideas of Carl Jung in respect of his psychoid concept, which is the subject of this book.

A further contemporary line of philosophical argument is provided by the phenomenologists, such as Edmund Husserl and the French philosopher Merleau-Ponty. Phenomenology as a theory of knowledge distinguishes between perceptual properties of objects and universal abstract properties or essences, reflecting especially on essences and their relations. We can perceive indirectly aspects of physical objects or directly, by intuition, their totality or essence. Acts of consciousness may also be reduced from acts of sense-perception to essences common to all such acts. Merleau-Ponty developed on these ideas and those of Descartes, by formulating a view of the world as the field of experience in which I find myself. He located access to the world in the body, neither as subject nor as object but as an ambiguous mode of existence wherein perception is primary.

This philosophical backdrop sets the scene for the present study. The present work, by contrast, originates and is grounded in clinical experience: not merely in a single analytic case, and not just in personal analytic practice, although the project stems from personal clinical work as its starting point. Such clinical origin drew attention to certain embodied phenomena, taken by the analyst to reflect the state of the analytic process, and has guided but was not the focus of a research project, generating at the outset the hypothesis that phenomena, combining experiences of body and mind in sensation at a psychic level, arise and are communicated to the analyst during periods of regression by the patient to states where issues concerning separation and bodily integrity are at the forefront.

The literature highlights a babel of theories, as well as a lack of coherent clinical description, language and theoretical elaboration, surrounding this clinical area, showing firstly that the area is not well delineated and secondly that it is difficult to establish a conceptual terrain. At the same time, there has been increasing interest in psychoanalytic circles, in recent years, on the role played by the body in psychoanalysis, whether in terms of the physical presence of the analyst and their embodied response to the patient or in terms of the ways in which the patient perceives and employs their own body in communications with the analyst, as evidenced by a proliferation of publications and conferences addressing this topic from a wide variety of angles. In all of these instances, a common issue is the question, how are we to think about and understand embodiment in psychoanalysis, the talking cure? There is, therefore, a manifest need for a mapping of the area and for specifying a conceptual terrain, and this is what the present book attempts to do, from a Jungian point of view.

In the clinical arena, the history of the issue of the relationship of mind and body reaches back to the beginnings of psychoanalysis and beyond, and the present project selects and tracks a single conceptual strand in the clinical debate, employing a form of conceptual research based on a methodology proposed by Dreher (2000), having an historical aspect and an empirical aspect. Jung's psychoid concept is selected as the focus, as a theoretical position relating to an ultimately unknowable area that is neither psychological nor physiological but that somehow partakes of both.

The historical conceptual research grounded in Jung's psychoid concept traces the origination and evolution of the concept to show how a present-day understanding has developed. The research locates the origins of the concept in the work on *Das Psychoid* of the biologist and neo-vitalist Hans Driesch (1903) around the turn of the nineteenth and twentieth centuries, and follows the development of this early thinking into *Die Psychoide* of Eugen Bleuler (1925), director of the Burghölzli from 1898 to 1927. Jung's adoption and extension of the ideas of both thinkers are set in the context of his own oeuvre and his relationship with the psychoanalytic movement. Trends in his own professional development, and comparisons from the work of other psychoanalytic sources, serve to clarify a characterisation of the psychoid concept according to Jung. Elaboration and refinement of this view is then achieved by contemplating subsequent developments by the post-Jungians. In this way, the book attempts to establish what was in Jung's mind when he conceived and formulated his psychoid concept, and to arrive at a contemporary understanding of events to be anticipated in clinical manifestations of psychoid processes.

This historical work does not confine itself to a narrow tracing of variations in the meaning of the psychoid concept. It also acknowledges influences on the thinking of Jung and his followers from other sources and employs a comparative approach based on ideas from other psychoanalysts, most notably Freud with his influence on Jung and Bion with his parallel development of his proto-mental concept. The result is a comparative contextual analysis.

Apart from the inherent historical interest of such an approach, the advantages of a comparative contextual model are the ensuing tightening of conceptualisation, something that is especially pertinent given the allusive style of writing adopted by Jung increasingly, following his *Red Book* work, in direct contrast to his scientific style in his early work on the Word Association Tests (WATs). Rowland observes that all of Jung's works after World War II "are devoted to finding a form of psychic healing that would avert the acting out of the apocalyptic myth", and so he experimented with "kinds of writing in which the word has the power to heal through appeal to more than rational understanding" (2005, p. ix). Thus, he came to a style combining aesthetic and scientific forms in a manner, described by Rowland as a "literary playing with metaphors", that seeks not merely to describe the psyche but also to "enact and perform it" (ibid., pp. 2–3). Jung's terminology is also constantly in flux, as can be seen from the fact that, whilst he employs the word "psychoid" in twenty-eight passages in the *Collected Works*, he refers inter alia to a psychoid *reflex-instinctual state* (1947/1954, para. 385), psychoid *processes* (e.g. 1947/1954, para. 380), psychoid *functions* (1947/1954, para. 382), a psychoid *factor* (e.g. 1947/1954, para. 417), a psychoid *unconscious* (e.g. 1955/1956, para. 787) and a psychoid *archetype* (1958, paras. 849/51), as well as describing the archetype as having a psychoid *nature* (e.g. 1958, para. 852), a psychoid *property* (1952, para. 947), a psychoid *form* (1945/1954, para. 350) and a psychoid *essence* (1958, para. 854). Accordingly, every contextual aid to the development of a more precise understanding of the concept is to be appreciated, whilst at the same time acknowledging that the ultimate unknowability of the psychoid unconscious, according to Jung, limits what can be said about it.

Having acquired an enhanced appreciation of the evolution of the psychoid concept from the historical first part of this book, a contemporary view is elicited using empirical techniques, in the form of expert interviews, as proposed by Dreher. Here, it has been necessary to devise a suitable methodology. Whilst Dreher describes the use of semi-structured interviews of analysts by analysts to elaborate the meaning and modes of employ of a concept, this approach to interviewing was felt likely to yield consciously constrained theoretical accounts, and hence to be too limiting for the present task. Rather, what has been sought in this research is a more unconscious formulation, such as arises in case discussion in response to clinical material through free association. Therefore, an interview design was formulated based on the process notes for a single session, actually the one that prompted early thoughts of the present research, and interviewees were asked to describe their *own* way of understanding and approaching the session, as well as their free associations in the face of the example given. The interviews were recorded, and the transcripts subsequently analysed by grounded theory techniques. It is to be emphasised that the transcripts, and not the process notes, constitute the data, and that grounded theory was selected in order to extract the personal models or theories of the interviewees, both conscious and unconscious, and to generate a set of parameters that could then be compared with the characteristics previously derived from the historical review of the psychoid concept. Jung's psychoid concept was thereby interrogated, by evaluating whether the contemporary views obtained from the empirical work matched the historical summary.

A comparative approach was again adopted, by selecting interviewees both from psychoanalysis and from analytical psychology. Since psychoid phenomena are a Jungian conceptualisation and are acknowledged in the language of analytical psychology, it was to be anticipated that the analytical psychologists would be more likely to generate accounts consistent with the historical psychoid formulation. By contrast, such phenomena are not recognised in the vocabulary of psychoanalysis, and therefore a finding of congruent phenomena, regardless of terminology, from any of the psychoanalysts would lend significantly greater weight to the validity of Jung's psychoid concept. Very surprisingly, some of the psychoanalysts did indeed also produce similar conceptualisations, effectively providing unexpected confirmation of Jung's psychoid concept, in the manner proposed by the philosophy of science of Popper.

This research has employed a methodology based generally on Dreher's model for conceptual research, but modified to suit the present project by:

(a) Adding a contextual dimension to the historical study, from the history of ideas in the twentieth century and from psychoanalysis generally.
(b) Interrogating rather than elaborating the selected psychoid concept in the empirical work, by undertaking clinical interviews and extracting theory from them, using grounded theory, and only subsequently assessing whether the extracted theory matches the psychoid concept as derived from the historical review.
(c) Supplementing the entire conceptual study, both historical and empirical, with comparative elements to clarify, push and refine definitions derived from the basic analysis.

Bifurcations

The trajectory taken by the research work and the manner in which at each stage the current position influenced the ongoing course of the project is of interest.

Once Jung's psychoid concept was selected as a focus for study, the work began with a review of Jung's writings on the subject, his main publications being *On the Nature of the Psyche* (1947/1954) and *Synchronicity: An Acausal Connecting Principle* (1952). Hans Driesch (1903) is acknowledged in the former, and a footnote directs the reader to *Die "Seele" als Elementarer Naturfaktor* for an early vitalist account of the psychoid. Following the initial review of Jung's own works, the conceptual line was traced back to its origins in the biological thinking and vitalist ideas of both Hans Driesch and Eugen Bleuler. The former published his accounts of *Das Psychoid* from 1903, and likewise gave lectures, most notably the Gifford Lectures, in both English and German on his experimental research that formed the basis for his psychoid concept (Driesch, 1907/1908). The latter also published in both languages, starting with his *Die Psychoide als Prinzip der Organischen Entwicklung* (Bleuler, 1925). Accordingly, a direct trajectory could be developed from these beginnings to Jung's writings in *On the Nature of the Psyche* and could be set in the context of ideas current in psychoanalysis during the same period.

As discussed below, and as evidenced by their correspondence, Jung mentions the psychoid to Freud in their famous 1907 meeting as a suitable designation for the unconscious, presumably, given the timing, referring to the biological ideas of Driesch (McGuire, 1991, p. 58). Based on this biological foundation, he goes on to develop a vitalistic understanding of the concept, as described in *On the Nature of the Psyche* to embrace a unified or monistic view of body and mind, designated "bodymind" herein.

According to this view, the psychoid constitutes an ultimately unknowable aspect of the unconscious, underlying the archetypes and linking body, mind and spirit in a purposive dynamic. The biology of instinct and the numinosity of spirit are both entrained in a teleological urge towards human development under the guidance of psychoid processes.

Jung's mature work also links the psychoid concept with synchronicity, his earliest recorded discussions of synchronicity arising in his *Dream Seminar* given in 1928–1930, when he developed a line of thinking from internal and external events that "synchronise", to the notion of "synchronism" in Eastern forms of thinking, to his invention of the term "synchronicity" to cover coinciding but unconnected events (1984). Subsequently, as a result of his collaboration with the Nobel Prize–winning physicist Wolfgang Pauli, he brings in a basis for his psychoid concept in quantum physics, as described in *Synchronicity: An Acausal Connecting Principle*, covering a panpsychic view of mind and matter generally.

At this point, it became apparent that Jung's account of the psychoid is derived from biology insofar as it concerns a monistic view of the body-mind issue, and from physics insofar as it concerns a panpsychic view of the matter-mind issue, and that chronologically he moved from the former to the latter. More especially, this move took him from a vitalistic base, wherein the origins of consciousness are embedded in living, organic matter, to an *unus mundus*, embracing mind and inorganic as well as organic matter. Although he presented his later ideas on the psychoid concept as an extension of his earlier ones, he did not offer an explanation for the traverse from the field of biology, applicable to his earlier thinking on the psyche-soma, to the field of physics, covering his later ideas on synchronicity. Actually, once he adopted his later thinking, he then applied it ex post facto to his understanding of the relation between body and mind, but he still omits an explanation for applying a principle from physics to a biological issue.

It was also apparent that Jung's earlier understandings of the psychoid and his later understandings of synchronicity are conceptually different. The former is considered as a teleological ordering factor immanent as potential in the stuff of the organism and creating an emergent dynamism by which the life process of the organism unfolds, as discussed in detail in Chapters 2 to 5. The latter, by contrast, is considered as a form of knowledge or meaning arising when two or more events that are not causally related nonetheless have a meaningful connection. The latter may arguably supervene on the former, but not underpin it, whereas the former may be usefully investigated without reference to the latter.

This same separation occurs also in the post-Jungian community, both theoretical and most especially clinical. Writers such as Dieckmann (1974, 1976, 1980), Clark (1996, 2006), Merchant (2006) and Stevens (1995) focus primarily on the biological approach to a monistic bodymind, whilst others, such as Fordham (1957, 1962), Aziz (1990, 2007), Von Franz (1992), Zabriskie (1995), Bright (1997), Meier (2001), Main (2004, 2007), Gieser (2005), Hogenson (2005), Cambray (2002, 2009), Colman (2011), Haule (2011), Giegerich (2012), Atmanspacher (2014), Atmanspacher & Fach (2013) and Connolly (2015) focus on an *unus mundus* embracing mind and matter, synchronicity, the occurrences of meaningful coincidences, their unknowability, and their associations with quantum physics. There is truly a proliferation of published work in this second arena, including a PhD thesis (Cadigan, 2007).

Gieser (2005) and Haule (2011) both contemplate specifically the issue of Jung's transition from a monistic to a panpsychic view.

Gieser (2005, p. 344) argues that Pauli believed in a unified science embracing psychology, physics and biology, and that Jung was influenced by his views on this. She notes Pauli's interest in evolution, his understanding that a "psychic factor in nature [. . .] has been present from the beginning in the building blocks of matter and life and [. . .] has evolved alongside and in interaction with them" (ibid., p. 306). And she postulates mathematics as "a genuine symbolic description of reality", the means of expressing universal processes, and the link between Jung's archetypes, physics and the mysteries of biological life (ibid., pp. 307, 310, 312).

Haule (2011, pp. 77, 81), similarly, notes Pauli's view of a potential connection between physics, biology and parapsychology, and accordingly contemplates synchronicity as a cosmic principle. In support of this, he lifts five lines of argument from Jung's correspondence with Pauli, referring to: synchronistic phenomena as knowledge not mediated by the senses; the fact that the archetype's psychoid nature makes it transgressive, allowing it to assimilate the physical and the psychic; the archetype as psychic probability, allowing it to bridge the psychic and physical realms; synchronicity as the numinous moment; and synchronicity as a universal dimension of nature supplementing the classical triad of space, time and causality.

Whilst both appear to propose the required link between biology and physics, and hence a justification for Jung's traverse from one to the other, it is not clear that either has proved one, and therefore this question remains open. It is beyond the scope of this research to settle this question.

Accordingly, a conceptual bifurcation exists, both originally in Jung's work and contemporaneously in the post-Jungian community. For a thorough understanding, it was clear that the biological conceptualisation of the psychoid must be explored first, before the conceptualisation linked with synchronicity and physics could be addressed, and that conflation of both would add an extra layer of complexity to an already complicated study, especially in view of the voluminous quantity of research and publication in the field of synchronicity.

The present book therefore focusses on one branch only, namely the earlier biological origination of the psychoid, and on the effects of these vitalistic roots on an understanding of the psychoid concept. The later branch relating to synchronicity is omitted, for the sake of focus and for the reasons given above. This also means that the history addresses primarily the forwards trajectory in Jung's thinking rather than the ex post facto reasoning, although it will be apparent in the empirical strand that some interviewees at least partially espouse this latter viewpoint.

This was the first and most significant bifurcation that arose in the evolution of the project, and it resulted in discarding one possible trajectory in the research. However, others more relevant *within* the subject of the research followed and were practically useful in setting up a differentiating function, and these were incorporated into the research methodology.

In particular, the data analysis in the empirical strand yielded an interesting bifurcation, in that two different models of the transference were located and isolated, namely a symmetrical model and an asymmetrical model, and were primarily but not completely aligned respectively with the different interviewee groupings of analytical psychologists and psychoanalysts. The symmetrical model presupposes a symmetrical field of unconscious interaction between patient and analyst during a session, whereas the asymmetrical model assumes that such field is weighted in the direction from the patient to the analyst. Analysts operating with a symmetrical model consider that patient and analyst contribute equally to an undifferentiated field of unconscious interaction. Of course, the fact that the analyst has had a training analysis, and is therefore better able to process and discriminate his or her own material, means that there is inequality in the analytic dyad at a personal and more conscious level, but nevertheless the unconscious field may be described as symmetrical. Analysts operating with an asymmetrical model consider the field between patient and analyst to be unequal and hierarchical, and for them the focus is on the patient and the patient's unconscious, the patient being seen as projecting onto or into the analyst, and the analyst whilst seeking to discriminate out their own material before making interpretations nonetheless viewing the dynamic primarily as being generated by the patient.

This particular bifurcation has been central in shaping the results of the empirical study, and in fact yielded the powerful and unexpected result mentioned above. Firstly, the analytical psychologists not only supported the symmetrical model, but they also linked it with the psychoid concept and demonstrated in their conceptualisations the embeddedness of the psychoid concept in current practise. The psychoanalysts, for whom there was a significantly lower probability of support for a similar conceptualisation, albeit employing alternative terminology, surprisingly produced powerful validating evidence for it, thus yielding an unexpected Popperian confirmation of the psychoid concept.

A further bifurcation manifested itself in the empirical strand, between a teleological organising function representing normal development through life and a chaotic fragmentation associated with psychosis, respectively associated in the empirical study with the symmetrical and asymmetrical fields of unconscious interaction. In the historical study, it became apparent that while Jung does acknowledge dissociation in his clinical work, and of course dementia praecox or schizophrenia in his early works, nonetheless he was generally more interested in the teleological view and individuation. This carried over into the empirical study, in which by and large the analytical psychologists conveyed more interest in questions of organisation and emergence, while the psychoanalysts focussed more on questions of splitting and schizoid states.

It became apparent that there are lacunae in Jung's ideas insofar as clinical applications are concerned, and that his account of his psychoid concept, whilst offering a foundation for understanding the purposiveness of individuation, lacks a detailed support for clinical work in borderline states. To address these lacunae, reference may be had to Bion for comparison, firstly because of a strong similarity between his proto-mental concept and Jung's psychoid concept in terms of understandings of the relationship between body and mind, and next because Bion focusses with his concept on psychotic functioning. Contextually, the experiential influences informing both concepts, as opposed to the theoretical ones, can be traced to World War I, and the difference of focus between the two concepts may at least partially be understood in terms of the utterly different war experiences of the two men.

One point needs addressing here: neither of the two concepts, psychoid and proto-mental, occupies a central place in the overall published work of their respective authors. There is evidence in the number of recent publications, however, that both concepts are increasingly becoming seen as clinically significant and are actually of fundamental importance.

Apart from these main bifurcations, other oppositions also became apparent during the course of the project, and were likewise absorbed into the results, as follows: instinctive and spiritual understandings of the archetype; developmental and archetypal experience; an organising function, and chaotic confusion; concrete behaviour, and symbolic capacity; and the individual and the group. Whilst the initial bifurcation of body-mind and mind-matter required a definitive choice for practical reasons of research capacity, the later ones presented themselves as differentiating aspects of the research work, to be evaluated and discussed in each instance, as aids to clarification and definition, appearing first in the historical strand of the research and later in varying guises in the empirical strand.

Chapters

This book presents the research in nine chapters, starting with the present Chapter 1, setting the context of the project and outlining its trajectory.

Chapter 2 introduces the historical strand of the research, by tracing the biological origins and vitalistic development of Jung's psychoid concept, based on the work of Driesch and Bleuler, set in the context of early debates between analytical psychology and psychoanalysis, which distinguish Jung's basic methodological approach to psychoanalysis from that of Freud. This provides a backdrop to Jung's account of the psychoid in *On the Nature of the Psyche*, and his discussion of the formation of instinctual images and archetypal images as products of psychoid processes, to yield an initial characterisation of the psychoid concept (1947/1954).

Chapter 3 considers the psychoid concept in the contexts of Jung's research, which embraced both scientific and hermeneutic approaches. His early Word Association Tests (WATs) are covered, as well as his subsequent self-experimentation leading to his initial theoretical conceptualisations foreshadowing the psychoid concept. Associated texts, including *The Red Book*, and two papers published, respectively, in 1916 and 1928 are reviewed for this purpose. A concurrent collective experiment by Jung with the aid of his contemporaries and analysands is brought in by reference to biographical accounts. This background provides a hermeneutic context for his psychoid concept, yielding additional vitalistic understandings of the same.

Chapter 4 compares Jung's psychoid concept with Bion's proto-mental concept, noting that their concepts have aspects in common in an underlying psychosomatic matrix. Starting from Bion's wartime experience and his work at the Tavistock Clinic, the development of *his* ideas is traced, in the light of his group work, and later shift into individual psychoanalysis, with respect to the nature of psychosis, projective mechanisms, and identification. A comparative element is introduced by considering common influences on the thinking of the two men, for example from the ideas of the French philosopher Henri Bergson, and by reviewing the intellectual climate in the Tavistock Clinic in the period covering Bion's employment there, during which time Jung delivered his Tavistock Lectures. This background helps to clarify the respective delineations of the two concepts, thereby also helping to refine the ambit of the psychoid concept.

Chapter 5 covers studies by certain post-Jungians, including especially Jacobi, Progoff, the Berlin Group, and Samuels, all of whose work extend on Jung's account of the psychoid concept. It is noted that the clinical research by the Berlin Group isolated two key themes, relating respectively to the notions of:

(a) A dialectic of undifferentiation/differentiation as aspects of individuation
(b) The transference

and that both themes are pertinent to a contemporary understanding of Jung's psychoid concept. A brief summary of one or two key pieces of clinical literature corroborates this, drawing links between the transference and the psychoid concept, and between active imagination and the psychoid concept. This chapter elaborates on the characteristics of the psychoid, according to the post-Jungian literature.

Chapter 6 introduces the empirical strand of the research, with an account of the interview process employed in the project, including the selection of interviewees, and the conduct of interviews with twelve individual clinicians from the United Kingdom and abroad, and a small group discussion involving six clinicians, having different affiliations. The parameters involved are discussed, in terms of demography relating to theoretical orientation, geographical location, gender and medical experience of the participants. The methodology for the interview process is described, including interviews based around the process notes for a single analytic session and a set of discussion vertices for guidance, and data analysis of the transcripts based on grounded theory techniques. This methodology also included field notes, recording the effects of the interviews on the interviewer and their implications, as well as the way that the overall process evolved and deepened as feedback from each subsequent interview was absorbed.

Chapter 7 gives an account of the use of grounded theory for the data analysis of one interview subject, by way of illustration. This example demonstrates the manner in which the data analysis, as it progressed, increasingly yielded (a) emergent metaphors and private theory for each interviewee and (b) conceptualisations of the interviewee relating to embodiment in analysis. A discussion about the relation of the same with public theory follows.

Chapter 8 introduces the results of the data analysis, isolating the main themes that emerged, especially concerning the transference models according to the private theories of the various interviewees. Two key transference models were isolated, namely the contrasting notions of a symmetrical and mutual transference field and an asymmetrical and hierarchical transference field, respectively congruent with and antithetical to the psychoid concept. The chapter classifies the findings into:

(a) Those that envisage a symmetrical field consistent with the psychoid concept, mainly from Jungian interviewees who have applied and moulded the psychoid concept in their own practices.
(b) Those of certain of the psychoanalysts who conceive aspects of their clinical work similarly, whilst yet employing different language and a different theoretical base.
(c) Those that envisage an asymmetrical transference field based around the notion of projective identification, in contrast or conflict with the psychoid concept, mainly from certain psychoanalysts.

Some interviewees combined features from both symmetrical and asymmetrical viewpoints, and these results are highlighted, in order to demonstrate the ways in which clinicians may in their private lived theories combine elements from different public theories, even to the point of introducing internal inconsistencies.

Chapter 9 summarises the results overall and compares the empirical findings and the previously established historical findings. This chapter notes how the study validates Jung's notion of a psychoid concept and shows that it holds value in present-day clinical work, offering a practical contemporary understanding, applicable both in the clinical setting and in terms of personal individuation. The chapter also considers the notion that the psychoid concept offers a methodology for monitoring progress in the clinical process on an ongoing basis. Finally, this chapter reviews the ambit of the research, and proposes avenues for further research.

Summary

The work undertaken in this research has shown conclusively the clinical usefulness of Jung's psychoid concept today, seen as a deeply unknowable aspect of the unconscious, manifest in the transference by a symmetrical field, characterised by an emergent dynamism, and in the countertransference by phenomena combining body and mind in sensation at a psychic level, often during periods of regression by the patient to primitive states of mind. Not only do the results show that the concept has relevance to the Jungian practitioner, which might be expected given familiarity with Jung's ideas, but that amongst the psychoanalysts there are those who, whilst employing different terminology, also conceive certain aspects of their work in a similar way.

The contents of this book are intended to elaborate on the foundations of the psychoid concept in Jung's thinking, and the development of that beginning in the hands of the post-Jungians, as well as provide an empirical account of the ways in which the concept is applied and applicable in clinical work currently. Most importantly, the book aims to provide an understanding of the significance today of the psychoid concept both theoretically and clinically.

Part I

Historical contexts

Chapter 2

Jung, vitalism and "the psychoid"

A historical reconstruction

Introduction

This chapter[1] begins the historical strand of the present conceptual study in detail, by looking at the origins of the psychoid concept, in an attempt to discover how the seeds of this concept arose and germinated in Jung's mind, thereby to gain a better understanding as to what he means when he refers to his psychoid concept to designate a deeply unconscious set of processes that are neither physiological nor psychological but that somehow partake of both. The primary aim in developing such a conceptual framework is to formulate an initial theoretical definition of the concept, but the history of this idea also sheds an interesting light on the relationship between Freud and Jung and on differences in their early epistemologies, and this offers additional comparative clarification.

The chapter begins with a comment in a letter of Freud to Jung dated 7 April 1907, very shortly after their first meeting in the spring of that year, in which Freud is responding to a suggestion, presumably made by Jung in their meeting, to give the unconscious the name "psychoid".

At first sight, this exchange may seem to be no more than a casual interchange between the two men, but it is here argued that in fact it contains far more significance than initially appears. Firstly, it shows that, in 1907, Jung was already contemplating an idea of a psychoid unconscious, although he did not adopt the expression "psychoid" into his own published theory until forty years later, in *On the Nature of the Psyche* (Jung, 1947/1954). Secondly, it points towards a divergence of approach right from the start of their collaboration, which highlights useful conceptual differences.

The reference in question is somewhat mysterious, since what Freud says is:

> I appreciate your motives in trying to sweeten the sour apple, but I do not think you will be successful. Even if we call the unconscious "psychoid" it will still be the unconscious, and even if we do not call the driving force in the broadened conception of sexuality "libido", it will

still be libido, and in every inference we draw from it we shall come back to the very thing from which we are trying to divert attention with our nomenclature.

(McGuire, 1991, p. 58)

Rather tantalisingly, the currently published records do not show in detail what passed between them in this first meeting, and so we cannot fully unravel the strands of their dialogue to get at their underlying intentions. However, we can surmise that it was Jung who raised the idea of calling the unconscious the "psychoid". We can also surmise that they were discussing Freud's theory of the unconscious, including his concept of "libido" with its sexual connotations, and that Jung was questioning his ideas. On the face of it, Freud is trying to neutralise a view alternative to his own, by claiming that the terms "unconscious" and "libido" carry within them the essence of *his* concepts, which already incorporate or supersede ideas offered by Jung.

It is to be borne in mind that, in the beginning, psychoanalysis was founded upon an interest in the links between psyche and soma. The pioneering work of Freud and Breuer (1892–1895), beginning with their *Studies on Hysteria*, traced a link between a precipitating psychic trauma on the one hand and sensory memory and experience on the other (later described by Freud as sensory hallucinations), that could be abreacted by bringing the memory of the original trauma to consciousness through analysis. The mechanism attributed to hysteria by Freud and Breuer involved the repression into the unconscious of unwanted ideas of a sexual nature, and thus their dissociation from consciousness, coupled with a conversion of the accompanying affect into somatic symptoms.

At the same time, Freud (1895[1950]) was writing his *Project for a Scientific Psychology* concerning the environment's impact on the human organism and the organism's reaction to it, in which Freud attempted to represent mental phenomena, including dreaming and hysterical compulsion, in terms of physiological processes.

Not much later, Jung (1907/1908) in his Word Association Tests (WATs) demonstrated through the use of a galvanometer, whose electrodes were placed in skin contact with the hands and feet of his subjects, that a physical reaction accompanies the manifestation of an affect-laden association of ideas or complex.

At this very early stage in the field of psychoanalysis, the ideas of Freud and his followers were founded primarily on empiricism and a search for causal mechanisms linking body and mind, following the prevailing influences including natural causality, Darwin's biology and the physiology of the Helmholtz school,[2] whose principles were physico-chemical. In *Freud's Models of the Mind*, Sandler et al. emphasise Freud's causal approach, stemming from his efforts to avoid metaphysical ideas, including teleology, in favour of an empirical orientation:

> In line with the dominant scientific ideas of the time, Freud systematically attempted to eliminate teleological explanations from his theories; that is, he saw mental functioning as being a form of adaptation to natural causes rather than having an ultimate and final "purpose".
>
> (1997, p. 17)

By the time that Freud and Jung met in 1907, Freud had moved to a more topographical theory of mind, in which conscious, preconscious and unconscious define different depth levels. The Unconscious was characterised by a very primitive mode of functioning according to which instinctual drives and wishes seek discharge, gratification and relief but are in conflict with the moral values of the Conscious and therefore subject to censorship. Freud linked these instinctual drives with the psychosexual development of the child, and conceptualised them as fluctuating quantities of energy seeking discharge. Such energy he termed libido.

Although, in the early years of their collaboration, Jung's attitude to Freud is popularly believed to have been based on an adherence to Freud's ideas, it is argued here that in fact Jung was from the very beginning in this first meeting proposing a completely different view of the unconscious: one that was embedded in the history of vitalism; and one that foreshadowed and laid the foundation for many of his later theories. More especially, it is asserted that, already, Jung had begun to formulate his own theory of the unconscious as it would ultimately be summarised forty years later in *On the Nature of the Psyche*, and that the implications in this first meeting were borne out by the subsequent unfolding of events.

This chapter, therefore, now traces Jung's interests at the start of his career, looking at his first case history and his early clinical work in the light of these interests, and then sets these themes against Freud's early views on hysteria. This will involve locating the psychoid concept within the history of vitalism, since a neo-vitalist notion of "a psychoid" had already been conceived by the biologist Hans Driesch (1903) prior to the meeting of Freud and Jung.

The subsequent development of the psychoid concept will then be considered, with a review of the extent to which Jung's more mature ideas developed out of the vitalist tradition and departed from those of Driesch.

Etymology

A consideration of the etymology of the word "psychoid" locates its roots in the Greek word *psyche*, meaning "spirit or soul", after the goddess Psyche, and "breath" or "breath of life"; and the Greek suffix *-oeide*, which is related to *eidos*, meaning "shape" or "form" or "what is seen". Interestingly, the Greek word *psycho*, meaning "I breathe", is onomatopoeic, representing out-breathing, followed by in-breathing.

The Greek *psyche* can be traced through the Latin *psyche* to later derivations in numerous languages. The Greek *psyche* also carries the meaning "mind", and *psyche* in the sense of mind may be opposed to the Late Latin (i.e. AD 180–600), *psychicus* having the meaning "materialistic" or "carnal".

Hence, the expression "psychoid" may express an attempt to convey something about the manifest shape or form of the spirit, soul or mind, animated by the breath of life. And yet, at the same time, the same root yields a derivation which is material and bodily.

Thus, such association points in both directions, towards mind and body, and also betrays some uncertainty concerning their relation, and in adopting the expression *psychoid*, the vitalists and Jung picked up on this association.

As this chapter will show, they tried to encapsulate the body-mind relation in a single unified idea that was based not on psycho-physical parallelism but on a conceptual unity.

Driesch's concept of *Das Psychoid*

The term *psychoid* was first employed in the field of vitalism to describe a particular teleological function of the human organism, having been coined by the neo-vitalist Hans Driesch,[3] biologist and philosopher (1903). Driesch studied at the University of Freiburg under Weismann, and at the University of Jena under Haeckel, Hertwig and Stahl. He received his doctorate in 1889, and began a series of scientific studies thereafter, establishing a significant body of scientific experimentation and publication, before turning to philosophy. He lectured both in the United Kingdom and Germany, and became president of the Society for Psychical Research in 1926.

Driesch was interested in the relationship between body and mind and was opposed to the notion of any deterministic connection between them, and to the mechanistic view that resulted from psycho-physical parallelism. According to Driesch, all living bodies have three primary characteristics, namely form, metabolism and the capacity for action.

In experiments conducted in 1892, he found that when an embryo of a sea urchin was at a very early stage, including only two or four cells (blastomeres), and all but one of those blastomeres were mutilated or destroyed, the single surviving blastomere still developed into a complete, though smaller than normal, whole. He concluded that the living organism aims at some sort of wholeness in terms of its form, and thus that the development of organisms is directed by a life force or unifying self-determining ordering principle.

Following a long line of philosophical thinkers from Aristotle onwards, he called this biological teleology "vitalism", and he used the term "entelechy" for the life force or ordering principle governing the process (as described in *Die "Seele" als Elementarer Naturfaktor* (1903) and *Der Vitalismus als Geschichte und als Lehre* (1905)). He went on to show that entelechy might

Jung, vitalism and "the psychoid" 19

also be found to account for the inheritance of characteristics from one generation to another.

He then turned to the third characteristic of the living body, namely action, in the sense of movement in response to a stimulus. Movement, he said, involves a functional adaptation through experience, when a stimulus is repeated over time. A mechanical cause and effect cannot be deduced, since the correspondence between an individualised stimuli and an individualised effect occurs on the basis of reaction that has been created historically. An individual stimulus has a "prospective potency" of possible fates, only a single one of which actually results; some innate faculty responds to the stimulus by acting to produce a specific combination of muscular movements based on history. This innate faculty he called *Das Psychoid* (i.e. a "psychoid"):

> This seems to be just the right place in our discussion to give a *name* to the "acting something" which we have discovered not to be a machine. We might speak of "entelechy" [. . .] but it appears better to distinguish also in terminology the natural agent which forms the body from the elemental agent which directs it. [. . .] I therefore propose the very neutral name of "psychoid" for the elemental agent discovered in action.
>
> (Driesch, 1929, p. 221)

Accordingly, Driesch considered that the psychoid served to regulate action, and it did so by employing the faculties of the brain as a piano player uses a piano.

He went on to postulate that, on the basis of future research into the nature of instinct, the psychoid might also be found to underlie instinctual behaviour, observing that, "if the analysis of instincts should help us some day to a true proof of vitalism, instead of offering only some indications towards it, it might also be said that a 'psychoid' is the basis of instinctive phenomena" (ibid., p. 221).

Driesch came to associate this innate faculty with unconscious "intrapsychical", as opposed to physical, states involving memory and association, and set about investigating the "relations between *my* conscious phenomena and *my* material body" (ibid., p. 304). He concluded:

> Seen from *a purely psychological side*,[4] entelechy, or at least that part of it which regulates action, i.e. our psychoid, is the same entity which is usually called *soul* or *mind*, being the ultimate foundation of the Ego, with all his experiences.
>
> (Ibid., p. 306)

Therefore, he defined his psychoid as an intrapsychic factor providing the unconscious ultimate foundation of the conscious ego and linking the conscious ego and the body-in-action. It is important to understand that overall Driesch saw his psychoid as neither body nor mind but as something occupying a third position in between and relating to both. This psychoid directs the brain in response to acts of volition from the ego to achieve individualised behaviour based on history, a process which he described as "I live my life" (ibid., p. 306). Further, this psychoid is teleological and purposive in the sense that it constitutes an ordering principle urging behaviour along paths of adaptation to the environment, based on intentionality of the ego and on historical experience.

Jung and vitalism

Returning to Jung, it is known from his very early work that he had a significant interest in vitalism. In *The Zofingia Lectures*, delivered as a student in the years 1896–1899, Jung rejected both "contemporary sceptical materialist opinion" (1896, para. 63) and metaphysics. He sought a third position lying between them, which he found in vitalism, asserting that "a pre-existent vital principle is necessary to explain the world of organic phenomena" (ibid., para. 63). He described the vital principle as a life force, which:

> [G]overns all bodily functions, including those of the brain, and hence also governs consciousness. [. . .] The vital principle extends far beyond consciousness in that it also maintains the vegetative functions of the body which, as we know, are not under our conscious control. Our consciousness is dependent on the functions of the brain, but these are in turn dependant on the vital principle, and accordingly the vital principle represents a substance, whereas consciousness represents a contingent phenomenon.
>
> (Ibid., para. 96)

He linked the vital principle with the purposeful and organisational activity of the soul, in what he described as the new empirical psychology:

> The new empirical psychology furnishes us with data ideally designed to expand our knowledge of organic life and to deepen our views of the world [. . .] Our body formed from matter, our soul gazing towards the heights, are joined in a single living organism.
>
> (Ibid., para. 142)

Accordingly, right from the outset and even as a student, Jung espoused in his psychology a purposeful, that is a teleological, approach directed towards goals of wholeness in the future, and in this he displayed the foundations of some of his much later ideas with their vitalistic basis.

This bias is also taken through into his early clinical work, as his first case study demonstrates.

Jung's dissertation

Jung's initial publication of clinical work was his dissertation on a case of somnambulism, defined as an hysterical illness often involving dissociation (1902).

The subject, designated Miss S. W., was in fact his cousin Helene Preiswerk although this was not at the time disclosed. She was a young girl who experienced states of "double consciousness", in which she held seances attended by the young Jung. Jung describes at some length so-called occult phenomena occurring in these states, without at any stage offering a view as to the reality of such phenomena. Rather, he adopts a position of enquiry into their psychological meaning for Helene.

In her somnambulistic "attacks", Helene would display an unnatural pallor and enact the behaviour and dialogue of other personalities foreign to that of her normal waking state. Jung (1902, para. 11) quotes Krafft-Ebing (1879, p. 498) that hallucinations of all the senses are not uncommon in somnambulism. Helene would display various kinds of automatic behaviour, including unconscious motor phenomena and automatic writing, prior to returning gradually to her waking state by way of a cataleptic stage.

Some of these other personalities were frivolous and childish but one, named Ivenes and identified by Jung as the somnambulistic ego of Helene, was a more mature woman, assured and influential. Jung (ibid., para. 116) considered that Helene "anticipates her own future and embodies in Ivenes what she wishes to be in twenty years' time – the assured, influential, wise, gracious, pious lady".

The mechanism of this double consciousness, as described by Jung, bears comment. Although he refers to the secondary personalities as dissociations from the already existing personality, mentioning Freud's *Interpretation of Dreams* (1900), nevertheless he explicitly avoids adopting Freud's theories on the ground that he has no means of judging how far the emotion in question was "repressed" (ibid., para. 97).

He also refers to the dream-states producing Helene's automatisms as hysterical, and links her periodic personality changes and splits in consciousness with hysteria, although again he avoids any idea of repression:

> Our patient differs essentially from pathological dreamers in that it could never be proved that her reveries had previously been the object of her daily interests; her dreams come up explosively, suddenly bursting forth with amazing completeness from the darkness of the unconscious. [. . .] [I]t seems probable that the roots of those dreams were originally feeling-toned ideas which only occupied her waking consciousness for

a short time. We must suppose that hysterical forgetfulness plays a not inconsiderable role in the origin of such dreams: many ideas which, in themselves, would be worth preserving in consciousness, sink below the threshold, associated trains of thought get lost and, thanks to psychic dissociation, go on working in the unconscious.

(Ibid., para. 119)

For Jung, then, repression is not a factor, but rather a "forgetfulness" in which *worthwhile*[5] content sinks below the threshold of consciousness.

This paves the way for a view contrary to the theory of hysteria based on repression favoured by Freud, a view according to which Helene's somnambulism has a teleological function:

It is, therefore, conceivable that the phenomena of double consciousness are simply new character formations, or attempts of the future personality to break through. [. . .] In view of the difficulties that oppose the future character, the somnambulisms sometimes have an eminently teleological significance, in that they give the individual, who would otherwise succumb, the means of victory.

(Ibid., para. 136)

In this very early piece of work, Jung achieves a remarkable synthesis, which is more in line with his earlier expressed interest in vitalism than with his acknowledgement of Freud.

Firstly, he offers a mechanism for explaining dissociation, in which body and mind co-operate to produce split off somnambulisms that are activated by unconscious motor phenomena and hallucinations, and that incorporate forgotten worthwhile content; and secondly he emphasises clearly both the psychological meaning of Helene's experiences and their teleological function in giving intimations of future possibilities and their form, as in the case of the personality of Ivenes.

A case of hysteria

During the next few years, Jung began to adopt some of Freud's ideas more overtly, most notably in his treatment of Sabina Spielrein, in which he employed Freud's method of working over childhood memories and associative material.

Sabina was admitted to the Burghölzli Clinic in 1904, when Eugen Bleuler was director and Jung had sole medical responsibility for patients. Although, in 1896, Bleuler had described Freud's *Studies on Hysteria* as "one of the most important publications of the last few years in the field of normal and pathological psychology", the hospital records give no indication of any clinical application yet of Freud's ideas (Minder, 1994, p. 111). Sabina was diagnosed with hysteria, and she was effectively the Burghölzli's first case to be treated using Freud's analytic method.

She suffered from compulsions, tics and other somatic symptoms, and according to notes taken by Jung, she reported feeling as if someone were pressing upon her, and as if something were crawling around in her bed. In her treatment with Jung, she confessed to a father complex, in which her father had beaten and humiliated her as a child. Jung wrote that he applied Freud's method with considerable success and her symptoms cleared up (ibid., p. 121).

However, while Jung acknowledged the efficacy of Freud's method, it is not so evident that he agreed with Freud's theory. Minder (ibid., p. 129) thinks that Jung was referring to Sabina in his paper *Cryptomnesia* (1905), in which Jung describes hysteria in terms of his own theories, according to which hysterical dissociation is brought about by a feeling-toned memory complex. The following year, in their early correspondence during October to December of 1906, Jung expressed directly to Freud doubts concerning various aspects of Freud's theory of hysteria and its genesis, writing that his scientific premises were utterly different from those of Freud (McGuire, 1991, p. 51). Papadopoulos (2006) sees in this statement a reference to significant epistemological differences from the outset.

In a lecture in Amsterdam in 1907 shortly after his meeting with Freud, Jung (1908, paras. 51–52) again referred to his work with Sabina, presented as a case of psychotic hysteria, describing her symptoms very much in the Freudian terms of infantile sexuality, repression and the consequent appearance of physical symptoms. Nevertheless, in the same lecture, Jung also criticises Freud's views, based on his own theory of complexes derived from his Word Association Experiments (ibid., para. 42), and he gives a very wide interpretation to Freud's understandings of "sexuality" and "libido", describing them respectively as "the instinct for the preservation of the species" and "any inordinate passion or desire" (ibid., para. 49). Therefore, it is quite possible that Jung tended to see the aetiology of hysteria more in terms of his own ideas concerning complexes and *their* links with dissociation and physical symptoms, rather than in terms of the mechanism described by Freud.

All of this suggests that Jung had definite reservations about Freud's ideas, and a clear view of his own scientific base, even at the stage of their first meeting.

Freud and Jung and their meeting

In the light of this background, Jung's suggestion to Freud to call the unconscious "psychoid" would seem to be no mere chance remark but one to carry within it a whole raft of already formulated ideas concerning the unconscious, in spite of the fact that the remark was tossed lightly aside by

Freud with the comment that Jung was simply "trying to sweeten the apple" (McGuire, 1991, p. 58). Given his already demonstrated interest in vitalism and his approach in his dissertation to the psychological experiences of his cousin Helene, Jung would almost certainly have contemplated an idea of the unconscious more in line with the vitalism of Hans Driesch than with the views of Freud, that is one that was teleological and aligned towards potential future forms, one having an organising function, and one whose drives were not solely sexual in origin. The contents of such an unconscious could then be seen as worthwhile and forgotten, as opposed to unwanted and repressed, and the dissociation and somatic symptoms of hysteria could be explained in terms of Jung's theory of complexes and the somatic thinking of Driesch.

Even at this early stage, therefore, it appears that Jung was contemplating a view of the unconscious that embraced something like the psychoid of Driesch to account both for the body-mind connection and for the teleological function that he attributed to Helene and her somnambulisms.

That this view is in fact probable may be demonstrated also by the references made by Jung to vitalistic ideas and works on vitalism in his later writings on his theory of libido, including *Symbols of Transformation* (1912), which proposed an idea of libido in non-sexual energic terms, and his essay *On Psychic Energy* (1928),[6] which sets out to explain the rationale for his ideas on libido.

Marilyn Nagy (1991, p. 128) draws attention to references to vitalistic ideas in *Symbols of Transformation*, commenting: "I am certain that what was really at stake between the two men in their struggle over the nature of psychic libido was the ancient mind-body problem as it surfaces in the biological sphere".

Actually, it is evident that the differences ran even deeper than this and were of an epistemological nature, since Freud, as stated above, espoused a biological-mechanical model in his initial work on hysteria and in the *Project* and located the origins of pathology in childhood sexuality, whereas Jung from the outset held to a vitalistic teleological approach, which continued to influence his thinking in one form or another throughout his life.

It is then no surprise that subsequent events led to a parting of the ways, as both Freud and Jung continued to develop their ideas along the lines already foreshadowed in their divergent initial epistemological approaches. In Jung's case, this meant that the influence of vitalism continued in the future evolution of his views concerning a psychoid unconscious, whilst Freud (1923, p. 15; 1925, p. 32) continued to dismiss such concept as being philosophical and representing something unknown.

Bleuler's concept of *Die Psychoide*

The next step in the background to Jung's mature ideas on a psychoid unconscious, derived from the field of vitalism, is provided by Eugen Bleuler,[7] professor of psychiatry at the University of Zurich, and director of the Burghölzli Asylum in the period 1898–1927. Jung was Bleuler's assistant from 1900 to 1909, and it is known, for example from Ernst Falzeder (2007), that the Burghölzli community was close knit and that ideas were freely discussed and exchanged. It is likely, therefore, that Bleuler was well acquainted with Jung's interest in vitalism, and he was certainly aware of Driesch, as his writings attest, although he dismissed Driesch's view of the psychoid on the ground that the underlying theory could be attributed to philosophy rather than science.

It was only considerably after Jung had left the Burghölzli that Bleuler (1925) published a concept of the psychoid in *Die Psychoide als Prinzip der Organischen Entwicklung*. In distinction from Driesch's concept "*Das Psychoid*", having the neuter gender, Bleuler called his the feminine "*Die Psychoide*". In a review in the *International Journal of Psychoanalysis*, Reich (1927) suggests that Bleuler does not satisfactorily distinguish his psychoid from that of Driesch, but the present discussion indicates that this shows an insufficient understanding of the two views.

By contrast with Driesch, Bleuler (1930, p. 35) described his psychoid in terms of a psycho-physical parallelism, in that he argued that "both physiology and the psyche act on similar principles" for motives that seek to achieve some final future orientation. In the case of the organism, the *instincts* are so ordered that life is maintained; and in the case of the psyche, *intelligence* acts as a guide to the same end. In both, adaptation occurs in response to experience and introduces new orientations accordingly. This approach suggests the idea of a psyche-soma split, whereas Driesch disputes such parallelism by proposing a third position for his psychoid between the two.

For example, in the case of the body, according to Bleuler:

> [T]he organism adapts itself a thousandfold to unusual needs, heat, cold, increased or diminished use of certain bodily organs, change of food etc. [. . .] It is as if the organism were "learning" to select the conditions most favourable to it. In any case, we are in the presence here of a function similar to human memory, which creates new connections.
> (Ibid., p. 36)

In another example, a new-born baby cries by reflex and finds that mother comes, which gradually leads first to an idea that mother comes in response to crying, which the baby likes, and then to the building of memory and psyche. The new-born has no ability to reflect, but his cry causes a reaction in that mother comes. This produces a change in his psyche so that an association is formed, and thereafter crying occurs on the mere inclination to have mother near.

In both cases, an influence causes a reaction and a permanent structural change, which shapes future reactions in a favourable direction. Since these are not conscious, Bleuler (ibid., p. 38) eschewed the expression "memory" in favour of "mneme" for the link between influence and reaction, and he allocated the expression "engramme" for the permanent change, borrowing his terminology from the psychologist Richard Semon. Thus, the mneme yields an adaptation, a "learning" of a purposeful action as if it already had a potential outcome in view, and the experiences are preserved in the form of engrammes that are later revived in the shape of actions, and in associations that determine the paths of our thought processes. In the body, this yields physical actions in response to nervous stimuli, and regeneration occurs following injury. In the brain, for example in the process of writing, it produces a perception of pen and paper, as well as engrammes of the writing movement and a conception of the ideas to be written that direct the writing action.

Thus, exactly the same elementary processes occur in the bodily functions as in the memory of the psyche. Both learn by experience and both comprise an integration of functions:

> The psyche – apart from its experience content – consists of a number of instincts [. . .] bound up as a unit. [. . .] Bodily functions, too, are integrated to a high degree, not only the nervous ones but all the others; all vegetative functions, digestion, circulation etc., are dependent on one another. [. . .] Hence, we have good grounds for bringing the bodily functions under one conception. This summary, the body soul, I have called the psychoid.
>
> As we ascertain in the psychoid, with the exception of consciousness, all the elementary functions that we find in the psyche, and in the latter all that are in the former, we cannot do otherwise than regard the psyche as a specialisation of the psychoid.
>
> (Ibid., p. 43)

Accordingly, the stage moves from the psychoid to the psyche at the point that consciousness sets in. Bleuler defines the psychoid as the capacity to respond and adapt in the face of stimuli, thereby creating permanent changes in the brain that shape future reactions. Out of this, he goes on to elaborate the functions of the psychoid in the development or evolution of the species.

For Bleuler, therefore, the psychoid is initially a bodily function that extends into the area of psychological growth, arising out of behaviour based on "what is favourable" and generating permanent changes in the body and in the brain through the experience. This leads Bleuler ultimately to see the psychoid as a causal agent of psychic development, as in the case of the infant who develops a pattern of behaviour as it learns that mother responds to its crying, and in this sense Bleuler's psychoid also has a teleological character.

Bleuler, by opposing psyche and soma, is forced to locate his psychoid in one or the other, and does so by placing it in the body rather than in the psyche, in distinction from Driesch's unifying psychoid having a third position. Nevertheless, Bleuler offers an elaboration not provided by Driesch, according to which his bodily psychoid is oriented towards psychic development based on a selection of that which has a favourable outcome. Thus, he supplies a mechanism of a causal nature by which psyche develops out of soma, which may be contrasted with the very deeply unconscious and life-enhancing process envisaged by Driesch. We may therefore see the psychoid of Bleuler particularly as a developmental agent, which fosters the development of mind out of the matrix of the body.

Jung's concept of "the psychoid"

This then is the background to the adoption by Jung of the same expression "psychoid" to describe a particular aspect of the unconscious in his paper *On the Nature of the Psyche* (1947/1954).

In the period between offering the name to Freud in 1907 and this time, Jung had been developing his own ideas concerning the structure and development of the psyche, in which he regarded instincts as a key factor. In his paper *Instinct and the Unconscious* (1919), he described instincts and archetypes as correlates of one another in the spheres of action and perception, the one regulating our conscious actions and the other determining our mode of apprehension:

> Just as instincts compel man to a conduct of life, which is specifically human, so the archetypes or categories *a priori* coerce his intuition and apperception to forms specifically human. I propose to designate the sum of such inherited psychic qualities as instincts and archetypes of apprehension by the words the "collective unconscious".
>
> (Ibid., p. 19)

A few years later, he arrived at a different view, according to which the archetypes are the forms which the instincts assume (Jung, 1927/1931, para. 339). By 1936, he was writing that the instincts are the chief motivating forces of psychic events:

> I regard the *compulsiveness* of instinct as an ectopsychic factor. None the less, it is psychologically important because it leads to the formation of structures or patterns which may be regarded as determinants of human behaviour. Under these circumstances the immediate determining factor is [. . .] the structure resulting from the interaction of instinct and the psychic situation of the moment.
>
> (1936, para. 234)

He called this process "psychisation".

This development in Jung's thinking is relevant to his views on the nature of psychoid processes, because of the way in which Jung links such processes with instincts and the archetypes. Acknowledging both Driesch and Bleuler, Jung dismisses Driesch's view of the psychoid as a "directing principle" on the ground that this approach is essentially philosophical, and observes that his own use of the term serves to delineate roughly the same group of phenomena that Bleuler had in mind, namely those subcortical processes concerned with biological adaptive functions (ibid., para. 368).

Jung defined his own use of the term "psychoid" thus:

> [F]irstly, I use it as an adjective, not as a noun; secondly, no psychic quality in the proper sense of the word is implied, but only a "quasi-psychic" one such as reflex-processes possess; and [. . .] it is meant to distinguish a category of events from merely vitalistic phenomena on the one hand and from specifically psychic processes on the other.
> (Ibid., para. 368)

Based on the enquiry "[H]ow do we define the psychic as distinct from the physiological?" (ibid., para. 376), he came up with precisely the view that the contents of the unconscious psyche contain undoubted links with the instinctual sphere, which may be thought of as physiological, the lower reaches of the psyche beginning where the psyche emancipates itself from the compulsive force of the instinct. The psyche then extends along a continuum from instinct in its lower reaches in the organic-material substrate to spirit in its upper reaches, and:

> Where instinct predominates psychoid processes set in which pertain to the unconscious as elements incapable of consciousness. The psychoid process is not the unconscious as such, for this has far greater extension. Apart from psychoid processes, there are in the unconscious ideas, volitional acts, hence something akin to conscious processes; but in the instinctual sphere these phenomena retire so far into the background that the term "psychoid" is probably justified.
> (Ibid., para. 380)

Having thus linked instinct with psychoid processes, he goes on to link instinct with his theory of archetypes, as follows:

> Instinct and the archaic [primitive] mode [of functioning] meet in the biological conception of the "pattern of behaviour". [. . . E]very instinct bears in itself the pattern of its situation. Always, it fulfils an image, and the image has fixed qualities. The instinct of the leaf-cutting ant fulfils the image of ant, tree, leaf, cutting, transport, and the little ant-garden of fungi. If any one of these conditions is lacking, the instinct

does not function, because it cannot exist without its total pattern, without its image. Such an image is an *a priori* type. It is inborn in the ant prior to any activity, for there can be no activity at all unless an instinct of corresponding pattern initiates and makes it possible. This schema holds true also of man.

(Ibid., para. 398)

He considered that this instinctual (i.e. primordial) image[8] represented the meaning of the instinct, and concluded that such patterns of behaviour constitute unconscious conditions acting as regulators and stimulators of the instinctual sphere. The resulting unconscious processes give rise to spontaneous manifestations in the form of new positions, and later dreams and other fantasy material of a consciously perceptible nature, in which can be seen certain well-defined themes and formal elements. As consciousness sets in, the archetypal image, seen as an extension of the instinctual image in the psychic arena, takes over. The unconscious processes thus act also as regulators and stimulators of creative fantasy-activity, which avails itself of the existing conscious material, so that the instinctual image, and then the archetypal image, stimulates mental activity generally. Consciousness, Jung wrote, is not only a transformation of the original instinctual image but also its transformer (ibid., para. 399). In this respect, it is here argued that Jung is describing and elaborating an emergent factor that arises whenever the instinctual image is fulfilled and that yields a new and synergistic result.

He goes on to say:

The archetypal representations (images and ideas) mediated to us by the unconscious should not be confused with the archetype as such. They are very varied structures which all point back to one essentially "irrepresentable" form. The latter is characterised by certain formal elements and by certain fundamental meanings, although these can be grasped only approximately. The archetype as such is a psychoid factor. [. . .] It does not appear to be capable of reaching consciousness.

(Ibid., para. 417)

By designating the archetype as such as a psychoid factor, Jung is suggesting that all archetypes possess this psychoid aspect, that is they are all underpinned by psychoid processes immanent in the structure of the organism, that may be conceived as emergent functions. This is the first time that he has specifically related archetypes to psychoid processes, and it results in an extension of his previous understanding of the archetypes, as generators of visual images and ideas, to embrace a new view, where their effect may be to generate phenomena *other than* visual images and ideas, which phenomena manifest psychically although being nearer in character to the physiology of the organism:

> In my previous writings, I have always treated the archetypal phenomena as psychic, because the material to be expounded or investigated was solely concerned with images or ideas. The psychoid nature of the archetype as put forward here does not contradict these earlier formulations; it only means a further degree of conceptual differentiation. [. . .] Just as the "psychic infra-red", the biological instinctual psyche, gradually passes over into the physiology of the organism and thus merges with its chemical and physical conditions, so the "psychic ultra-violet", the archetype, describes a field which exhibits none of the peculiarities of the physiological and yet, in the last analysis, can no longer be regarded as psychic, although it manifests itself psychically.
>
> (Ibid., paras. 419–420)

Consequently, for Jung, the psychoid nature of the archetype is a way of linking psyche and soma through a continuum extending from an instinctual or "psychic infra-red" pole to a spiritual or "psychic ultra-violet" pole. We can see that, for him, body and mind do not stand in a parallel relation but are two different aspects of one and the same thing, represented in his notion of the psychoid unconscious.

In Jung's model, psychoid processes underlying the archetypes are immanent at an instinctual level in the matrix of the organism and are so deeply lodged that they are incapable of being made conscious. Such processes through their links with the instincts give rise to activity within the psyche that produces emergent forms of an archetypal nature, which contribute to the development of consciousness and of structure within the psyche, both transforming the existing structure and then being transformed by the new structure:

> The archetype itself (nota bene *not* the archetypal representation!) is psychoid, i.e. transcendental and thus relatively beyond the categories of number, space, time. That means, it approximates to oneness and immutability.
>
> (Adler, 1976, p. 318)[9]

Speaking of the "gripping" quality of the archetype, Jung writes:

> This remarkable effect points to the "psychoid" and essentially transcendental nature of the archetype as an "arranger" of psychic forms inside and outside the psyche.
>
> (Ibid., p. 22)[10]

When, therefore, the psychologist explains genuine conscience as a collision of consciousness with a numinous archetype, he may be right. But he will have to add at once that the archetype *per se*, *its psychoid essence*, cannot be comprehended, that it possesses a transcendence which it shares with the unknown substance of the psyche in general. The mythical assertion of conscience that it is the voice of God is an inalienable part of its nature, the foundation of its numen.

(Jung, 1958, para. 854)

Discussion

Interestingly, both Bleuler and Jung dismissed Driesch on the grounds that he was a philosopher and that his ideas were based merely on philosophy, in spite of the fact that, of the three of them, Driesch was the one with the strongest record of scientific experimentation, publication and scientific claim.

In viewing the evolution of the psychoid concept through its various incarnations in the hands of the three men, they adopted different positions in regard to the nature of the linking mechanism between body and mind, with Driesch and Jung both arguing that body and mind are different aspects of the same thing, and Bleuler taking a view based more on a psycho-physical parallelism. A common theme in each case, however, was a notion of the psychoid concept as a teleological factor, and here each of them developed the ideas of their predecessor further towards an hypothesis of a specific methodology by which such teleology might be expressed.

Driesch postulated a unifying psychoid situated between psyche and soma, such psychoid directing and organising behaviour, in the sense of the body-in-action, towards goals of wholeness lying in the future. His psychoid was to be seen as a directing principle in a living body. Bleuler's advance over Driesch was to elucidate a view of the psychoid as an unconscious, adaptive bodily process by which psychic learning takes place in response to physical stimuli, as in the case of the infant who develops a pattern of behaviour as it learns that mother responds to its crying. Haule (2011, p. 75) considers that Jung wanted to locate his psychoid somewhere between Driesch and Bleuler.

However, it is argued here that Jung developed his description of psychoid processes a long way beyond the ideas of both Driesch and Bleuler. Nonetheless, the fact that he chose to adopt the same terminology suggests that he still wished to retain a vitalistic base for his ideas, in spite of the fact that he eschewed the entirely vitalistic notion of Driesch, saying that his definition of psychoid processes is not intended to embrace merely vitalistic phenomena within its scope.

The key aspect of Jung's advance lies with his linking of psychoid processes with his theory of archetypes. This enabled him to draw connections with the function of instincts, and with his notion of the instinctual image with its many components combining together into one single outcome. This connection is a very interesting one, whose full implications may be far-reaching. As Jung observes, *all* of the elements must be present before *any* outcome arises, but at the moment when they all come together something entirely new emerges. In his example, the instinctual image of the leaf-cutting ant, all of the ant, tree and so forth, must coincide to produce the leaf-cutting behaviour natural to the ant. No previous experience of leaf-cutting behaviour is required for the ant to know what to do, and no learning takes place; rather the instinct is complete in its specificity from the very first occurrence. The instinctual image is therefore complex and multivalent. It is also purposeful, teleological and directed towards the survival of the organism in bringing about the next developmental stage. In this manner, we can see that each succeeding stage supervenes on the previous one, neither being caused by, nor reducible to, the factors in the previous stage.

A pattern of elements, in their multiplicity, coincide and an entirely new and more complex position emerges, in which all the elements are combined not simply as an independent collection or collocation but as an interacting whole, in which the interaction is not predictable from the individual parts.

Furthermore, the instinctual image with its pattern of elements is immanent as a potential in the basic structure of the organism. It exists as potential inherent within the organism, but it can only be brought to fruition when external circumstances arise to fulfil the instinctual image. The internal potential must be met by the external circumstances for the next stage to emerge. Hogenson (2001, p. 600), noting that Jung made reference to both Baldwin and C. Lloyd Morgan and their ideas on evolution, observes that "the archetypal is always embedded in a context", which is equally as important as any structure. Such context constitutes "instances of actually occurring entities that place adaptive demands on the organism", and thus the archetypes may be seen as emergent properties of a dynamic developmental system involving organism and environment (ibid., p. 607).

As Jung says, what holds true for the instinctual image of the ant is a schema that also holds true for man. And indeed it can be seen in the newborn infant who, when laid on her mother's breast, has been found to seek out the nipple and start to feed. Here, infant, mouth, tongue, mother, breast, nipple come together, and in this moment the infant instinctively suckles and milk starts to flow.

However, Jung does not stop at the behavioural level of instinct. He goes on to apply this schema to the development of consciousness, linking such development with the dynamism of instinct and the instinctual image at one end of the spectrum and with the aspiration of spirit and the archetypal image at the other, the archetypal image being described by Jung as "the dominants that emerge into consciousness as universal ideas" (ibid., para. 423). Hence, it is to be noted that he discriminates archetypal images from instinctual images.

This suggests that he is depicting a mechanism by which consciousness not only emerges from the matrix of the body under the pressure of the dynamism of instinct, in co-operation with the elements of the instinctual image, but also how consciousness may become increasingly sophisticated by developing to ever further levels by the same kind of process. It also suggests that this process in its early stages requires a duality, in which the instinctual image as potential meets the elements of the instinctual image as objects, for new forms to arise, and points to the significance of relationship in the development of the psyche, the "other" being required to fulfil aspects of the instinctual image in the early stages of physiological development and of consciousness.

The process of emergence of new forms of instinctual image will thus gradually give rise to consciousness, to internal representations of the "other", to fantasy material concerning self and other perceptible to and interacting with consciousness, and eventually to forms of archetypal image. In advanced stages, internal representations of the other, including fantasy material, provide elements of the archetypal image, and the process of emergence will be at least in part an intrapsychic one. This fits with Jung's comments that consciousness is not only a transformation of the original instinctual image but also its transformer.

Conclusion

Based on the above, this research argues that Jung is giving us a model of psychoid processes in terms of the primordial or instinctual image, which he describes as a pattern of behaviour in relation to the leaf-cutting ant. When a particular set of conditions is fulfilled, then these processes are initiated and the instinctual sphere is stimulated to activity. However, such set of conditions can only be fulfilled in the human sphere in relationship, at which point psychoid processes respond and lead first to connection, communication, and in time to the development of psychic structure. Accordingly, Jung's psychoid processes link the physiological and instinctual spheres with the growth of the psyche, and lead to the emergence of ever new and more complex psycho-physical and psychic structures.

To return now to the point where this chapter started, with Freud's letter of 7 April 1907 to Jung, and the suggestion put forward by Jung in their meeting that the unconscious could be called "psychoid", it now seems evident that even at this early stage Jung had in mind some idea of an unconscious more aligned with the biological thinking of Driesch than with the views of Freud. Further, it appears that, even in their meeting, the groundwork had already been laid in the mind of Jung for an idea of the unconscious based on a teleological outlook directed towards the possibility, and even character, of future potential. Such a view implies that the two men had wholly different epistemological approaches from the outset. Certainly, this was borne out in the unfolding of events between Freud and Jung. Importantly, however, it also feeds in to the way in which Jung's more mature ideas took shape and asserted themselves, as discussed in the next chapter.

Thus, the next chapter continues the exploration of Jung's ideas on his psychoid concept, by pursuing another strand in his early thinking, based on his researches into the vision-making process, including his self-investigation in his *Red Book* work, and his consequent theoretical conceptualisations.

Notes

1 This chapter is based on a paper published by the researcher as "Jung, Vitalism and the 'Psychoid': An Historical Reconstruction", *Journal of Analytical Psychology*, 54, pp. 123–142.
2 In connection with the association between Freud and the School of Helmholtz, Cranefield (1966) reacts against the position that Freud was a mechanist/materialist, a view which was attributed to Bernfield (1944).
3 1867–1941.
4 Author's italics.
5 Author's italics.
6 Partly written in 1912, although only published in 1928.
7 1857–1939.
8 His use of the word "*image*" is confusing in this paper, since he employs it on the one hand to refer to a complete set of criteria composing the primordial or instinctual image, and on the other to refer to the more usual context of a visual representation.
9 Letter to Enrique Butelman, July 1956, Letters II.
10 Letter to Dr. H., 30 August 1951, Letters II.

Chapter 3

Jung's psychoid concept
A hermeneutic understanding

Introduction

Jung's thinking about his psychoid concept spans most of his working life, from his early discussions with Freud in 1907 (McGuire, 1991) to his relatively late publication of his account of synchronicity (1952). It is not one of his most publicly acclaimed ideas, and yet it provides a fundamental underpinning to his entire model of the psyche, relating as it does to an ultimately unknowable area of the unconscious from which emerge the archetypes and all that is associated with them.

From a theoretical point of view, the evolution of the psychoid concept may be situated within the field of vitalism, commencing with the biological ideas of Hans Driesch, neo-vitalist, and his experiments on sea urchins. Driesch demonstrated a teleological drive of the organism towards goals of wholeness in the future, and in man an organising function having a morphogenetic aspect and a motor function (instinctual) aspect. Subsequently, the concept came to embrace the developmental ideas of Eugen Bleuler, director of the Burghölzli Clinic, who postulated the adaptation of the human infant, in response to experience, in a direction fostering favourable future orientations, and eventually consciousness. Ultimately, this led to Jung's notion of the psychoid as a factor providing an archetypal base to experience, linking psyche and soma, and self and other.

In each instance, the more advanced conceptual understanding elaborated further refinements on the less advanced one, in terms of the nature of the purposive development of the organism in directions of growth, consciousness and spirituality, and in terms of the issue of the body-mind relation.

Vitalism afforded Jung a matrix of thinking allowing him to develop new ways of seeing a purposive unfolding of the psyche-soma throughout the life cycle, and thus it offered a foundation for his notions of a psychoid factor underlying the archetype as such. Addison (2009) argues that the archetype as such can be seen as a potential in the psychoid unconscious for organising and shaping elements of an instinctual or imaginal character to engender new and more complex emergent positions depicted as the instinctual image or the archetypal image, respectively. As a result of the psychoid nature of the archetype, these images may emerge in embodied form anywhere along the psyche-soma continuum between instinct and spirit, and thence become conscious.

This terrain offers a theoretical approach to understanding the psychoid concept, located in an historical ground.

Acknowledging this theoretical background, the present chapter follows a different root, situating the psychoid concept in a hermeneutic field through a review of Jung's personal and clinical experience, including his *Red Book* work.

Such depiction yields another insight into the psychoid concept, one that is more clinically oriented, relating to states of immersion in an undifferentiated unconscious field, commonly known as participation mystique, and to imaginal processes fostering individual realisation of archetypal forces through a dialectic between participation mystique, or undifferentiation, and analytic processing, or differentiation. Such a dialectic has a bearing on regression and progression in the consulting room, in the particular sense of regression to states of unification of body and mind, and self and other, and progression to states of increasing emancipation of mind from body, and self from other.

The present chapter explores this hermeneutic background, and then attempts to bind the resultant understandings together with the more formal view of the psychoid concept derived from the matrix of biological thinking established in the theoretical history, so as to reach a more clinically useful viewpoint.

Accordingly, the chapter first traces a trajectory from Jung's experimental researches, in his scientific study of word association, generating knowledge of autonomous processes in the personal unconscious, to his self-investigation of the human vision-making function, yielding understandings of archetypal processes in the collective unconscious. This will lead on to his early conceptualisations foreshadowing the psychoid concept. Finally, the chapter will review how this history affects our contemporaneous view of Jung's psychoid.

Jung's studies

1. Early work

Enrolling at Basel University in the spring of 1895, Jung decided to specialise in medicine, and therefore his early direction was very much concerned with the medical model of his day, by which a Cartesian duality presided over body and mind, and symptoms were to be treated as organic. In 1898, whilst preparing for his final examinations, he opened Krafft-Ebing's textbook on psychiatry and became taken by his description of psychiatry as a subject in an incomplete state of development, embracing diseases of the personality (Krafft-Ebing, 1904, p. iii). Concluding that he had found "the empirical field common to biological and spiritual facts", including hysteria and dementia praecox, Jung embarked on his psychiatric career at the Burghölzli Clinic (1963, pp. 129–130).

As part of the pioneering research taking place at the Burghölzli Clinic under the aegis of Eugen Bleuler at the beginning of the twentieth century, Jung (1904–1907, 1910) produced his major scientific study on the Word Association Tests (WATs) applied both to normal subjects and to subjects displaying hysteria and other psychopathological conditions, such as dementia praecox. The experimental procedure involved recording the reactions of individual subjects to a series of stimulus words, including the subject's spontaneous word association and their reaction time. The recorded observations were classified in a variety of different ways, according to logical-linguistic criteria and temporal delay, and the resultant categories were scrutinised to ascertain patterns and locate empirical laws. Jung discovered that characteristic disturbances of association arise in connection with emotionally charged personal events: clusters of associative feeling-toned ideas constellate in the personal unconscious around these events and produce delayed reactions times in the subjects undergoing the test (1905/1906, para. 637). He adopted the term "complex" for such constellation of feeling-toned ideas (Jung and Riklin, 1904/1906, para. 167).

An extension of the original research into the psycho-physical domain involved additionally measuring the skin resistance of the subject in reaction to the stimulus words, employing a galvanometer whose electrodes were placed on the palms of the hand or the soles of the feet. The results demonstrated that the same feeling-toned ideas that generated delayed reaction times also produced physical effects associated with the sympathetic nervous system (accumulation of sweat and reduction in skin resistance yielding increased current flow) (Jung, 1907/1908, paras. 1046/9). In an example of word association in a normal subject, the stimulus word *stupid* produced the association *am I* and a peak in galvanometer reading, and Jung wrote, "the subject had a clear egocentric complex" (ibid., para. 1104). Accordingly, emotion and physical reaction were seen to be intimately combined in relation to complexes.

A further application of this research was in a study of families, in which Jung and Fürst administered the WAT to all members of twenty-four families (Jung, 1909b). The findings showed remarkable similarities in patterns of response amongst certain sub-groupings within the families, including close correlations of association between mother and daughter in one family, father and two daughters in another, and respectively (a) two sisters living together, and (b) a further sister and her husband, in a third. As Papadopoulos notes, "in effect, this research indicated that within families there must be certain formations that are organising structures which are collectively shared" (1996, p. 130).

These studies, carried out under Jung's direction in the period from 1902 to 1910, are described in numerous papers, published in Volume 2 of *The Collected Works* (1973) and elsewhere, and they provide scientific evidence in support of:

(a) A theory of complexes, defined as collections of unconscious ideas bound together by a common emotional feeling tone;
(b) The fact that activation of unconscious complexes affects individuals concurrently both on a psychic level and on a physiological level; and
(c) The hypothesis that, in certain categories of people, psychic organising and structural affinities exist between individuals in their responses when complexes are activated.

Jung's psychiatric career at the Burghölzli Clinic also involved the clinical treatment of cases of hysteria, where blocked or repressed affect occasioned by emotional trauma was converted into symptomatology involving a wide variety of physical characteristics and sensory phenomena, and in which he employed Freud's method, as discussed in Addison (2009).

Hence, from the outset of his working career, Jung was investigating the unconscious dynamics in personal complexes and addressing the relationship of psyche and soma when psychic facts and physiological facts are combined.

Whilst his psychiatric work and his collaboration with Freud form one backdrop to his early ideas concerning the unconscious and its relations between mind and body, there is another background element, namely his personal experiment into the process of vision-making, commencing in the lead-up to World War I. Shamdasani describes this study as hermeneutic science, by contrast with the traditional view of science as applied in the WATs (Jung, 2009b, p. 32). Through this investigation, published as *The Red Book* (2009a, 2009b), Jung's understandings of the unconscious entered a new phase, with his discovery of the technique of active imagination. His focus also shifted from the personal unconscious to a deeper level, which he came to call the collective unconscious.[1]

His self-investigation and his early theoretical conceptualisations proceeded in tandem, the one providing the platform for the other. Accordingly, the self-investigation will be described first, and the theoretical deductions elucidated afterwards.[2]

2. The Red Book

Within Jung's oeuvre, *The Red Book* is successor to *Symbols of Transformation* (1912), where he contrasted two forms of thinking, namely directed rational attention and undirected fantasy attention. His researches for *Symbols* brought him to an awareness of symbolic thinking, when he realised that he had been projecting his own process onto Flournoy's description of the visions of his patient, and hence that he had been "analysing [his] own fantasy function" (2012, p. 29). As Shamdasani notes, this was the start of the work of *The Red Book* (Hillman and Shamdasani, 2013, pp. 39–40), in which it is possible to see Jung elaborate a dialectic between these two forms of thinking, namely conscious and unconscious, through symbolisation.

A few years later, in response to intense psychic pressure, Jung began to assess his entire life, and thus commenced his self-investigation. Observing that the games of his childhood still had an emotional charge, he set about a form of play, constructing model buildings, a church and a village (Jung, 1963, p. 198). This brought forth further psychic material and developed into a self-analysis, through a method of shaping the unfolding fantasy into creative form, followed by critical observation. It is to be noted that introspection and self-investigation were respectable methods in psychology at the time (Casement, 2010, p. 39). Further, Jung was aware of earlier examples of self-experimentation from Herbert Silberer's investigation of hypnagogic states in 1909, and Ludwig Staudenmaier's experimentation with self-induced hallucinations in 1912 (Jung, 2009b, p. 21).

In the autumn of 1913, there arose two dreams of a terrible sea of blood, and a flood of unconscious fantasy was unleashed (ibid., p. 199). From December 1913, he began his "most difficult experiment" of *actively*[3] engaging with the unconscious, by plunging himself into his fantasies, deliberately soliciting them, and then entering into dialogue with them (2009b, pp. 22/4). He recorded the visions occurring in the short few months from October/November 1913 to February 1914, seeing those entries as the records of an experiment, in which the scientific question was "to see what happened when he switched off consciousness" (ibid., p. 24). Thereafter, he commenced a series of retrospective reflections, elaborating the original material in a lived method of metaphorical evocation, including mythopoeic writing, calligraphy and painting, which he later termed active imagination (Hillman and Shamdasani, 2013, pp. 9/14). The extent and thoroughness of these reflections is not to be underestimated, since it involved repeated re-working over many years.

Jung employed no conceptual terminology in his retrospective reflection, preferring instead to stay with experience-near language evoking the power of the emotional undertaking, although elsewhere he was already using terms such as "complex" and "collective unconscious" (1917a, pp. 377, 432). Jung regarded this period as absolutely crucial in his later conceptualisations:

> The years of which I have spoken to you, when I pursued the inner images, were the most important of my life. Everything else is to be

derived from this. [. . .] Everything later was merely the outer classification, the scientific elaboration, and the integration into life.

(Shamdasani, 2012, p. 366)

Although, in 1930, he moved on to alchemy, Jung continued his retrospective reflection in further orders of re-working for the remainder of his life, in himself personally embodying the lessons that he had learnt, in his analytic work, and in translating the original experience conceptually into a scientific psychology, including his psychoid concept, as discussed below. His concept of active imagination is an important aspect of these developments.

3. Active imagination

The Red Book presents Jung's active imagination as: a polyphonic interweaving of inner voices from different aspects of his personality; different texts generated at different times; and different narrative forms. The process was profoundly multi-layer. Visions recorded directly in his Black Books are supplemented by poetic elaborations from a year and more later, re-worked repeatedly in the various different drafts of *Liber Primus* and *Liber Secundus* existing amongst the extant manuscripts for *The Red Book* (2009b, p. 105). Jung also made a calligraphic transcription, and added his own paintings.

In the published work, the original material from the Black Books is presented as Layer 1. Here, a series of dramatic personifications unfold, commencing with a dialogue between Jung and his soul, who leads him to a hot desert, where he confronts two principles: the spirit of this time and the spirit of the depths. Various key figures appear, amongst them Siegfried, the hero; Elijah and Salome, the old man and the maiden; the Red One, the devil; Izdubar, the warrior with bull-horns; the magician; and the prophetic figure, Philemon. According to Hannah (1997, p. 117), the figure of Philemon was the most important in all of Jung's exploration. The later re-working, involving interrogation of the personified figures of Layer 1, and a dis-identification with their various voices through the reflective dimension of mythopoeic narrative and depiction in plastic form, is presented as Layer 2 (Hillman and Shamdasani, 2013, pp. 19–20). Jung struggles between the spirit of the time, which draws him towards scientific knowledge and practical value, and the spirit of the depths, the location of the soul in time immemorial. Especially, there was a need to distinguish himself from the prophetic voice of Philemon, and it is through this differentiation that he came to understand that it was not he who created his own visions but that the figures had an independent existence and represented an objective reality of his psyche (ibid., p. 122). Layers 1 and 2 together may respectively be conceived as the practice of the image and the metaphorical way (ibid., pp. 42–43).

By 1916, Jung (1916/1957) was already beginning to conceptualise the process of active imagination in his essay *The Transcendent Function*. He was not as yet employing the expression, but in a prefatory note, added in 1959, he refers to the essay as a description of the method of active imagination. In this essay, he discusses his "constructive or synthetic method of treatment" for assisting the patient to gain insight into the meaning of their disturbance, by seeking a union of conscious and unconscious contents in a new position transcending and integrating the content of both (ibid., para. 145). He proposed starting from the emotional state of the patient:

> The emotional disturbance can also be dealt with [. . .] by giving it visible shape. Patients who possess some talent for drawing or painting can give expression to their mood by means of a picture. It is not important for the picture to be technically or aesthetically satisfying, but merely for the fantasy to have free play. [. . .] There are others again [. . .] whose hands have the knack of giving expression to the contents of the unconscious. Such people can profitably work with plastic materials. Those who are able to express the unconscious by means of bodily movements are rather rare.
>
> (Ibid., para. 168)

This quote foreshadows Jung's later account, in which he attributes a role to psychoid processes in meaning-making through the embodied elaboration of unconscious imagery, the practice that he himself developed in *The Red Book*:

> And so it is with the hand that guides the crayon or the brush, the foot that executes the dance-step, with the eye and the ear, with the word and the thought: a dark impulse is the ultimate arbiter of the pattern, an unconscious *a priori* precipitates itself into plastic form. [. . .] Over the whole procedure there seems to reign a dim foreknowledge not only of pattern but of its meaning. Image and meaning are identical; and as the first takes shape, so the latter becomes clear.
>
> (1947/1954, para. 402)

According to Jung, such amplification elicits and *personalises*[4] the mythological motifs contained in the original images, and encourages a spontaneous manifestation of a purposive unconscious process (ibid., para. 400). No matter what plastic form is selected for the living embodiment of the original fantasy image, new material drawn from the unconscious becomes available to the conscious mind for assimilation and integration, with the form and the process acting as a container to facilitate and hold this work. *Just as the effects of archetypal processes manifest in embodied images within the psyche-soma continuum, so also may embodied experience feed back into the archetypal organising process.*[5] The result enriches and vitalises the personality, bringing to conscious realisation the personalised effects of the archetype, and setting in train the coming-to-be or purposive unfolding of the Self, which Jung called individuation.

Such conceptualisation flows out of Jung's own active imagination. Specific examples of his active imagination, and of the accompanying theorisation, demonstrate this, and foreshadow his later account of the psychoid concept.

a. The seven sermons

One theme that appears repeatedly in different guises in *The Red Book* is the mystery and meaning of God. For example, in *Mysterium Encounter*, Jung's "I" reflects on the essence of God in Layer 1, through a vision of Elijah and Salome (2009b, pp. 174–177). In Layer 2, he contemplates the mystery play as a deep place like the crater of a volcano, pushing out a fiery molten mass of the unformed. He who enters the crater, as someone formed and determined, melts and the formed in him dissolves and becomes smelted anew in the primordial beginning (ibid., pp. 178–183). The Layer 1 vision took place on 21 December 1913, but the date of the Layer 2 reflection is not mentioned.

This example prefigures the series of visions over the short period, from end January to beginning February 1916, that were to become the seven sermons to the dead (ibid., 507–536). Jung published these separately from the rest of *The Red Book*, circulating them privately amongst his circle in 1916 as *Septem Sermones ad Mortuos*, and ascribing them to Basilides in Alexandria, a Gnostic sage from second century AD. An English translation by H. G. Baynes was printed in 1925, and is the translation discussed here, although others have been produced subsequently.

Jung's reference to Gnosticism was deliberate, because the seven sermons are arguably derived from the Gnostic mythologem of a demiurge, in the form of Abraxas, who appears in the second sermon; and the work makes use of a Gnostic style and employs Gnostic vocabulary. Jung's debt to the Gnostics is acknowledged, and is the subject of discussion and disagreement, by a number of scholars, including Hoeller (1982), Quispel (1992), Ribi (2013), and Segal (1992), amongst others, as well as being the subject of criticism by Buber (1952). Ribi notes that Gnosticism[6] may be thought of as "a primordial psychic experience" (2013, pp. 32/8), and that "Jung's conception of Gnosis permeates the entirety of his systematic psychology" (ibid., pp. 168–169).

Jung turned to the accounts of the Gnostics seeking support for his own observations of the mythopoeic depths underlying consciousness. Hannah records that Jung told her "more than once that the *first* parallels he found to his own experience were in the Gnostic texts, that is in the *Elenchos* of Hippolytus" (1997, p. 114). As Jung (1951, para. 169) stated in *Aion*, "for the Gnostics – and this is their real secret – the psyche existed as a source of knowledge", and this is precisely how he approached his active imagination.

In the seven sermons, Jung elaborates the themes above from *Mysterium Encounter* in terms of Pleroma and Creatura.

The Pleroma is described as nothingness or fullness, both differentiation and undifferentiation, whose qualities are undifferentiated pairs of opposites, such as living and dead, light and dark, time and space, good and evil. Although not specifically mentioned, the Pleroma must thus also include the undifferentiated opposites of subject and object, as well as body and mind. As Ribi (2013, pp. 188–189) observes, Jung has borrowed a well-known Gnostic term, which he later designates the *unus mundus* or unknowable psychoid substratum of the collective unconscious. Creatura on the other hand is not in the Pleroma but in itself and confined within time and space; Creatura is distinct, and its function is to differentiate or discriminate. In Creatura, the Pleroma is rent and the opposites are separate. Creatura is distinguished, here, from created beings, or man, and is changeable or capable of transformation.

Man's nature is distinctiveness, and the danger for man is to fall into the Pleroma or undifferentiated state and become submerged in nothingness. His fight to achieve differentiation leads to the "Principium individuationis". Ribi (ibid., pp. 196–197) thus considers that Creatura should be regarded as the universal principle of individuation, which emerges from the Self and is the cause of individual consciousness, stating that something can only become conscious when it is separated out of the Pleroma. He notes that the Gnostics see the Pleroma as the origin of the individual (ibid., 180). Jung later wrote of individuation that, "in general, it is the process of forming and specialising the individual nature; in particular, it is the development of the psychological individual as a differentiated being from the general, collective psychology" (1923, p. 561).

b. Systema Munditotius

Around the same time that he was writing seven sermons, Jung was also drawing his first mandala, which he termed *Systema Munditotius*, shown surrounded by "Pleroma" and including Abraxas at its base (Jaffé, 1979, pp. 75–76). Later, in 1955, Jung wrote:

> It portrays the antimonies of the microcosm within the macrocosmic world and its antimonies. . . . Abraxas . . . represents the *dominus mundi*, the lord of the physical world, and is a world-creator of an ambivalent nature.
>
> (2009b, p. 560)

Jeromson (2005/6, p. 10) indicates that there is evidence that the first sketches pre-date the seven sermons in 1916, and sees the seven sermons and *Systema Munditotius* as mirroring one another, joint symbolic products of Jung's self-exploration, leading towards the Self. Jung himself later interpreted mandala as symbols of individuation and the Self.

4. Concurrent theorisation

These imaginal or symbolic accounts may be compared with Jung's conceptual papers *The Conception of the Unconscious* (1917b) and *The Relation between the Ego and the Unconscious* (1928b), as well as with various later statements made by Jung about psychoid processes.

The former essay is the text of a lecture, given in 1916 to the Zurich School of Analytical Psychology, on the effects of assimilating the unconscious in the service of individuation. It makes sense to read this essay and the seven sermons in tandem, not only because of their coincidence of timing but also because of their complementary content, the one employing only mythopoeic language, the other only conceptual terminology. Although this difference means that no definitions exist for the mythopoeic expressions, it is possible to deduce counterparts in the conceptual terminology, as discussed below.

In this essay, Jung designates two layers in the unconscious, a personal unconscious and a collective or universal psyche inhabited by primordial images, the latter referring to what he later came to call the collective unconscious with its archetypal images.[7] Assimilation of the collective unconscious tends to produce a certain quality of "god-almightiness", an "all-compelling binding to and identification with the collective psyche" that disregards the different psychology of the other (Jung, 1917b, pp. 450/4). "A dissolution of the pairs of opposites sets in", often accompanied by peculiar symptoms, such as physical sensations of being too large for one's skin, or hypnagogic feelings of endless sinking or rising, or of enlargement of the body or dizziness (ibid., pp. 452/8). A release of fantasy, including audio-visual and physical hallucinations, is common. Jung describes the freeing of the individual from the collective unconscious, through processing fantasies hermeneutically as symbols, leading increasingly to a differentiation (separating out) of psychological function and individual corporeity (ibid., p. 465). We may assume from this description that he is equating the individual and his personal corporeity with the created beings or man of the first sermon, and is linking the collective unconscious and its dissolved opposites with the Pleroma, as noted by Ribi (2013, pp. 188–189).[8]

The 1916 text thus complements Jung's seven sermons, with its account of Pleroma and Creatura, and of undifferentiation and differentiation, and its early reference to individuation. It effectively conceptualises Jung's own process of self-experimentation in *The Red Book*, and provides a context for his 1916 account of the transcendent function. More importantly, however, this essay describes the clinical process of regression, as mentioned above, to a state in which the physical fact and the psychic fact coincide, and self and other are not separate, and progression, as differentiation occurs in the individuation process, corresponding respectively with the process, set down in *Mysterium Encounter* and the seven sermons, first of dissolving in the undifferentiated state of the collective unconscious, and then of being "smelted anew" (Jung, 2009b, p. 183).

The later paper constitutes an updated version of the 1916 text with a fuller account of the collective unconscious. Jung (1928b, p. 150) warns of the attractive power of the archetypal image, and of the consequent dangers of inflation, wherein the whole personality is dissolved and splitting of the mind ensues. Strict separation from the collective unconscious is needed for the development of the personality, since a partial or blurred differentiation can result in the individual imposing their views on their fellows, and even obliteration of difference in the entire community (ibid., p. 158).

Jung's, 1928 essay also describes the process of individuation as "a gradual differentiation of functions which in themselves are universal" and further develops the idea of symbolic representation of such process (ibid., p. 184). He gives an example here of a transforming vision experienced by woman patient after a long period of active ego participation[9] in her fantasy life:

> I climbed the mountain and came to a place where I saw seven red stones in front of me, seven on either side, and seven behind me. [. . .] I tried to lift the four stones that were nearest to me. In doing so I discovered that these stones were the pedestals of four statues of gods which were buried down in the earth. I dug them up and so arranged them around me that I stood in the middle of them. Suddenly they leaned towards one another so that their heads touched. [. . .] I fell to the ground. [. . .] Then I saw that beyond, encircling the four gods, a ring of flame had formed. After a time I arose from the ground and overthrew the statues of the gods. Where they fell to earth four trees began to grow. And now from the circle of fire blue flames shot up which began to burn the foliage of the trees. [. . .] I stepped into the fire. The trees disappeared and the ring of fire contracted to one immense blue flame that carried me up from the earth.
>
> (Ibid., pp. 246–247)

Jung described this dream as the symbolic expression of the process of individuation. As he says, "our individual conscious psychology develops out of an original state of unconsciousness, or in other words, a non-differentiated condition (termed by Levy-Bruhl, '*participation mystique*'). [. . .] Discrimination is the essence, the *condition sine qua non* of consciousness" (ibid., p. 226).

The effect of this is described by Boechat (2017, p. 19) as the human need to reach our basic instinctive roots and overcome dissociation through aesthetic configuration, by recovering and personifying the archetypal images instantiated in the psychoid unconscious through a dialectic between the ego and these inner figures. Such process grounds the ego in organising symbols and their meaning.

Subsequently, in *The Philosophical Tree*, Jung (1945/1954) employs the symbol of "the tree" to represent the process of individuation symbolically, observing that, "in so far as the tree symbolises the opus and the transformation process 'tam ethice quam physice' (both mentally and physically) it also symbolises the life process in general" (ibid., para. 459). Being an archetypal image of universal character, its full range of meaning for a particular individual may be difficult to establish, since "the psychoid form underlying any archetypal image retains its character at all stages of development, though empirically it is capable of endless variations" (ibid., para. 350).

Ribi (2013, pp. 41–42) brings this back to Gnosticism, describing the psychoid nature of the archetype as a mystical concept that provides "the interface in the psyche where the mental and the physical meet" and that "manifests itself precisely in human relationships".

In *On the Nature of the Psyche*, Jung (1947/1954, para. 367) brings in the analogy of a scale, contemplating the psyche extending at one end into the physiological sphere of instinct and at the other into a spiritual form, so that psychoid processes underpinning the collective unconscious therefore relate both to instinct and spirit, and to body and mind. He asserts, the "psychoid nature of the archetype contains very much more than can be included in a psychological explanation. It points to the sphere of the *unus mundus*, the unitary world" (1958, para. 852). Emancipation or differentiation of psychic function from the psychoid realm through the organising and integrative process of individuation leads increasingly to consciousness and true individuality. All of this is foreshadowed in the seven sermons and the associated conceptual texts from 1916 and 1928 onwards.

Jung's own process, and the examples given above, each contemplates a dialectic between the individual ego and figures in the imaginal material emerging into consciousness to foster personal development. Both of these two conceptual essays also bring in the notion of transference.

In the 1916 text, Jung discusses the case of a young woman experiencing attacks of night terror and nervous asthma. Investigation uncovered a history involving an unhappy parental marriage, with a mother subject to hysteria; a series of incidents surrounding first her father and then a young Italian man, when she could see in their eyes a terrifying animal lust; and, finally, following the birth of her own second child, a discovery that her husband was entangled with another woman. Jung noted that her libido was unconsciously fastened in unadapted form on the young Italian, but that her fantasies transferred in the course of treatment to the physician himself (Jung, 1917a, pp. 385/408). He wrote that if the doctor accepts the situation, a natural channel for overcoming the neurosis is created, but that, if he fails to understand the phenomenon, the patient is liable to break off the relationship with the doctor (ibid., p. 408).

There follows a description of the normal progression of the transference from a projection onto the physician of personal material, in this instance relating to the young Italian and the father, to the projection of more fantastic material based on mythological themes, such as magician, demoniacal criminal, and saviour, none of which relate to the actual person of the physician. This later phase involves the projection of archetypal images based on inherited links to the potentialities of the human imagination:

> We have therewith now found the object selected by the libido when it was freed from the personal-infantile form of transference. Namely, that it sinks down into the depths of the unconscious, reviving what has been dormant there from immemorial ages. It has discovered the buried treasure out of which mankind from time to time has drawn, raising thence its gods and demons.
>
> (Jung, 1917b, p. 411)

Through the relationship with the doctor, this may hopefully lead to a differentiation in the unconscious of the personal and the impersonal (i.e. collective) unconscious, something which is necessary to avoid pathology.

> In order to differentiate the psychological ego from the psychological non-ego, man must stand upon *firm feet* in his ego function, that is, *he must fulfil his duty towards life completely, so that he may in every respect be a vitally living member of human society.*
>
> (Ibid., pp. 416–417)

The 1928 paper contains a shift in emphasis over the 1916 version. Jung (1928b, p. 131) brings in another example of a woman with a father complex, writing that they had reached an impasse, and he found himself unable to dissolve the transference. Accordingly, he turned to her dreams, "since the psyche is a vital process . . . a purposive process with a final orientation, so that we might expect the dream" to provide indications as to what is going on (ibid., p. 131). In these dreams, the active figures were unmistakably herself and himself, so that he knew she had transferred onto him a father imago. But, in each case, he was misrepresented, having a body of supernatural size or being extremely old, while she was tiny or very young. The contrast was quite fantastic. He understood that she could distinguish the actual reality from the unconscious position, and concluded that "the energy of the transference is so strong that it gives one the impression of a vital instinct" (ibid., p. 133). He asked himself whether this was the "most real meaning of this purposeless love that we call transference?" (ibid., p. 133). Gradually, the patient evolved an unconscious super-personal guiding point, and was eventually freed of her father complex sufficiently to form a new personal attachment. Through the dreams, her unconscious was able to achieve a widening and a deepening of her psychic position that produced a living effect. Jung described this as the function of a reactivated archetype in the collective unconscious.

In this way, Jung describes an important aspect of the analytic process and makes a connection between the transference, the relationship with the analyst, and individuation.

5. The collective experiment

Throughout the period when Jung was conducting and conceptualising his own active imagination, he also continued his private practice, and, according to Shamdasani, he extended his self-investigation of the vision-making process into a wider empirical research study, based on his practice:

> Jung's self-experimentation was in part a collective experiment, involving his patients. Jung encouraged his patients to engage in active imagination and attempted to see to what extent the process of development he had undergone could be replicated and had typical phases.
> (Casement, 2010, p. 41)

This is corroborated by an observation made by Tina Keller, one of Jung's analysands, to the effect that Jung "was after all experimenting just like a surgeon who is trying out new methods" (Swan, 2000, p. 100). Swan (2000, 2011) gives accounts of Keller's two analyses, with Jung and Toni Wolff, indicating that she used automatic writing and painting to elaborate her fantasies in her initial analysis with Jung, and embodied them through dance and movement in her subsequent analysis with Wolff. Keller described a session with the latter in the following terms:

> Following my body tensions, I formed a crude dance. I, or rather a young fantasy-woman in me, felt imprisoned in stone. [. . .] The contours of her body were clear, yet she must with great exertion free herself from the stone walls. It took a good part of the session until at last I stood upright and free. This session seemed to me much more satisfying than sessions where we merely talked.
> (Swan, 2011, p. 31)

It is also corroborated by the fact that Jung encouraged his patients to make copies of the pictures created in their own active imaginations, and to donate them to him for his private collection. The collection is now housed in the

Picture Archive at the Jung Institute in Zurich, which contains approximately four thousand pictures produced by Jung's analysands and approximately six thousand pictures produced by those of Jolande Jacobi. Both Jung and Jacobi presented and published extensive examples of such active imaginations; see, for example, Jung's *A Study in the Process of Individuation* (1934/1950) and *Visions: Notes of the Seminar Given in 1930–1934 by C. G. Jung* (1997),[10] and Jacobi's *Symbols in an Individual Analysis* (1964).

6. Summary

The above discussion demonstrates a complete change of direction between Jung's earlier psychiatric, science-based WATs, applied to the relationship of body and mind, and his subsequent hermeneutic understanding and approach, although he makes use of the latter to build on knowledge derived from the former. He is now coming at his theoretical ideas firstly from self-experimentation and secondly from the empirical base of his own analytic practice and patients. He has arrived at a hermeneutic method of symbolic elaboration by means of active imagination, a technique uniquely combining body and mind in a creative process, which as early as 1916 he had linked with the transcendent function, defined here as a meeting of opposites to create a living third or new situation. This gives a symbolic dimension to the psychoid concept.

Such discussion also shows how, in the period from 1913 to 1930, Jung was grappling with notions of individual and collective, and differentiation and undifferentiation having regard to self and other, as well as body and mind, and he was doing so both in an empirical sense, within his own self-experimentation and his collective experiment, and in a conceptual sense, in his evolving attempts to produce theoretical accounts from this work. He has developed a notion of individuation, starting from an undifferentiated state, a participation mystique, peopled by typical forms or archetypal images, corresponding in analysis with a particular form of regression to unified states of body and mind, and self and other. He has conceived the need for the individual to discriminate his psychological function and his individual corporeity increasingly from the collective, through personalisation of these archetypal images, and he has proposed a process of symbolic reflection or active imagination, involving both body and mind, in order to achieve this progression. Further, not only has he worked out his notion of regression to, and progression from, undifferentiated states and, in his 1928 essay, conceived the view that consciousness proceeds from a *participation mystique*, he has also demonstrated the application of these specific ideas to an early notion of the transference developing in analysis from a personal to an archetypal process.

Here, we have the empirical basis for these ideas, and its conceptual working out. Further, as discussed, these ideas pre-figure his later accounts of the psychoid unconscious.

Discussion

This chapter has described various historical scientific and empirical research studies, serving to establish the psychoid concept practically and ground it in a clinical setting. Empirically, the notions of a psychoid unconscious and of psychoid processes are confirmed by Jung's own experiments, personal and collective. These accounts offer hermeneutic insight into the psychoid concept, and demonstrate how Jung shifted from an approach founded on a scientific base in the biological experiments of Driesch[11] and his own WATs, to one founded on a hermeneutic base in his own self-experimentation and later conceptualisations. It is believed that this shift could only take place because of the solidity of Jung's earlier foundation in his scientific work, in which the WATs provided evidence not only of the connection between psyche and soma, but also, in the family studies, of the existence of collectively shared organising structures. This base enabled Jung to be open to the emergence of ideas of a monistic body-mind and the existence of "participation mystique" from his hermeneutic investigations.

These investigations yield two related strands to incorporate in an understanding of the psychoid concept.

Firstly, Jung's hermeneutic research proposed ways in which psychoid processes link individual man to the *unus mundus*, and in which the individual develops in the process of individuation from an undifferentiated state towards increasing differentiation from the collective through the personalisation of archetypal images. This process has a numinous quality and serves to distinguish the individual personally in terms both of his psychological function and his corporeity. Jung conceived the method of active imagination for this personalisation, demonstrated by his own example and by those of his analysands, as conceptualised in various theoretical papers. Such approach is heavily weighted towards metaphorical reflection, and psycho-physical forms of symbolic functioning, implying that working with imagery and spiritual experience in all areas of the body-mind continuum is an important aspect of the analytic process.

The other key theme, implied but not overly fully discussed, is the manifestation of psychoid processes in the transference in an undifferentiated or symmetrical unconscious field, in which analyst and patient are mutually immersed. The psychoid processes then have an effect in ordering the material emerging into consciousness, and in generating an archetypal arena, where archetypal images may arise and be personally mediated through active imagination.

This leads to a clinically meaningful understanding of the psychoid as a deeply unknowable realm, thereby limiting what can be said about it, and as an area of undifferentiation, where psyche and soma are monistic, and self and other are in a participation mystique, from which the individual differentiates himself in the process of individuation. Here, a purposive, structuring and organising principle gives rise to psychic patterns having emergent properties, by which the psyche is differentiated out of the body-mind matrix and new individual positions come to be realised. Such patterns link instinct and spirit symbolically by means of instinctual and archetypal images, and impart meaning. They also manifest in the transference relationship between analysand and analyst, so that the analytic dyad may together engage with the archetypal process in a manner designed to foster transformation.

Conclusion

This chapter has endeavoured to trace the hermeneutic background to Jung's psychoid concept, in order to highlight his search for living meaning in the unknown depths of the psyche, and the conceptualisations that arose out of this search. The advantage of uncovering this history is the demonstration, by example, of a dialectical method of engaging with archetypal material through the symbolic, in a manner engendering a series of transformations from undifferentiated and universal states to increasingly differentiated and personalised states in the process of individuation.

Notes

1 Defined here as a universal psyche inhabited by primordial images; see page 12 herein.
2 His vocabulary evolved as his ideas matured, and the original or early term will be supplemented by the more well-known, later term, which thereafter will be employed exclusively.
3 Author's italics.
4 Author's italics.
5 Author's italics.
6 In the second and third centuries AD, Gnosticism assimilated itself to emerging Christianity (Ribi, 2013, pp. 29/40).
7 In his 1928 essay, he describes primordial images as archetypal images.
8 See also Hoeller (1982) and Segal (1992).
9 Jung is not yet employing the expression "active imagination"; see page 41 above.
10 Based on the visions of Christiana Morgan.
11 Addison (2009).

Chapter 4

Jung's psychoid concept and Bion's proto-mental concept

A comparison

Introduction

Jung and Bion were both interested in the relationship of body and mind, and respectively developed the psychoid concept and the proto-mental concept to account for a combined body-mind, a monism, in which body and mind are seen as different aspects of the same thing. Both concepts situate such monism in a deeply unknowable unconscious stratum, from which distress may manifest as much in physical as in psychic form.

The present chapter considers the background to their shared conceptual terrain, reviewing the claim that this commonality arises from the same source of vitalist ideas in philosophy, including the work of Henri Bergson, and that Jung's ideas exerted a direct influence on Bion, whilst noting the ultimate evolution of the two concepts in fundamentally different directions.

Jung's opus

A vitalist strand permeates Jung's entire opus, beginning with his assertion in his Zofingia lectures as a student that "a pre-existent vital principle is necessary to explain the world of organic phenomena" (1896, para. 63). His initial representation of "the psychoid"[1] is founded in *Das Psychoid* of the biologist and neo-vitalist Hans Driesch (1903), whose experiments on sea urchins demonstrated teleological aims of the organism towards wholeness.

In 1913, just before the onset of World War I, Jung began to have a series of visions that became the foundation of a prolonged self-experimentation, and his subsequent conceptualisation of almost all of his theories, including the psychoid concept. *The Red Book* (2009) records his investigation, including his technique of active imagination as a process for symbolically elaborating the vision imagery to reveal an underlying pattern and meaning. This led him to early understandings of a universal and collective level of the mind (1916).

Such background promoted a biological view of the collective unconscious and its archetypal foundation, culminating eventually in his notion of the psychoid unconscious as a deeply unknowable area of the unconscious, forming a base to archetypal experience (1954). Jung linked this area with primitive experience, prior to the differentiation of self and other and of psyche and soma, and with a structuring and organising principle giving rise to emergent properties yielding instinctual and archetypal images of a psycho-physical nature, by which the individual personalises the archetypes to separate self from other and mind from body. In the clinical setting this evolving experience may manifest in the transference.

A later phase in Jung's thinking, stemming from his collaboration with Wolfgang Pauli, the Nobel Prize–winning physicist, extended the psychoid concept into physics and the mind-matter arena, which generated his notion of synchronicity as an acausal connection between psychic events and physical events, founded on a psychoid substrate (1952).

Bion's opus

By contrast, Bion's proto-mental concept is firmly grounded in his early career, in his World War I experience as a tank commander near the front line, his subsequent employment at the Tavistock Clinic, and his group work. The conceptualisation largely precedes his psychoanalytic phase, in which he subsequently developed his ideas on psychotic mechanisms regarding the conversion of undigested sensual impressions or beta elements through alpha functioning or reverie, and his transformational concept of "O", the unknowable thing-in-itself.

Bion's experiences in World War I alerted him to the effects of war on soldiers, rather loosely described at that time as nerve strain or shell shock (later as battle or war neurosis).[2] As a commander of one of the early tanks[3] on the front line, Bion witnessed, and in all probability himself experienced, shell shock. As he wrote in his diary for 26 September 1917 at Ypres:

> All our nerves were in an awful state, and we tried not to think of what was coming. The waiting was awful and seemed to be almost a physical pain – a sort of frightfully "heavy" feeling about one's limbs and body.
> (Bion, 1997, p. 29)

Later, for 8 August 1918 at Amiens, he wrote, "these considerations and the anxiety of my job rather crushed me. I sat still and numbed with an almost physical pain, which made movement difficult" (ibid., p. 120).

After the war, Bion attended Oxford University and then underwent a medical training. From 1927 to 1935, he was in therapy with James Hadfield, who worked at the Tavistock Clinic and who was an authority on war neurosis (Hadfield, 1942a & 1942b). Possibly through the influence of Hadfield, Bion himself came to work there in 1933, remaining until 1948.

As a result of his experiences in World War I, Bion was asked in 1942 to cooperate with Eric Trist in setting up War Office Selection Boards (WOSBs) for the selection of future officers. Bion was largely instrumental in devising the Leaderless Group technique for the WOSBs (Harrison, 2000, p. 90), in which unstructured group interactions were employed to test the performance of potential officers and discover who would emerge as a leader. Then, in 1943, he joined Rickman in setting up the Northfield Experiment in group psychotherapy at Northfield Military Psychiatric Hospital. After World War II, the Tavistock Clinic began to look at group methods for treating people with psychological difficulties, and Bion was invited to develop his interest in groups already fostered by the WOSBs and the Northfield Experiment. Based on this work, he published a series of papers, and subsequently a book, entitled *Experiences in Groups* (1961).

Bion refers to the proto-mental system as a concept that transcends experience, describing it in terms of group dynamics. His initial definition sets the proto-mental system as a fundamental matrix, in which psyche and soma are undifferentiated and which is activated in the individual by his participation in the group, where a number of basic assumptions prevail, so that the individual expresses a group pathology. Basic assumption activity, according to Bion, requires no experience or mental activity; it is instantaneous and instinctive. Development out of the proto-mental matrix occurs when the group perceives the need for a less magical form of thinking, and emotions become expressible in psychological terms.

Subsequently, as a result of his work with Melanie Klein, Bion modified his thinking on groups, and began to apply his understanding of psychotic mechanisms to the group process. From this point it becomes possible to set his ideas on the proto-mental concept in the context of his later psychoanalytic thought.

Influences

1. The Tavistock Clinic

The Tavistock Clinic was founded in 1920 by Hugh Crichton-Miller to implement in civilian life a programme of treatment that he had learnt as part of a team adapting Freud's method for treating shell-shocked soldiers in wartime. A number of members of staff had seen and treated shell-shock victims, both fresh from the line and in hospitals at home, and they brought to their practices an understanding of psychosomatic disorders occurring in battle conditions (Miller, 1940).

Under Crichton-Miller, the Tavistock Clinic aimed at a unified psychosomatic approach to diagnosis and treatment (Armstrong, 1980). Hinshelwood (2013b, p. 46) writes that "Bion arrived at the Tavistock during a time when a certain psycho-physical integration was probably still a prevalent idea".

Crichton-Miller (1920, p. 4) placed emphasis on what he described as a binocular approach that paid attention to physical factors as well as mental factors of a given neurosis, noting that "the physician who has been trained to regard disease solely from the organic point of view, and the psychotherapist who has become accustomed to think exclusively in terms of mind, are both employing only monocular vision".

In the 1930s, the Tavistock Clinic also represented a school of psychotherapy dedicated to an integrative practice combining both Jung and Freud (Hinshelwood, 2013b, p. 45). The atmosphere in the clinic was biased towards Freud's theoretical models of hysteria and psychogenic disease, but Dicks (1970, p. 23) observes that Jung's ideas found representation amongst the Tavistock staff, most notably in Crichton-Miller himself and in Maurice Nicol, a British pupil of Jung.

According to Dicks (ibid., p. 67), Hadfield, Bion's analyst, favoured a reductive clinical attitude, seeking to discover dynamic links between the symptom and its causes in the past, the "nuclear incidents", generally a Freudian approach. However, Hadfield was also influenced by the work of the social theorist William McDougall (1908, 1920), who developed a theory of the group mind. McDougall established a system of hormic psychology, which placed emphasis on the dynamic and purposive aspects of the mind, and which inclined more towards Jung's understanding of libido than Freud's. It would appear, therefore, that Hadfield's leanings placed him somewhere between Freud and Jung in his theoretical stance.

Thus, Bion would certainly have been well exposed to Jung's ideas in his daily work.

It is interesting to note that Bion's daughter, Parthenope, had intended before her untimely death to write an account of Bion's intellectual formation, and left brief notes on this project on the website: www.sicap.it/merciai/parthenope.parthenope.htm. Although the site closed down in 2010, these notes, dated 1 February 2001, have been copied and published by Torres and Hinshelwood (2013, pp. xvi–xvii) and describe plans for a three-part biography, entitled *Bion and his Books*, in which the second part, designated "Groping towards Psychoanalysis", included section headings "Tavistock" and "Jung". Therefore, Bion was not only exposed to the ideas of Jung, but was undoubtedly influenced by them.

2. Bergson and vitalism

The French philosopher Henri Bergson was also influential in the Tavistock Clinic. During a continuous period of at least twelve years from 1915, the list of corresponding members of the Society for Psychical Research includes key contributors to the psychoanalytic thinking of the time, amongst them Freud, Jung and Janet, as well as Bergson, while McDougall was president of the Society in 1920 and Driesch was president of the Society in 1926. The hormic psychology of McDougall, who influenced Hadfield, owed much to Bergson's *élan vital*. And, while Jung's psychoid concept owes a debt to the vitalism of Driesch,[4] his writings also contain numerous references to the vitalistic ideas of Bergson.

Bergson published the French edition of *Creative Evolution*, acknowledging the neo-vitalism of Driesch,[5] in 1907.[6] It is known that Jung had a copy of the 1912 German edition in his library (Shamdasani, 2003, p. 227). Further, writing to Hans Schmid on 24 June 1915, he indicates that he had read it two years previously (Beebe and Falzeder, 2013, p. 48). Both Shamdasani (2003, p. 227) and Gunter (1982, p. 639) note that, by 1913, Jung was comparing his own notion of the libido with Bergson's *élan vital*.

The minutes of the Zurich Psychoanalytical Society, Psychological Club, Zurich for 20 March 1914, show that, following a presentation by Keller of a paper on Bergson's theory, Jung responded that this discussion of Bergson was long overdue since he was saying everything that they had not yet said. And, in 1916, in a paper on the psychoses, Jung observed:

> I realise that my views are parallel with those of Bergson, and that in my book the concept of libido which I have given, is a concept parallel to that of "élan vital"; my constructive method[7] corresponds to Bergson's "intuitive method". I, however, confine myself to the psychological side and to practical work. When I first read Bergson a year and a half ago I discovered to my great pleasure everything which I had worked out practically, but expressed in consummate language and in a wonderfully clear philosophic style.
>
> (Jung, 1916, para. 351)

Jung also acknowledged an influence on his typology in a letter of 4 June 1915 to Schmid, writing that "it was Bergson who gave me the notion of the *irrational*. What I like is the unmistakable *hypostasization* of this notion. As a consequence we get two intimately connected, mutually dependent principles: the *rational* and the *irrational*" (Beebe and Falzeder, 2013, pp. 41–42). Jung was not yet employing these terms in his typology, but they came to be applied with reference to his rational functions, thinking and feeling, and his irrational functions, sensation and intuition.

Thus, by his own admission, Jung acknowledged the influence of Bergson on his notion of libido, his synthetic method and his typology. Bergson's descriptions of instinct and intuition also lend themselves to comparison with Jung's descriptions of the same, and point towards Jung's accounts of the archetypes and thence of his psychoid unconscious.

For example, Kerslake (2007) compares Bergson's theory of instinct and Jung's instinctual or primordial image. Bergson (1907[1911], pp. 181–183) describes the paralysing instinct of certain species of Hymenoptera (wasp), which, prior to laying their eggs, sting their victim to the point of paralysis but not death, in order to ensure a living supply of fresh food for their larvae. He describes this as the wasp having a *sympathy* for its victim. They are no longer considered as two organisms, but as a relation of one to the other wherein the mere presence of the two together is sufficient for the wasp to respond by instinct.

Jung (1919, para. 18) gives an example of the refined instinct of the yucca moth, which once only in its lifetime lays its eggs in the yucca plant on the one single night that the plant is open, making a link with Bergson's philosophy and his notion of intuition. He draws an analogy between instinct as a purposive impulse to carry out a highly complicated action, and intuition as the unconscious purposive apprehension of a highly complicated situation, citing Bergson:

> Bergson's philosophy suggests [a] way of explanation, where the factor of intuition comes in. . . . Just as instinct is the intrusion of an unconsciously motivated impulse into conscious action, so intuition is the intrusion of an unconscious content of an "image" into conscious apperception.
>
> (Ibid.)

Jung (ibid., pp. 22–23) goes on to relate this to his own notion of a primordial image and to Bergson's conception of *durée créatrice*.

This leads us to the question of the body-mind relation addressed by both Bergson and Jung. Bergson refuted the idea of psycho-physical parallelism and gives an account of life as an undivided unity, in which intelligence and instinct are turned in opposite directions, the former towards inert matter and the latter towards life:

> In reality, life is a movement, materiality is the inverse movement, and each of these two movements is simple, the matter which forms a world being an undivided flux, and undivided also the life that runs through it, cutting out in it the living beings along its track. Of these two currents the second runs counter to the first, but the first obtains, all the same, something from the second. There results between them a *modus vivendi*, which is organization.
>
> (Bergson, 1907[1911], p. 243)

Bergson, then, is promoting a panpsychic view of mind-matter relations, consistent with Jung's monism in his psychoid concept.

It is evident from the above that Jung was influenced by Bergson in the development of his early ideas generally, and in the development especially of those concerning his psychoid concept. There is also evidence that Bion was so influenced, as Torres (2013b) discusses.

According to Torres (ibid., p. 20), Bion possessed in his library a copy of Bergson's *Matter and Memory* (1896[1911]),[8] which is marked with Bion's manuscript comments. Based both on the evidence of this book and on the parallels that can be drawn between their respective ideas, Torres argues that Bion was influenced by the metaphysics and process philosophy of Bergson, specifically in the formulation of his proto-mental concept.

As discussed above, Bergson's ideas were current with Freud, Janet and other psychoanalysts through the Society of Psychical Research, and certainly influenced Jung. In the Tavistock Clinic, Crichton-Miller (1933, pp. 33, 138, 185) himself wrote that Jung's ideas bear a fundamental resemblance to Bergson's, and also that Jung's use of the term *libido* is exactly analogous to Bergson's *élan vital* or to McDougall's *hormé*, while noting that McDougall described Jung's scheme as entirely reconcilable with the conception of creative evolution. Undoubtedly, Bion too would have been well acquainted with Bergson's philosophy at the Tavistock Clinic.

In *Matter and Memory*, Bergson (1896[1911]) sought to review the relation of spirit and matter through a study of memory, or aphasia, reaching the conclusion that memory constitutes the intersection of mind and matter. He describes pure reality and intuition as an undivided continuity, which we break up into elements laid side by side, corresponding in the one case to *words* and in the other to independent *objects*, in adaptation to the exigencies of life (ibid., p. 239). For him, man exists in "pure duration, of which the flow is continuous and in which we pass insensibly from one state to another: a continuity which is really lived, but artificially decomposed for the greater convenience of customary knowledge" (ibid., p. 243). *Durée*, or true reality, is thus an endlessly indivisible temporal succession, and a living unity or panpsychism.

Bergson here describes the birth of consciousness:

> The progress of living matter consists in a differentiation of function which leads first to the production and then to the increasing complication of a nervous system capable of canalizing excitations and of organizing actions: the more the higher centres develop, the more numerous become the motor paths along which the same excitation allows the living being to choose, in order that it may act. An ever greater latitude left to movement in space – this indeed is what is seen. What is not seen is the growing and accompanying tension of consciousness in time. . . . [F]reedom always seems to have its roots deep in necessity and to be intimately organized with it. Spirit borrows from matter the perceptions on which it feeds, and restores them to matter in the form of movements which it has stamped with its own freedom.
>
> (Ibid., p. 332)

Such statements from *Matter and Memory* evidence a vitalist approach to the bodymind, and it may be assumed that this work influenced Bion in his understanding of an undifferentiated layer as a function of his proto-mental system. Indeed, Torres draws a connection between Bergson's panpsychism, as conceived in *Matter and Memory*, and Bion's proto-mental matrix as a monism.

It would, therefore, appear that Jung and Bion were both influenced by the vitalistic conceptions of Bergson, insofar as their two concepts designate a deeply unconscious stratum, combining body and mind in an undifferentiated field from which consciousness arises.

This is reinforced by evidence from Jung's *Tavistock Lectures*, which suggest a direct influence of Jung on Bion.

3. Jung's Tavistock Lectures

In 1935, Jung was invited to deliver a series of five lectures at the Tavistock Clinic. Bion attended at least the first three on 30 September, 1 October and 2 October, bringing his patient Samuel Beckett[9] to the third.

The first lecture was on psychological types, in which Jung (1935, paras. 20–25) described the four functions of sensation, thinking, feeling and intuition as "ectopsychic" functions, meaning that they concern a system of relationship between the contents of consciousness and environmental data discerned through the senses. He next described the "endopsychic" functions, concerning a system of relationship amongst the contents of consciousness, and postulated processes in the unconscious, designated as the four functions: memory, the subjective components of conscious functions, emotions/affects and invasion or something that breaks through from the unconscious.

In the ensuing discussion, questions, including one by Bion, were put concerning the links between the ectopsychic function, feeling, and the endopsychic function, emotion or affect. By way of response, Jung made reference to his Word Association Tests,[10] demonstrating the physiological manifestations of emotion. Asked about the connection between affect and physiology, he replied that the relationship between body and mind is a difficult question:

> All we can know empirically is that processes of the body and processes of the mind happen together in some way which is mysterious to us. It is due to our most lamentable mind that we cannot think of body and mind as one and the same thing; probably they *are* one thing, but we are unable to think it. . . . In the same way, the so-called psycho-physical parallelism is an insoluble problem. . . . Body and mind are two aspects of the living being, and that is all we know. Therefore I prefer to say that the two things happen together in a miraculous way, and we had better leave it at that, because we cannot think of them together. For my own use, I have coined a term to illustrate this being together; I say there is a peculiar principle of *synchronicity* active in the world so that things

happen together somehow and behave as if they were the same, and yet for us they are not.

(Ibid., para. 70)

In the second lecture, Jung described his model for the structure of the mind, including a personal unconscious having personal contents and a collective unconscious containing traces of the archaic mind, with its archetypes, archetypal images and mythological motifs. He observed:

> The deepest we can reach in our exploration of the unconscious mind is the layer where man is no longer a distinct individual, but where his mind widens out and merges into the mind of mankind – not the conscious mind, but the unconscious mind of mankind, where we are all the same. . . . On this collective level we are no longer separate individuals, we are all one. You can understand this when you study the psychology of the primitives. The outstanding fact about the primitive mentality is this lack of distinctiveness between individuals, this oneness of the subject with the object, this *participation mystique*, as Levy-Bruhl terms it.
>
> (Ibid., para. 87)

He described this layer as "the ultimate kernel which cannot be made conscious at all – the sphere of the archetypal mind. Its presumable contents appear in the form of images" (ibid., para. 92). He also observed that "when the collective unconscious becomes really constellated in larger social groups, the result is a public craze, a mental epidemic. . . . [T]hese movements are exceedingly contagious" (ibid., para. 95).

In the discussion following this lecture, Bion referred to Jung's observations on body and mind from the previous evening, and to a recently published article titled "A case of 'periventricular epilepsy'" (Davie, 1935). In that case, the patient, a man in his middle forties, had served in the war and been severely wounded in 1918 with subsequent sepsis. Some fourteen years later, he fell prey to attacks of loss of consciousness, involving disturbed breathing, movements of the jaw and pallor, apparently unconnected with his wartime wounds. He was treated by his doctor, who considered the possibility of links with the patient's wartime experience and of "an anxiety neurosis in the Freudian sense" (ibid., p. 295). In view of this, the doctor conducted a dream investigation, and Jung was called in rather than Freud, since:

> I do not recollect that Freud has diagnosed organic maladies by dream analysis, but readers of Jung will recall instances of this. . . . It has been suggested that the diagnosis of such cases by Jung is the outcome of his intuition. . . . Jung, however, seems to reach his conclusions solely by symbol interpretation.
>
> (Ibid., p. 296)

In the dream, some machinery needed oiling and milk was suggested as the best lubricant, although the dreamer felt that oozy slime was preferable. Then, a pond was drained and amid the slime were two extinct animals, one of which was a minute mastodon. Jung immediately diagnosed an organic disturbance, interpreting the drainage of the pond as the damming up of the cerebrospinal fluid circulation.

Bion observed that, if this case had been correctly reported, it made a very important suggestion, and wondered whether Jung considered there was some closer connection between the two forms of archaic survival, that of the body and that of the mind.

Jung responded that this also related to the controversial problem of psycho-physical parallelism:

> As I tried to explain yesterday, the two things – the psychic fact and the physiological fact – come together in a peculiar way. They happen together and are, so I assume, simply two different aspects of our *mind*, but not in reality. We see them as two on account of the utter incapacity of our mind to think them together. Because of that possible unity of the two things, we must expect to find dreams which are more on the physiological side than on the psychological, as we have other dreams that are more on the psychological side than on the physical side.
> (Jung, 1935, para. 136)

Continuing, he brought in Janet's *abaissement du niveau mental*, and the nature of Tao, including the way the Chinese mind experiments with "being together" and "coming together at the right moment", an experimental method that is not known in the West (ibid., para. 144). "I use another word to designate it", he said. "I call it *synchronicity*"[11] (ibid., para. 143).

In the remaining three lectures, Jung covered the Word Association Tests, dream interpretation and active imagination. No further observations were made by Bion, although we know that he was present with Beckett at one of these at least, when Jung interpreted two dreams from a small child of five in terms of images of the sympathetic nervous system (ibid., paras. 202–203); and the mythological dreams of another child as prognostic of her death, something which followed a year later from an infectious disease (ibid., para. 205).

In these 1935 lectures, Jung refers to his notion of "synchronicity" as a way of describing the body-mind connection, although he had not yet reached the idea of associating synchronicity with quantum physics.[12] Here, Jung confines himself to a rejection of the notion of psycho-physical parallelism in favour of the radical idea of body and mind being two aspects of the same thing linked in a way that is not causal. He describes the psychic fact and the physical fact as different aspects of the mind, coming together at the right moment and behaving as if they are the same, even though in reality they are not. In other words, he brings in the notion of a dual-aspect monism.

He specifically refers to synchronicity in terms of Janet's *abaissement du niveau mental*, associated with a deeply unconscious layer in the mind, an ultimate kernel, which cannot be made conscious at all and which is undifferentiated, archetypal and primitive in the sense that subject and object come together in a *participation mystique*. He also links the constellation of this deep layer of the collective unconscious, in groups, with contagion, public crazes and mental epidemics.

These encounters between Bion and Jung demonstrate a striking overlap of interests in 1935, both focusing on the nature of the relationship between body and mind in a deeply unknowable archaic layer of the unconscious, something that foreshadows aspects of Jung's psychoid unconscious and Bion's proto-mental concept.[13]

4. Conclusion

The above discussion yields some very interesting conclusions, suggesting that both men were influenced by the same source of vitalist ideas in philosophy, namely Henri Bergson, and further that Jung's ideas influenced Bion directly. Both the psychoid concept and the proto-mental concept profit from a similar debt to vitalism with a conceptual notion of an ultimately unknowable, deeply unconscious layer, in which the individual has no distinctiveness and body and mind are undifferentiated. This layer is a source of very primitive states, that may manifest as much physically as psychically, and out of it organisation and a differentiated consciousness arise.

However, the two men ultimately developed entirely different accounts of the clinical situation associated with such a layer. Jung went on to expand this vitalist background in his search for living meaning in his psychoid concept, while Bion developed his proto-mental concept in his group work towards an understanding of psychosis.

Jung's mature thinking

It is interesting to note that Jung's psychoid concept originated in his early interest in vitalism and his investigation of vision-making, including his own active imagination, as demonstrated in *The Red Book* and discussed in the previous chapter. This started Jung on an imaginal approach to his own unconscious psychic material, and later to the unconscious in general, something he elaborated further with his subsequent studies of the *I Ching* and Eastern thinking (beginning with his association with Richard Wilhelm), and his study of alchemy. It was a trajectory that led him to a realisation of a transcendent reality, and to a psychoid concept emphasising the prospective function, living meaning and numinous aspects of a deeply unknowable unconscious realm.

Bion's group work

Bion, by contrast, effectively went on to elaborate on his early war experience. Torres and Hinshelwood (2013) cite various influences on Bion's thinking, including Wilfred Trotter, whom Bion encountered during his medical internship at University College Hospital. As Francesca Bion writes in her introduction to *The Long Weekend*, Trotter played a very great part in Bion's intellectual development (Bion, 1982).

At this time, towards the end of the 1920s, Trotter (1916) had long published his acclaimed work *Instincts of the Herd in Peace and War*. He drew his ideas on groups from biology, citing the bee as an example of instinctual behaviour with its sensitivity to the hive. In this work he not only identified a clear link between individual and group behaviour, describing the two fields of the social and the individual as absolutely continuous (Trotter, 1916, p. 12), but also attributed to man three primary instincts: self-preservation, nutrition and sex, plus in addition a herd instinct (ibid., p. 97). He noted the extent to which man embodies the voice of the herd, with his tendency to affirm beliefs sanctioned by the herd, no matter how far such beliefs may be opposed by the evidence (ibid., p. 39). Such wholesale acceptance of non-rational belief is:

> invariably regarded by the holder as rational . . . while the position of one who holds contrary views is held to be obviously unreasonable. . . . The difference is due rather to the fundamental assumptions of the antagonists being hostile, and these assumptions are derived from herd suggestion
>
> (Ibid., p. 37)

Trotter pointed out that sensitivity to the group leads to mental instability (ibid., p. 64).

Torres (2013a, pp. 17, 19) notes that the influence of Trotter's vitalistic work on Bion's ideas is plain.

Both Trotter and McDougall with their studies of groups, large and small, formed a backdrop to Bion's understanding of group dynamics, as he described in the series of papers and the book entitled *Experiences in Groups* (1961). The papers divide into three sections, containing chronologically different accounts, published respectively in 1943 (*Intra-Group Tensions in Therapy*, written with Rickman), 1948–1951 (*Experiences in Groups I-VII*) and 1952 (*Group Dynamics: A Re-View*). These sets of papers contain Bion's evolving ideas concerning group processes, starting in the first section with observations from his work with Rickman at Northfield Hospital.

In the second section, he includes an account of his work with therapeutic groups at the Tavistock Clinic. And, in *Re-View*, the third section, he applies ideas from psychoanalysis, particularly the theory of Melanie Klein, to his earlier views on group dynamics.

During the second period, he came to classify different groups based on "group mentality", meaning the "unanimous expression of the will of the group", which ensures that group life proceeds according to one of a certain number of basic assumptions from which emotional reinforcement is derived (Bion, 1961, p. 101). He identified three such basic assumption mentalities, namely the fight-flight group, the pairing group, and the dependent group.[14] He saw each basic assumption mentality as modelling itself unconsciously on a structure suited to the relevant assumption and as being associated with related emotional states, and each as excluding the emotional states associated with the other two basic assumptions. Basic assumption activity, according to Bion, requires no experience or mental development: it is instantaneous, inevitable and instinctive.

He observed that basic assumption mentalities tended to be opposed to learning by experience and to alternate, rather than conflict, with one another. However, as soon as it is perceived that there is a need to develop rather than rely on the efficacy of magic, a more sophisticated group comes into being, which privileges the value of a rational and scientific approach to problems and displays a more differentiated level of consciousness. Bion called this the "work group", and described it as one that learns by experience. Such a group is associated with one of the basic assumptions and mobilises the associated emotions in an attempt to cope with those of the others, which it suppresses, and this gives rise to conflict.

Conflict manifests at an individual level, since the individual is faced with the choice of identifying himself with the unconscious emotional state of the group or, in his wish to develop as an individual, with the more sophisticated conscious approach of the work group. Persecutory distress may arise when an individual finds himself caught in this conflict.

Bion postulated the existence of the proto-mental system, in which body and mind are undifferentiated, to account for the dynamics then occurring. He described the proto-mental system as a matrix, from which spring phenomena constituting prototypes of the three basic assumptions and also precursors to the emotional states respectively associated with the basic assumptions. Those basic assumptions that are excluded by the particular one that is operating in a given work group are confined to the proto-mental arena, since it is only the basic assumption associated with the work group task that has been able to develop freely. Proto-mental events cannot be understood by reference to the individual alone, being predicated on the dynamics of individuals meeting together in a group; these events are therefore a function of the group. Thus, the origins of such phenomena must be sought in two places, namely the relationship of the individual with the group as a participant in the group work, and the basic assumptions that are excluded by the task of the group (ibid., pp. 102–103).

As Bion says of the proto-mental system, "since it is a level in which physical and mental are undifferentiated, it stands to reason that when distress from this source manifests itself, it manifests itself just as well in physical forms as in psychological" (ibid., p. 102). This is the source of group diseases having physical and psychological components, even though they may manifest in an individual alone. According to Bion, in this second stage of his thinking, the undifferentiated area is activated in the individual by his participation in the group, and the individual expresses a group pathology.

Bion then goes on, in the third section, to apply ideas developed from his psychoanalytic training and his analysis with Melanie Klein to his thinking on groups. He had foreshadowed this step by stating in the second section that the apparent difference between individual psychology and group psychology is an illusion (ibid., p. 134). The forward to *Experiences in Groups*, written after the original papers in the second section with the benefit of hindsight, confirms this view, stating "I am impressed, as a practising psychoanalyst, by the fact that the psycho-analytical approach, through the individual, and the approach these papers describe, through the group, are dealing with different facets of the same phenomena" (ibid., p. 8).

In the third section, Bion relates stability in a group to work group functioning and to Freud's view of the family and neurotic patterns, and instability to basic assumption functioning and to psychotic patterns. In the initial 1952 version of this paper, he refers to Klein's account of schizoid mechanisms to describe the obliteration of individuality and automaton-like behaviour in a basic assumption group; and the use of splitting and projective identification in such a group in the face of pre-verbal psychotic anxiety, with the accompanying persecutory feelings and bizarre elements (Bion, 1952, pp. 242–247). In a later version, he describes basic assumption formations as secondary to an extremely primitive primal scene that is much more bizarre than the classical account offered by Freud, and that is worked out on a level characteristic of the paranoid-schizoid position of Klein, in which primitive oedipal conflicts manifest on a "foundation of part-object relationships" (Bion, 1961, p. 162). According to Bion, the adult in the group regresses to mechanisms typical of the earliest phases of mental life, in which a primitive primal scene appears to be operating and "a part of one parent, the breast or the mother's body, contains amongst other objects a part of the father" (ibid., p. 164). He suggests that these psychotic dynamics apply not only to a sick group, but rather may be found in every group (ibid., p. 181).

In this respect, the association of theories from psychoanalysis with ideas concerning groups leads to a view of the analytic encounter as a group of two people, a link Bion makes himself (ibid., p. 131). He attributes a group mentality to the individual alone, describing the individual as having a group mentality or "groupishness", in the sense that the social instinct exists whether or not the individual is present in a group situation (ibid.).

The real importance of this, although not specifically stated in *Experiences in Groups*, is that it points to Bion's subsequent ideas on psychosis for further explication of the proto-mental system, particularly to publications where he elaborates on Klein's work on the paranoid-schizoid position and on the mechanisms of projective identification and splitting.

This is confirmed by: first, the parallel, just mentioned, that Bion himself draws between the functioning of the group and the individual (1952); second, a chronological interweaving of his papers on psychosis and on groups; and third, his own observations in *Re-View* that primitive mechanisms, peculiar to paranoid-schizoid functioning, occupy a central position in group dynamics (1952, pp. 245–247). Not only did he indicate that the same psychotic phenomena arise in individual psychoanalytic work and in group work, but also he was already generating clinical writing (*The Imaginary Twin*) on his analytic work before he had published the final paper of the second section and his *Re-View* of the third section (Bion, 1950c, 1951, 1952).

In *The Imaginary Twin*, Bion describes certain psychotic mechanisms based on splitting and introjection and projection, stating that he found it impossible to interpret the clinical material,

> as a manifestation of purely psychological development divorced from any concurrent physical development. . . . If this is so, we would have to ask ourselves if these psychological developments . . . come close to the first four months in the individual's life.
>
> (1950c, pp. 21–22)

A comment such as this helps us to see why psychoanalysts such as Grotstein (2007, pp. 192, 258) have sought to make links between Bion's proto-mental system and his subsequent ideas concerning beta elements, which are described by Bion (1967, p. 22) as elements "partaking of the quality of psychic object and inanimate object without any form of distinction between the two".

In *Re-View*, Bion (1952, pp. 246–247) describes the basic assumption group in terms of psychotic anxiety and obliteration of the individual, in which splitting dynamics and schizoid mechanisms apply. Bion's subsequent papers in *Second Thoughts* (1967) describe such psychotic mechanisms in detail, discussing the distinctions between the non-psychotic personality or part of the personality and the psychotic personality or part of the personality. The latter has a hatred of reality and resorts to excessive use of projective identification in order to rid itself of the perceptual awareness of sense impressions, and becomes persecuted by the expelled fragments and feels surrounded by bizarre objects. Although Bion does not designate the bizarre objects as proto-mental phenomena, nevertheless he describes them in terms of an undifferentiated psyche and soma and unmanageable distress (emotion), thereby suggesting that he is thinking of them in the same way.

Likewise, in his group work, Bion links proto-mental phenomena with intense emotion belonging to one of the basic assumptions, with primitive anxiety, and with the psychotic parts of the personality. Therefore, it would seem fair to assume that his later description of psychotic functioning in *Second Thoughts* is relevant to such phenomena.

In summary, Bion's account of proto-mental phenomena associates them with groups, group mentality, instinctive basic assumption functioning, including intense primitive and often persecutory emotion, and psychotic mechanisms.

However, he notes that a development out of the proto-mental matrix leads into emotional experience and psychological states. In other words, although he linked proto-mental phenomena with psychotic elements and anxiety, he does also see them as a function of all group situations, both pathological and healthy.

Conclusion

The above discussion highlights a common vitalistic foundation to Jung's psychoid concept and Bion's proto-mental concept. Both offer a panpsychist or monistic account of a deeply unconscious realm, where body and mind are undifferentiated and in which the individual has no distinctiveness, out of which organisation and a differentiated consciousness arises. Likewise, both designate this layer as ultimately unknowable, seeing it as a source of very primitive states, that may manifest as much physically as psychically, and may be encountered in regression.

However, from this origin and out of their lived preoccupations, the two men ultimately developed entirely different accounts of the clinical experiences associated with such a layer.

Jung's thinking evolved further along the abstract lines of his vitalistic forebears, expanding on a biological understanding of instincts into his instinctual image, and thence his archetypal image.[15] His psychoid concept links body and mind, instinct and spirit, with the imaginal and the symbolic, emphasising the teleological aspect of its organising function in the service of individuation. Although he pursued the association of body and mind in his early work, he later came to be more interested in the numinous and the spiritual, and accordingly imported a more transcendental aspect into his psychoid concept.

Bion, by contrast, linked his proto-mental concept directly with fragmentation and psychosis, and with associated clinical factors. Since, in World War I, he was viscerally concerned with the chaotic, fragmentary and undoubtedly claustrophobic experience of being a tank commander near the front line, it is no surprise that this experience informs his proto-mental concept.

This difference in background is very important, because it highlights the experiential roots of the two concepts, and the associated marked differences in their application to clinical work. There is a pronounced development in opposing directions, firstly in terms of Jung's more abstract and universal conceptualisation versus Bion's more clinical and applied application, and secondly in terms of Jung's emphasis on a teleological organising function versus Bion's on fragmented psychotic mechanisms.

A comparison of the two concepts is fruitful, however, not only for furthering understandings of both, but also because each highlights theoretical developments absent in the other, and potentially useful avenues for expanding clinical knowledge.

Notes

1. See Freud's letter of 7 April 1907 (McGuire, 1991, p. 58).
2. Now Post-Traumatic Stress Disorder (PTSD).
3. Displayed at Bovington Museum, Wool, Dorset, and commonly known as a Mother Mark IV.
4. Addison (2009).
5. Bergson (1907[1911], p. 45). The reference is from the English language version, quoted in this paper.
6. The same year that Jung offered to Freud the term "psychoid" to designate the unconscious (Addison, 2009).
7. This reference by Jung alludes to a distinction, made in a presentation entitled *On Psychological Understanding* before the Psycho-Medical Society in London in 1914, between Freud's method and his own (Shamdasani, 2003, p. 64). Based on a view of Freud's method as a causal tracing back to antecedent elements, as compared with his attempt to grasp living meaning through synthesising the symbol into a universal and comprehensible expression, he described Freud's method as reductive and his own as constructive. Later, he came to call his method the synthetic method.
8. The French original was published in 1896.
9. Beckett sought analysis presenting psychosomatic issues, including painful physical symptoms and panic attacks.
10. 1907/1908.
11. Jung's italics.
12. This only followed later, after comments made by Pauli in 1937 to the effect that "modern physics offers a symbolic representation of psychic processes" (Meier, 2001, p. 19) and in 1947–1948, in letters to Jung, and an unpublished essay on Kepler, that "background physics" is of an archetypal nature affording psychological interpretation (ibid., 32–35, p. 180).
13. Bion did not acknowledge this influence.
14. Note the similarity to Trotter.
15. Addison (2009).

Chapter 5

The post-Jungians and the psychoid concept

Introduction

The post-Jungians have developed Jung's ideas concerning the psychoid concept in a considerable variety of directions. It is beyond the scope of this chapter to explore all of them, and therefore a single main theme will be selected, relating to a biologically based understanding, founded in the ideas of the neo-vitalist and philosopher Hans Driesch. Some background sets this strand in context.

Background

Jung's main writings on the subject of his psychoid concept are in *On the Nature of the Psyche* (1947/1954) and *Synchronicity: An Acausal Connecting Principle* (1952).

Hans Driesch (1903) is acknowledged in the former, and a footnote directs the reader to *Die "Seele" als Elementarer Naturfaktor*, in which Driesch published an early vitalist account of his experimental researches on sea urchins. His experiments demonstrated a teleological urge in the organism towards goals of wholeness in the future, and formed the basis for his concept *Das Psychoid*. From this point, the history traces the evolution of the concept through its vitalist development in the further ideas of Hans Driesch and in those of Eugen Bleuler, director of the Burghölzli Clinic. Driesch published accounts of *Das Psychoid*, and likewise gave lectures, most notably in the annual series on natural theology, the Gifford Lectures, in both English and German (1907/1908), and Bleuler also published in both languages, starting with his *Die Psychoide als Prinzip der Organischen Entwicklung* (1925).

Jung took up the concept early in his career, first referring to the psychoid in the famous 1907 meeting with Freud as a suitable designation for the unconscious, presumably, given the timing, referring to the nomenclature of Driesch (McGuire, 1991, p. 58). Based on this original foundation, Jung went on to develop a vitalistic understanding of the concept in terms of his archetypes of the collective unconscious, embracing an unknowable dimension characterised by a unified or monistic view of body and mind ("bodymind") in a teleological field. The evolution of the psychoid concept in his work took place in two phases: namely an initial phase, dating from the 1907 reference, grounded in biology and vitalism and addressing the relationship of body, mind and spirit; and a later phase, dating from 1937, associated with quantum physics and addressing the relationship of mind and matter. Jung's mature work links the psychoid concept with synchronicity, his earliest recorded discussions of synchronicity arising in his *Dream Seminars*, when he developed a line of thinking from internal and external events that "synchronise", to the notion of "synchronism" in Eastern forms of thinking, to his invention of the term "synchronicity" to cover coinciding but unconnected events (Jung, 1928–1930). Subsequently, Jung began his collaboration with the Nobel Prize–winning physicist Wolfgang Pauli, who suggested in 1937 that "modern physics offers a symbolic representation of psychic processes" (Meier, 2001, p. 19); and in 1947–1948 in letters to Jung, and an unpublished essay giving rise to two lectures to the Zurich Psychological Club on Kepler, that "background physics" is of an archetypal nature affording both psychological interpretation and a basis in modern physics (ibid., pp. 32–35, 180). Together, Jung and Pauli then conceived a development of the psychoid concept based in quantum physics, covering a panpsychic view of mind and matter generally.

Thus, Jung's account of the psychoid is derived from biology insofar as it concerns a monistic view of the body-mind issue, and from physics insofar as it concerns a panpsychic view of the matter-mind issue, and chronologically he moved from the former to the latter, in both instances, however, situating the psychoid in the unknowable and irrepresentable depths of the unconscious. This move took him from a vitalist base, wherein the origins of consciousness are embedded in living, organic matter, to an *unus mundus*[1] embracing mind and inorganic as well as organic matter. He presented his later ideas on the psychoid concept as an extension of his earlier ones, and, once he had adopted his later thinking, he then applied it ex post facto to his understanding of the relation between body and mind.

It is to be noted, however, that Jung's earlier understandings of the psychoid and his later understandings of synchronicity are conceptually different. The former may be conceived as a teleological ordering factor, immanent as potential in the stuff of the organism, serving to create an emergent dynamic by which the life process of the organism unfolds. The latter, by contrast, pertains to a form of knowledge or meaning arising when two or more events that are not causally related nonetheless have a meaningful connection. The latter at least arguably supervenes on the former, but may not underpin it, whereas the former may usefully be understood without reference to the latter.

This same division occurs also in the post-Jungian community, both theoretical and most especially clinical. Writers such as Dieckmann (1974, 1976,

1980), Clark (1996, 2006), Merchant (2006) and Stevens (1995) focus primarily on the biological approach to a monistic bodymind, whilst others, such as Fordham (1957, 1962), Aziz (1990, 2007), Von Franz (1992), Zabriskie (1995), Bright (1997), Meier (2001), Main (2004, 2007), Gieser (2005), Hogenson (2005), Cadigan, (2007), Cambray (2002, 2009), Colman (2011), Haule (2011), Giegerich (2012), Atmanspacher (2014), Atmanspacher & Fach (2013) and Connolly (2015), focus on an *unus mundus* embracing mind and matter, synchronicity, the occurrences of meaningful coincidences, their unknowability, and their associations with quantum physics.

Accordingly, a conceptual bifurcation exists, both originally in Jung's work and contemporaneously in the post-Jungian community, one aspect of which characterises the psychoid as a deeply unknowable layer of the unconscious instantiating processes that are neither physiological nor psychological but that somehow partake of both (Jung, 1947/1954). This aspect, concerning a living relation of body and mind founded in biology, has given rise to an associated corpus of theory and practice in the post-Jungian community, in which Jung started a rigorous and fertile tradition of research. It is this latter aspect which is the focus of the present chapter.

The biological conception of the psychoid

There are a variety of different strands within this research tradition. A number of scholars amongst the post-Jungians have focused on Jung's model for the archetypes, including respectively their nature, their function, both in infant development and in social structuring, and their manifestations as archetypal images, while other researchers have respectively focused more on clinical issues, including dissociation, active imagination, the transference and technique. These studies are discussed below, acknowledging that there is considerable overlap between them. Clinical references are also included, since knowledge advances on the basis of clinical experience as well as study.

1. Research on archetypes and the psychoid concept

a. The social implications of archetypes

Scholarly accounts by Progoff (1953, 1959) and Gray (1996) review the social applications of Jung's archetypes, starting with the early developmental environment of the infant.

Working towards his doctoral dissertation on the social meaning of Jung's psychology, Progoff (1953) submitted a copy to the Bollingen Foundation, and Cary Baynes, one of the Foundation's advisors, forwarded it to Jung, asking her daughter Ximena de Angulo to record Jung's comments. The transcript of their discussion was placed in the archives of the Foundation and discovered nearly twenty years later (Jung, 1977). Throughout, Jung repeatedly emphasised the experimental, empirical nature of his work. He referred to Levy-Bruhl's conception of *participation mystique* as the manner by which society contains the individual in a state still undifferentiated from others, and to individuation as a natural process of differentiating a piece of the archetype out of the *participation mystique* (ibid., pp. 215–216).

The thesis of Progoff,[2] incorporating Jung's comments, refers to the history-making function of the psyche that takes up the symbol alive in the depths of the unconscious and adapts it to the cultural time and place in which the individual lives, the motifs that emerge expressing the basic phases of the process of individuation (1953). Every psychic process is related to the fact that the human being has a body, and psychic factors emerge out of a physiological context. Progoff points out that:

> [Jung] is not thinking in terms of an inter-relationship between the physical and the psychological, and not of a parallelism either. When we go one step back beyond psychology, and when we go one step back beyond biology, we reach a point at which they are not differentiated from each other and at which neither biologic nor psychologic characteristics can be specifically discriminated. We come to a third category which is neither biological nor psychological, but in which the rudiments of each are contained.
>
> (Ibid., pp. 190–191)

When the primal element in man begins to differentiate itself, it breaks into biological and psychological aspects. The thesis does not refer to the psychoid unconscious, although the above is a good description, but in a later work Progoff elaborated some interesting ideas on the vitalist nature of the psychoid realm (1959).

Based on the ideas of Jan Christian Smuts on man's place in biological evolution, Progoff noted that the development of personality is to be understood "in terms of a single dynamic principle present in the seed of the organism and working towards unfoldment, the ultimate goal being to develop a scientific understanding of the creative, emergent nature of human personality" (ibid., pp. 100–101). He also borrowed from the work of the biologist Edmund Sinnott, for whom the primary material of the life process is *protoplasm*, seen not as a substance but as a system, a guiding principle inherent in every organism (ibid., pp. 116–118). Acknowledging both Jung and Driesch, he observed that there is a purposiveness implicit in the structure of the organism, a "psych-like"[3] activity of growth leading to dawning consciousness:

> Mind and body are both expressions of protoplasm moving towards a purpose in terms of the nature of a particular organism.
>
> (Ibid., p. 121)

This led Progoff to conceptualise a protoplasmic image directing the human organism, both individually and as a species, in its basic drive towards individual wholeness and the preservation of life, such imagery having two functions, namely to provide *in potentio* the instinctive spontaneous patterns of behaviour that represent the basic life tasks of the human organism and to provide the underlying patterns by which man apprehends and gives life meaning. The former drive the growth of the infant, its instinctive careseeking behaviour and gradual acquisition of tasks, and dramatise themselves in the way in which the individual chooses to live out his individual life; and the latter provide his source of creativity in the symbolic forms that emerge into consciousness and impart meaning to his life both individually and on a cultural level, ultimately embracing art and civilisation.

Accordingly, Progoff adopts the vitalist views of Jung with respect to the archetype, and with his protoplasmic imagery embraces both Jung's instinctual image and his archetypal image.

Acknowledging Progoff as a major influence, Gray locates the fundamental ground of the archetype in the psychoid unconscious, defined as a "foundational biological state or condition below the level of the psyche that gives rise to psychic contents" (1996, p. 287). He notes Jung's description of the archetypes as psychoid elements originating in the living patterns of the organism and embarks on an analysis of the nature and meaning of archetypal images, commenting, "it is at the psychoid pole nearest the biological that we can best discover the roots of archetypal activity" (ibid., p. 17).

For Gray, the archetypal image is "an emergent property of the interaction between psychoid and biological processes occurring at the lower levels of integration", expressing the biological and psychological needs of the organism (ibid., pp. 51, 54).

According to Gray, Progoff's protoplasmic image encompasses within itself the goal, the energy necessary to reach that goal, the outer stimuli upon which that end depends, and the pattern of behaviour needed to reach the end, all occurring on a level far below consciousness in the biological history of the individual (ibid., p. 160). Gray also acknowledges affect images described by Redfearn (1973), which may include a characteristic pattern and level of energy; and evocative and recognitive memory according to Fraiburg (1969), which reactivates the affective tone of earlier experience including muscle tonus, visceral response and physical state. In Gray's view, these are all associated with the psychoid realm of the unconscious, including even further a level of reflex movement and physiological response, and an organ level featuring tropisms, accommodations and assimilations responsive to stimuli (ibid., pp. 52–54).

Hence, Gray posits different *levels* of archetypal patterning, starting from a most basic psychoid level rooted in the rhythmic movements and genetically determined characteristics of the organism, out of which emerge first instinctual and reflex actions, and then the instinctual patterns relating to the significant events of life, such as birth, death, kinship, sexuality and so forth (ibid., pp. 72–75). He links this with human development, suggesting that, in the early months of life, psychoid processes give rise to an archetypal psychic core, through a pairing of the innate biological element with the environmental encounters with the parents. These interactions feed back into the biological system and become the visual, affective, visceral and bodily foundation for the archetypal image (ibid., pp. 62–63). Such images become available to our conscious perception to be registered and assimilated. In this way, the psyche of the infant first emerges and then interacts with both the environment and internal experience, as a social being.

As can be seen from the above review, Progoff and Gray adhere to a developmental/emergent view of archetypes, seeing them as having an organising function giving rise to instinctual patterning and archetypal imagery. And an underlying psychoid factor, present in a unitary and unknowable psycho-physical reality, is seen as the origin of this dynamism.

b. The nature of archetypes

More recently, Stevens (1990, 1995, 2006), Knox (2003) and Merchant (2006, 2012) have linked Jung's theory of archetypes with research in other fields, the first and the last incorporating observations on his psychoid concept. Knox omits any reference to this concept but is useful for her rigorous approach to a contemporaneous understanding of archetypes.

Stevens (1995, 2006) holds an evolutionary view of Jung's ideas, considering that archetypes are the deposits of our ancestral experience embedded as predisposition in the inherited dynamic system, and are thus made manifest through the body. He contemplates the evolutionary history of our species, relating the archetypes to universal patterns of behaviour and drawing parallels with ethology, evolutionary psychology and evolutionary psychiatry. Describing the archetypes as possessing a fundamental duality, psychic and non-psychic, spirit and body, he envisages their psychoid aspect as the bridge between the opposing elements, inherent in the underlying unitary reality of the *unus mundus*.

Knox (2003, p. 24) reviews Jung's various accounts of the archetypes and observes that he offers four different models: biological entities hardwired into the genes for instructing mind and body; organising mental frameworks of an abstract nature; core meanings containing representational content; and metaphysical entities that are independent of the body. She takes issue with a view of the archetypes as innate and points out that these different definitions give rise to confusion, something which detracts from the value of Jung's ideas. She also takes Stevens to task for the same ambiguity. Her own study makes links with attachment theory and neuroscience, positing that "mind and meaning emerge out of developmental processes and the experience of interpersonal relationships" (ibid., pp. 10–11). She concludes that the archetypes emerge out of a developmental interaction between genes and environment to organise day-to-day experience and create patterns or image schemas forming the foundation for the growth of core meanings (ibid., p. 8).

Merchant (2006, 2012), making links with anthropology in a study of Siberian shamanism, also proposes a developmental understanding of the archetype. He refers to Knox (2003) and her emergent/developmental approach, which understands archetypes as developmentally produced mind/brain structures, providing implicit "internal working models", and thus sees archetypes as an emergent phenomenon and not innate. In his view, her approach provides a way to explain the psycho-physical nature of Jung's psychoid factor underpinning the archetypes, wherein archetypal imagery arises out of neural bio-structures laid down in early infancy as a result of developmental experience.

Merchant highlights the way in which these internal working models are initially produced, and later activated, by intense affectivity, the later activation "in terms of imagery and numinous affect [being] due to the similarity of the person's current emotional experiences with those which formed the mind/brain structure in the first place" (2012, p. 156). Because the origins are so early, and the affectivity so intense, the opposite poles of the archetype split. Applying this to a case study from the Siberian Sakha (Yakut) tribe, he isolates a proto-borderline aspect resulting from trauma in the early mother-infant dyad, as a result of their societal practices and customs. This leads him to a view of Siberian shamanism as a display of expressions of such developmentally produced archetypal mind/brain structure.

All of the above researchers give psycho-physical accounts of the archetypes and their relationships with living processes and meaning, and most of them locate the archetypes in relation to an underlying psychoid reality.

2. Clinical perspectives on the psychoid concept

These theoretical accounts supporting the biological base of Jung's psychoid concept are elaborated clinically by Jacobi (1959) and others associating the psychoid concept with dissociation, and are followed by various further clinical accounts, which shed light on the ways in which the psychoid concept is employed contemporaneously in the analytic setting with respect to human development. Particularly, Jacobi (1959), Kalsched (1996), Sidoli (2000) and Proner (2005), respectively, make links with dissociation and anxiety in early development. Redfearn (1973) discusses the early formation of archetypal imagery, and Moore (1972, 1986) and Schaverien (2005, 2007) relate the psychoid concept to archetypal imagery and active imagination. Gordon (1993) and Clark (1996, 2006) bring in a vitalist view associated with early development and the transference, and Dieckmann (1974, 1976, 1980) and Samuels (1985a) focus specifically on the countertransference.

a. Dissociation

Jung (1902, para. 5) initially linked dissociation with hysteria, when body and mind co-operate to produce split-off somnambulisms.[4] Later, he generalised his views, describing how little it takes to shatter the unity of consciousness and form a state of secondary consciousness, representing:

> [A] personality component which has not been separated from ego-consciousness by mere accident, but which owes its separation to definite causes. Such a dissociation has two distinct aspects: in the one case [. . .] an originally conscious content [. . .] was repressed on account of its incompatible nature: in the other case, the secondary subject consists essentially in a process that never entered into consciousness because no possibilities exist there of apperceiving it.
> (1947/1954, para. 366)

Jacobi (1959) was in a unique position to elaborate on Jung's ideas, being for many years his close associate, in that she studied and had an analysis with him, and was one of the founders and directors of the C. G. Jung Institute in Zurich.[5] She saw such personality components representing a secondary consciousness as an expression of hidden complexes appearing first as symptoms, and by elaborating on their origin in the psychoid realm, she succeeded in moving the psychoid concept into the clinical arena (Jacobi, 1959, pp. 118–121). Unconscious contents connect the conscious mind in one direction with physiological states and in the other direction with numinous experience. Jacobi points out, however, that in referring to the "psychoid" realm as instinctive or spiritual, "one is making a statement about something concerning which, because it is unconscious, no statement can be made. One can only describe the effects that emanate from it" (ibid., p. 61n).

Describing the archetype as such as beyond apprehension, belonging to the psychoid realm only as a structural factor and potentiality (ibid., p. 119), she noted that, in certain constellations present from birth, the archetype brings forth particular "patterns". Emerging from the psychoid background, the archetypes have an ordering effect on psychic processes and also on the contents of consciousness, generating psychic manifestations of a biological, psychobiological or ideational character, including psychic and/or somatic symptoms (ibid., p. 34) and living symbols pregnant with meaning (ibid., p. 72).

Significantly, the archetype as such is present in the healthy and the sick alike. The content, with which the archetype when constellated becomes filled, may suffer a variety of fates, being assimilated to a greater or lesser degree. In the case of a healthy ego, the resulting disturbances can be resolved and integrated and employed as a catalyst for psychic development; the archetype is thus neutralised. In the case of a weak ego, the content is rejected by the ego to become an autonomous splinter psyche, producing symptoms and hallucinations, as in psychosis. The determining factor is not the content of the archetypal image but the state of consciousness confronting it (ibid., p. 122).

Thus, in Jacobi's account, psychoid processes promote archetypal activity, producing living symbols when the constellated material is integrated, and dissociative states when the ego becomes overwhelmed by archaic affects arising out of the constellated material. This is an important clarification of the effects of psychoid processes, emphasising their links with body and mind dependent on the critical function of the ego.

Kalsched (1996) relates this with infant development, proposing that the infant world is composed of sensations of comfort and discomfort, interspersed by primitive affects that assail the vulnerable infant psyche like volcanic storms. The infant relies completely on his mother for mediation of their effect and, when mothering is satisfactory, the infant's experience is metabolised and gradually converted into an ego capable of containing such affects. Without mediation, the infant psyche becomes overwhelmed and forms a "total" defence to protect a fundamental aspect of his being. An internal agency steps in and dismembers the psyche in order to encapsulate and keep separate unmanageable experience. Kalsched observes that both extremes of the body-mind spectrum, that is, the instinctual and spiritual archetypal poles in the psychoid unconscious, tend to carry the dissociation in this case.

Sidoli (2000, pp. 52, 92) associates Jung's psychoid concept with psychosis originating in early infancy. When there is a failure of maternal reverie, opposing archetypal forces of a psychophysiological nature, that are unmanageable for the young infant, split the two poles of archetypal experience into body and psyche, and archaic bodily elements remain lodged in the body as symptoms and do not reach mental representation. She notes that these primitive elements often manifest in analysis as unintegrated psychotic pockets.

According to these sources, therefore, psychoid processes promote archetypal activity in the face of constellating events, and generate dissociative states when the ego of the individual becomes overwhelmed by archaic affects arising from the constellated material.

Proner (2005) focusses on anxiety, contemplating the relationship between physical and mental states of anxiety. He refers to Jung's comment to Bion in the Tavistock Lectures that "the psychic fact and the physiological fact come together in a peculiar way" (Jung, 1935, para. 136), and links this with Jung's representation of the archetypes by the electromagnetic spectrum and conceptualisation that they have a psychoid pole that is outside mind (Proner, 2005, p. 313). He then considers how somatic states in the consulting room may be mediated to become thought, since psychosomatic phenomena do not readily respond to verbal interpretation of content, and the emotional experience that cannot be dreamt must be discovered. He gives an example from a week of sessions, in which the patient progresses from a focus on pains in the gut, through desolate longings for physical contact that result in weeping, to painful verbal expressions and representations of anxiety. Noting a psychotic quality to the defences, he proposes that change takes place through meaningful emotional experience within an I-Thou relationship, in which a trend can be discerned, "from 'proto-mental' sensations with (painful) physical facts, to physical facts with meaning, on through to meaningful-painful emotional experience and mental representation" (ibid., pp. 321, 325).

b. The archetypes and development

Further review of the links between the psychoid unconscious and development, in normal circumstances, comes from Redfearn (1973, 1994) and Gordon (1993), for example.

Redfearn (1973, 1994) links Jung's psychoid processes with the pre-reflective level of the primal or infant self, where bodily experience is archetypal. In his view, frustration, arising when there is a less than perfect fit between the organism and the environment, triggers such processes and promotes spontaneous psycho-physical events and primordial images. Interaction between archetypal bodily activity and the individual's conscious adaptation to the here-and-now generates affective experience that ultimately shapes itself into patterns and images. Redfearn (1973, 1994) describes the archetypal image as the imaginal aspect of affective or emotional behaviour and experience, and, on this ground, he refers to it as an *affect-image*. Affect-images are activated by unintegrated parts of the self when libido is blocked, and thereby emerge and become conscious and available for integration. Hence, archetypal imagery may be considered to relate to an emergent part of the Self (1973, p. 128).

Gordon (1993) associates psychoid processes with a normal developmental stage prior to the differentiation of psyche and soma, describing Jung's psychoid concept as a reference to the basic substance which, in the course of development, both personal and collective, differentiates into body and mind. She suggests that such processes are the expression of the basic drive towards fusion and wholeness, experienced first of all between mother and baby. They manifest particularly in projective identification, which has as its goal the undoing of boundaries and separateness between people to produce shared experience.

c. Archetypal imagery and active imagination

Jung's practice of active imagination, by which archetypal ideas are explored and personalised through creative physical expression, has also engendered a fertile post-Jungian research tradition, as described, for example, by Dieckmann (1971, 1974, 1976, 1980), Moore (1972, 1986), Schaverien (2005, 2007) and Swan (2000, 2008, 2011).[6] Likewise, clinical accounts of active imagination in analysis are given by a number of post-Jungians, including Cwik (1991, 2011), Davidson (1966), Fordham (1955, 1977) and Schaverien (2005, 2007).

Jung applied the practice of active imagination in his own analytic work, as described in *On the Nature of the Psyche*, where he notes the manifestation of certain well-defined themes and formal elements, arising as if guided by unconscious regulators (1947/1954, para. 401):

> And so it is with the hand that guides the crayon or brush, the foot that executes the dance-step, with the eye and the ear, with the word and the thought: a dark impulse is the ultimate arbiter of the pattern, an unconscious *a priori* precipitates itself into plastic form, and one has no inkling that another person's consciousness is being guided by these same principles at the very point where one feels utterly exposed to the boundless vagaries of chance. Over the whole procedure there seems to reign a dim foreknowledge not only of pattern but of its meaning. Image and meaning are identical; and as the first takes shape, so the latter becomes clear. Actually, the pattern needs no interpretation: it portrays its own meaning. There are cases where I can let interpretation go as a therapeutic requirement.
>
> (1947/1954, para. 402)

Later, he described his method as:

> [A]t bottom, a purely experiential process in which hit and miss, interpretation and error, theory and speculation, doctor and patient, form a *symptosis* . . . or a *symptoma* . . . – a coming together – and at the same time are symptoms of a certain process or run of events.
>
> (1947/1954, para. 421)

These early accounts are considered by Davidson (1966), who proposed that the transference itself, and the entire unconscious drama of the analysand enacted through the transference, could be seen as active imagination. She points out that the patient may be unable themselves to symbolise, being able only to project onto the analyst as carrier. In these circumstances, the analyst must process the unconscious projection through practising their own active imagination.

Moore (1972) develops this further in a study of countertransference. Contemplating the analyst's part in the process of change in analysis, she (Moore, 1972, 59) suggests that ego development involves "the gradual separation out of the archetypes, which are at first experienced in terms of bodily feeling and later on in play, make believe and fairy-tales", in the presence of an adequately containing environment.

In a study of 129 analytic sessions from 15 patients, recorded over a period of four weeks, she monitored the transference process, her introspections, and her interpretations, whereby to investigate how the Jungian notion of amplification[7] affects the transference process (Moore, 1986). She begins with a personal account of a visit to the Yad Vashem memorial to victims of the Holocaust, and of an experience of feelings of nausea, physical symptoms and primitive body sensations. Her approach to managing this was to seek associations of a cultural, collective and mythological nature, until these led her to childhood sense memories of soft fur and blackness. She noted that this process of amplification rendered the unmanageable manageable. She applied this in her clinical study, observing that it is fruitless to make clinical interpretations when concrete somatisation occurs in the countertransference. Instead, she takes a "self" or "non-ego" position, which may be related to Jung's notion of an *unus mundus*,[8] associated by Jung with the psychoid nature of the archetype (Jung, 1958, para. 852). She works this through in her own mind, making use of her own introspections and referring back to the personal individual body basis of her own earliest maternal relationship, until symbols begin to emerge. Thus, the analyst's somatic concretisation may give way to symbolisation, at which point interpretations can be made.

Schaverien (2007) describes active imagination as emerging spontaneously within the imaginal field in between patient and analyst and, likewise, proposes that the analyst employ a method of active imagination to mediate emergent consciousness in the patient. She gives a clinical example, in which the analyst faced by a stuck and silent patient could not shake off a visual image of a wolf, quite the opposite of the apparently mild woman facing her. Through personal amplification of the image, the analyst became aware of the deadness of the silence, the unspoken anger in the patient and the aliveness of the wolf image. This eventually enabled interpretation and movement in the analytic session. In another example, where the patient was able to follow their own imaginative process, the analyst experienced a perceptual distortion, feeling the consulting room as a vast cavern with herself and the patient tiny figures dwarfed within it. She was able to respond from this countertransference, speaking to an infant aspect of the patient and allowing the transference to develop further, which freed the patient. Thus, the analyst employed active imagination in each instance. Even when the patient lacks the capacity to symbolise, the analyst through active imagination may effect a shift from the concrete to the symbolic in themselves on behalf of the patient, and thereby shift the patient's internal attitude.

These accounts emphasise the importance of creative imagination on the part of the analyst in mediating the psychoid unconscious and archetypal processes for the patient. Further, the examples given demonstrate how the technique of active imagination has been adopted as a significant therapeutic instrument.

d. The transference

Various post-Jungian researches have specifically addressed the transference and its relationship with the psychoid concept. One empirical research project of especial interest is the transference study of the Berlin Group (Dieckmann, 1974, 1976, 1980, 1991), which provides evidence for the existence of a very particular type of transference associated with the psychoid concept, wherein the processes of analyst and analysand are synchronised in terms of both body and mind, and a symmetrical dynamic[9] may be seen to be occurring. Another relevant research study is that of Samuels (1985a).

I. BERLIN RESEARCH GROUP

The Berlin Research Group conducted a clinical study between 1969 and 1974. The group, consisting initially of four Jungian analysts, all men, and, after two years, including also a fifth Jungian analyst, a woman, set out to investigate the countertransference "in a situation with proper scientific controls" (Dieckmann, 1974, p. 71). They met for regular fortnightly meetings, each lasting three hours and in each of which one member of the group presented a single analytic session, bringing also the content of the preceding session and the subsequent development of key themes. Thereby, they conducted a regular review of clinical material based on process notes from individual analytic sessions.

The method involved assuming a particular attitude to the transference, neither that of Freud involving "emptying oneself" and focusing solely on the patient and his unconscious by "holding up a mirror to him" nor that of Jung and his example of the rainmaker who is thrown into disharmony by the outer world (the patient's unconscious) and who focuses exclusively on his own reactions to restore inner harmony (ibid., p. 71). Rather, the aim was to find a middle way, and to note side by side in the correct temporal sequence both the analyst's observations of the patient and his observations of his own unconscious processes, since the group wanted to capture their "highly charged emotional thoughts" and also fantasies and "the psychosomatic affects arising from the unconscious" (Dieckmann, 1976, p. 25).

A selection criterion was employed to choose the session to be discussed: In a first research phase, the criterion was an archetypal dream displaying highly charged emotional activity. In a second phase, a random choice was made, selected from a complete series of recorded sessions of the presenting analyst from a given week, irrespective of content. In all, thirty-seven patients contributed to the first phase, and twelve patients contributed to the second phase.

Two examples are given here, demonstrating the manner by which psychic processes of patient and analyst coincide, even in the somatic arena. The fact that such coincidences of process and timing arose repeatedly led the group to certain conclusions discussed below.

The initial example, from the first research phase, concerns a woman of thirty-seven with a borderline condition and a psychotic mother (Dieckmann, 1974, p. 73). The patient brought a dream in which she was wearing a robe, like a devil's, a god's or a king's, or one that might have been worn by Death. She wanted to cast aside the evil, which was represented by the robe. Her friend came, and in her fear she wanted to cling to him, but when she said, "Get thee behind me, Satan", she thought he might think she meant him. She felt terribly afraid, and was beset by doubt and fear whether it really was her friend. This woke her up.

Without emotion, the analyst associated to Mephistopheles, and a scene where Faust thinks he has caught the devil but the devil escapes. The patient then continued that she could never sleep in the same room with her mother without terrible fear, since she imagined her mother would kill her with an axe. At this, the analyst became filled with vital emotion. He re-experienced viscerally his own early childhood fears of death, dying and extinction, all connected with the figure of Faust and *his* entry into another life. Next, the patient went on to speak of her evacuation and complete uprooting as a child. Surprisingly, the analyst saw in his mind's eye a mediaeval city nestling behind the security of its walls, and felt that he had found within himself an emotional stronghold from which to overcome the conflict. *At this very same moment*,[10] the patient reported that, during the evacuation, she had found a safe place of refuge in a local barn. Simultaneously, therefore, analyst and patient found within themselves a safe enclosure from which to face the problem of fear. It is to be noted that this entire scenario took place without interpretation on the part of the analyst.

In the ensuing group discussion of this particular session, the group contemplated the issue of fear between patient and analyst in the transference, and how it was worked out by passing from a confrontation at the level of the personal unconscious, in which the fear was unconsciously transmitted to the analyst through activated personal childhood memories and emotion, to an archetypal encounter, in which both patient and analyst simultaneously experienced the security of a primitive archetypal refuge (mediaeval city). They noted the sequence: archetypal amplifications occur to the analyst around the unsuccessful banishment of the devil, corresponding visceral emotions from childhood become activated in his personal unconscious, and the chain of associations passes into the actual situation. The patient meanwhile stays in her own history, exposed to her severe childhood fears. Then, both the patient and analyst find an archetypal refuge from the distress.

They concluded that the processes of both patient and analyst were somehow simultaneously guided and organised to arrive *in the same moment*[11] at a place of symbolic safety.

The second example, probably, although not explicitly, from the second research phase, demonstrates more clearly these different levels to the transference (Dieckmann, 1976, p. 33). The patient is a twenty-one-year-old woman, suffering from a borderline personality disorder and certain addictions. At the beginning of the session, she recounted a vision of a tramcar standing in the woods. She was obsessed and horrified by it, because she felt it represented an image of a destroyed world. The analyst, by contrast, could not engage with the horror, since to him a tram situated in the woods surrounding Berlin was a natural and commonplace sight.

The patient began repeating the story of the tramcar in a stereotypical fashion, using the same words but with a different emotional inflection. Gradually, this stereotyped repetition engendered in the analyst a memory of a holiday with a friend years previously in a deserted area in the mountains in Turkey. They had driven all day without encountering a soul, when they rounded a corner to find three men with dark suits and top hats in the road, all carrying musical instruments. The incongruity took their breath away. The analyst began to experience a participation in the patient's horror, and *at precisely this moment*[12] the patient uttered, "I can't adapt to this destroyed world. I would rather suffer under it" (Dieckmann, 1976, p. 34).

The analyst then had another memory, this time of a dream brought by another young woman patient from her own earlier adolescence: She was in the street leading to her school, and in front of her was a crowd of people surrounding a young woman of her own age, naked and shivering. They were attacking her body with needles, pens and nails, pinning pieces of paper to her flesh. She looked at the dreamer with a face full of blood and tears, and the dreamer began to cry aloud, because the face was her own.

At this, the analyst became really connected to the sense of horror and destruction, and considered that the patient felt understood. No interpretation had been made.

In this example, Dieckmann writes, the initial part of the session had taken place mainly on the personal and projective level for both analyst and patient, and they had occupied opposed positions of adult/parent and child/daughter. The regulated and conventional adult world was opposing the chaos of youth. The repetition of the imagery by the patient had, however, awoken in the analyst a more archetypal understanding. This enabled the analyst and patient then to enter a participation at a deeper collective level and arrive synchronously at a common understanding from the vital position of youth.

These examples, but most especially the second, give illustrations of two different forms of transference field, respectively in which analyst and patient relate differently, namely through projective processes at the level of the personal unconscious and through participation mystique at the level of the collective unconscious. In the latter, their processes are intertwined and synchronous, and the transference may thus be described as mutual.

The group, attributing the latter transference effects to "unconscious participation", noted repeatedly an extraordinary degree of correspondence between the associations of the analyst and those of the patient in these moments. As one member of the group remarked, "the patients continually say what I am thinking!" Conversely, the group often found amazing similarities between what the patients were saying and the analysts' associations (Dieckmann, 1974, p. 73).

Dieckmann writes:

> What has impressed us most [. . .] is that the usual causal model of transference and countertransference, i.e. of action and reaction or influence and counterinfluence, has not sufficed as a means of grasping the phenomena in question. In a deeper layer underlying the analytical situation there is a synchronistic process regulated by the self.[13]
>
> (1971, p. 83)

Referring to von Franz, the research group divided the transference into a primary archaic (archetypal) level where a primitive identity exists and a projective or personal level (ibid., p. 30). Based on their observations of synchronisation, they concluded that at the archetypal level the psychoid unconscious is organising the dynamics in the analytic dyad in a manner that is entirely mutual and characterised by common unconscious factors. The term *participation mystique* is not employed but would appear to be appropriate.

Dieckmann reported on the research findings:

> When Jung formulated his conception of the archetype *per se*, he characterised this sphere, belonging to the transcendent nature of the archetype, as psychoid. In a letter written in 1951[14] he stated that this transcendent nature of the archetype has the effect of an "arranger" of psychic patterns inside and outside of the psyche. I think we can hardly find a better proof for this concept than through our method of studying the processes of transference and countertransference.
>
> (1976, p. 30)

A footnote to the letter defines the term "psychoid" as a reference to "quasi-psychic 'irrepresentable' basic forms", belonging to the transconscious areas where psychic processes and the physical substrate touch (Adler, 1976, p. 22).

The outcome of these experimental investigations demonstrated that, "the basic foundation of the analytic situation [. . .] is governed by the archetype of the self which is synchronising the chains of associations, that means all the psychic events between two persons" (1976, p. 31).

We also see from the above examples that somatic experiences of emotion arise between patient and analyst. Specifically, the group noted amongst the reported countertransference reactions certain symptoms, including:

> [S]omatic reactions of the analyst in the vegetative as well as the motor sphere, such as pounding of the heart, feeling of strain, tension, fatigue, yawning, scratching, etc. Without exception an area of unconsciousness common to both analyst and patient could be found behind these symptoms.
>
> (Dieckmann, 1974, p. 73)

Whilst Jung developed his understanding of the psychoid concept and its links with the body-mind connection from vitalism and his self-experimentation, he did not specifically extend his findings into the clinical aspect of the transference. The research of the Berlin Group especially addresses this, and yields two important findings.

Firstly, they note two different kinds of transference, according to whether the dyad is in a personal transference field or an archetypal transference field. And, in the case of the latter field, the research demonstrates the existence of a *participation mystique* in the analytic dyad, and the organisation and synchronisation of the processes of analyst and patient throughout the psyche-soma. Here, analyst and patient are in a condition of common understanding and identification, in other words in a symmetrical transference. These findings are of particular interest in their application of the psychoid concept quite directly to the clinical setting, with the extension of the psychoid concept into the arena of the transference.

II. SAMUELS

Another empirical investigation of the transference was also conducted by Samuels (1985a), employing a sample of thirty-two qualified psychotherapists, of unspecified orientation. They were asked to report a few examples of countertransference, classifying the examples according to one of two specified types, defined respectively as: a reflective countertransference, effectively reflecting a mood or state of the patient, as in feeling unaccountably depressed in the session then learning that the patient is in a depressed state in the here and now; and an embodied countertransference, incarnating the patient's emotional experience of a significant other and constituting "a physical, actual, material, sensual expression in the analyst of something in the patient's inner world", for example becoming depressed in a manner echoing the patient's depressed mother (ibid., p. 52). Instances of a neurotic countertransference that might be due to the analyst's own pathology were to be excluded. Twenty-six replies, covering seventy-six examples from fifty-seven patients were received. Of these examples, 46 percent were held by the participants to relate to embodied countertransference and 54 percent to relate to reflective countertransference.

The results were collected, collated and evaluated, and classified into fantasy responses, feeling responses and bodily and behavioural responses. An overall pattern emerged, including a further form of countertransference embracing the imaginal.

Two examples make this plain. The first comprises an embodied fantasy response in a session with a patient who was extremely controlled and watchful of the therapist's slightest reaction. The therapist interpreted the patient as beginning to trust what was inside the therapist, and had a visceral image of a huge black pot with a big belly. Continuing, the therapist said it might be like having a pot to put things in. The patient instantly responded that it was like a wall against which something had been violently hurled. The therapist next had a visceral image of projectile vomiting against a wall (ibid., pp. 55–56). The next comprises a reflective bodily response. The therapist noted she was wearing clothes similar to her woman patient, presenting like a little boy in a school sweater and muddy shoes. The patient had never felt able to relate to her mother. She had allowed herself to be "Daddy's girl" but had avoided incestuous involvement by a little boy strategy, and the therapist had unconsciously picked this up (ibid., p. 56).

These examples bring in the analyst's body, and confirm the aspect of Dieckmann's research demonstrating the way that the body and the mind are bound up with one another, not only in a monistic relationship together in the individual, but also between self and other. Samuels concluded that the analyst may be subject to "bodily visions" in the countertransference "based on the psychoid unconscious in which distinctions between psyche and soma do not apply" (ibid., p. 65). He proposed a theory of a *mundus imaginalis*,[15] defined as a "level of reality, located somewhere between primary sense impressions and more developed cognition and spirituality" (ibid., p. 58). Such an area functions as a mutual relationship between patient and analyst, in line with Jung's transference diagram[16] of a *quaternio* and is thus to be distinguished from projective identification.

III. EMBODIED COUNTERTRANSFERENCE

These researches are supplemented by accounts, from a significant number of post-Jungians, writing about embodiment in the transference, including: Plaut (1956), Fordham (1957), Dieckmann (1974, 1976, 1980), Moore (1972, 1986), Samuels (1985a), Clark (1996, 2006), Proner (2005), Connolly (2015) and Martini (2016), some of whom have already been mentioned above. Stone (2006) has undertaken a research study of embodied forms of countertransference, referring to Dieckmann (1974), McLaughlin (1975),

Field (1989), Schwartz-Salant (1989), McDougall (1989) and Spiegelman (1996). More generally, Sassenfeld (2008) offers a review of approaches to the body in analytical psychology, citing inter alia Sidoli (1993) and Redfearn (2000) on psychosomatic disturbances, Samuels (1985a), Redfearn (2000) and Cambray (2001) on embodied countertransference, Chodorow (1999) and Greene (2001) on body and mind as a monism, and Chodorow (1999) on active imagination.

A number of these, but not all, make specific reference to psychoid processes; others refer more generally to archetypal activity and are included here, since they elaborate the contributions of those who refer to Jung's psychoid concept.

Plaut (1956, pp. 16–17) writes of an archetypal transference, in which the analyst takes on the "image of the archetypal contents" of the transference, becoming the image "bodily" so as to "incarnate" it for the patient. Fordham (1957, pp. 144–145) describes such incarnation as a state of primitive identity, in which the image can be expressed either by the analyst or by the patient. Samuels (1985a, pp. 53, 60), as discussed above, describes this as an "embodied countertransference", in which the analyst experiences "a physical, actual, material, sensual expression" of an internal object of the patient, implying that the analyst's body has become a medium for the patient's transference communications and the analyst may thus be subject to "bodily visions".

Various authors address this embodied countertransference clinically.

Clark (1996, 2006) describes primitive sensations and psychosomatic events experienced between patient and analyst:

> [T]he psychoid level of experience is not only personal, subjective and intrapsychic but vitally it is also interpsychic, between and together, belonging to an intimate mix-up. It is effective in the communications and meta-communications at the level of the autonomic nervous systems as moved and shared between persons in mutual symbolic sensations. As, for example, deeply and at a visceral level, between mother and baby, or in regressive transferences.
>
> (1996, p. 349)

In his model, the patient is operating at a pre-verbal, part-object infantile level, and the transference produces in the analyst psychosomatic sensations and symptoms, as well as imaged body parts and experiences, possibly even making the analyst ill. Clark discusses several clinical examples relating to borderline patients, "for whom developmental lacks and failures have caused an inability to distinguish or differentiate between fantasy and reality, inside and outside, self and other, and who are in a chronic and acute state of body-mind confusion" (2006, p. 68). As he emphasises, however, this area is not only pathological, it is also a normal and necessary pre-differentiated state, which is a natural archetypal aspect of human nature. He sees it as the analyst's parental job to differentiate out his/her reactions, to "help the patient – (and the analyst) – to a new psyche-soma co-ordination" (1996, p. 365).

Greene (2001, p. 566) writes about embodied processing of the countertransference, noting that activated complexes are rooted in bodily reactions "in the psychoid unconscious, that dark place where psyche and soma intersect so profoundly". Using her body as an instrument of perception, by noting her own somatic cues, such as posture, hunger, sleepiness, muscle constriction and breathing rhythms, she seeks to transform sensation into emotion or image, and hence into symbolic understanding. In one example, she repeatedly had the sensation of floating upwards and of being unable to inhabit her own body (Greene, 2001, p. 572). The patient finally revealed that she had recurrent dreams of floating off into outer space, and they could then link this to a lack of binding with a cold, distancing mother. This may be seen as a form of active imagination.

Connolly (2015), referring to Atmanspacher and Fach (2005) and their notion of categorial, non-categorial and acategorial states representing varieties of ordering system, describes different states in the analyst from a categorial state based on a stable ego consciousness to a non-categorial state in regression representing a return to earlier levels of differentiation and integration involving more fluid boundaries between representations of self and other, to acategorial mental states of an unstable or transitive nature. She gives an example from a session where the patient had spoken of a physical sensation of a weight like earth on her stomach (Connolly, 2015, p. 170). Connolly experienced a series of responses in the form of an olfactory image involving the smell of damp earth, a haptic image of earth pressing on a face, and a visual image of a freshly dug grave. She saw this as a move from a categorial to a non-categorial state of mind, enabling her to experience a kind of reverie created in the intersubjective space *between* the two participants (ibid., p. 174).

Martini (2016, p. 7) also contemplates the dialogic aspects of somatic manifestations in the unconscious relationship between analyst and patient, which arise from the level of existence defined by Jung as "psychoid" where "psychic and somatic dimensions co-exist in a substantial unity". He offers the notion that these manifestations may appear in any of three possible ways, namely: as an impediment to the imaginative capacity of the analyst in an attack on linking; as a communication of split-off complexes of the patient; and as a dynamism on the archetypal level having as objective transformation (ibid., p. 10).

An interesting aspect of these studies is the way that the authors are increasingly seeking to classify and describe different forms of transference and different kinds of countertransference response in the realm of embodiment in analysis.

Conclusion

This chapter has described various pieces of scientific and empirical research, and a number of clinical references, serving both to flesh out understandings of the original psychoid concept as proposed by Jung and to ground it in the clinical tradition. This is especially important, because Jung's rather elusive writings on the psychoid concept now become accessible, applied to actual cultural and clinical situations with illustrative examples.

Most especially, the post-Jungian literature addresses the relationships between: archetypal processes arising from the psychoid unconscious and dissociation; active imagination and the integration of archetypal content through the embodied countertransference of the analyst in the service of meaning; and the processes of analysand and analyst in the dialectic that is analysis. Various forms of transference, countertransference and receptive state of mind in the analyst are envisaged.

One key theme, isolated by the Berlin Research Group, is the extent to which psychoid processes manifest in a specialised form of archetypal transference, in which analyst and patient are mutually immersed in an undifferentiated or symmetrical unconscious field. The psychoid processes then take effect in ordering the material emerging into consciousness, in synchronising the associations of analyst and analysand, and in sharing visceral experience between them, in the service of the analytic process. This particular extension of Jung's ideas into the clinical arena helps to elaborate ways of thinking and ways of working with psychoid processes that are not envisaged in his original writings. Later writings, such as those by Samuels (1985a), Connolly (2015) and Martini (2016) supplement this early study by classifying such countertransference in a variety of different ways.

This leads to a contemporary and clinically meaningful understanding of the psychoid concept, as a designation for a deeply unknowable area, thereby limiting what can be said about it, and for an area of undifferentiation, where psyche and soma are monistic, and self and other are in a participation mystique, from which the individual differentiates himself in the process of individuation. In this realm, a purposive, structuring and organising principle engenders psychic patterns symbolically linking instinct and spirit by means of instinctual and archetypal images, thereby imparting meaning. Such principle has emergent properties, by which the psyche becomes differentiated out of the body-mind matrix and new individual positions come to be realised. It manifests in a symmetrical transference, in the synchronising of associations of analysand and analyst, in terms of physiological and psychic facts, and so fosters the analytic process in ways that enable the more experienced analyst to facilitate the dialectic and track progress moment by moment through their self-processing and containment.

In this fashion, Jung's psychoid concept effectively offers a model for the analytic attitude, and a methodology for the analyst's approach to his own work, guiding the analyst towards respect for the unknowable and into a receptive attitude of mind that receives, contains and processes emergent phenomena, in the form of instinctual and archetypal images of psychic and/or physical character, and allows them to inform the process.

Notes

1 Defined as a unitary world, in which mind, body and matter are undifferentiated.
2 Progoff studied with Jung from 1952 to 1955, and thereafter became director of the Institute for Research at Drew University from 1959 to 1971.
3 In a footnote, Progoff notes "psych-like" means psychoid.
4 Corresponding to complexes.
5 Jacobi also taught in Zurich University, and conducted research at the Zürichberg Clinic.
6 The process of active imagination also forms the theoretical foundation for Sandplay Therapy (Friedman and Mitchell, 1994), for Jungian art therapy (Schaverien, 1991), and for the Jungian practice of drama and movement therapy (cf. Chodorow (1991), Whitehouse (1979) and the Sesame Approach taught at the Central School of Speech and Drama, London (Lindkvist, 1998)). Chodorow (1991, p. 3) refers to "the mysterious interface that mediates between body and psyche", designated the psychoid level by Jung, and notes that emotions are the stuff of this interface, being made up *both* of bodily innervations and expressive physical actions *and* of mental images and ideas. There is a vital link between the moving body and memory, enabling embodied links to our past to be retrieved and offering a possibility for healing trauma, and she practices sandplay and dance therapy as means of accessing this interface.
7 Defined as using images and associations that are historical, mythological or religious to elaborate experience.
8 Defined as a unitary world, in which mind, body and matter are undifferentiated.
9 This term, introduced by the author, is to be distinguished from Matte-Blanco's use of the same term.
10 Author's italics.
11 Author's italics.
12 Author's italics.
13 It would seem that this should be "S"elf, although the English translation shows a small "s".
14 To Dr H, dated 30 August 1951 (Adler, 1976, p. 21).
15 Corbin is acknowledged as originator of the term *mundus imaginalis*.
16 Jung, 1946, para. 422.

Chapter 6

Interrogation of the psychoid concept

An empirical study

Introduction

The previous chapters have contemplated Jung's psychoid concept, its origins and evolution, in a variety of different contexts, both in the thinking of Jung himself and in the thought of selected post-Jungians.[1] The aim has been to shed light on different aspects of the concept in order to clarify the scope of possibility covered within its ambit, hopefully to develop a more rounded understanding than has hitherto been available.

The present chapter and those following address another context, namely contemporaneous clinical applications of the concept. Although certain clinical publications have referred to Jung's thinking on the psychoid as a theoretical explanation for some clinical event or other, very few have enquired how the psychoid concept may assist our clinical understanding in a general way and how it may be applied to the clinical method. An exception in this respect is the paper by Bright (1997) looking at synchronicity as a basis of analytic attitude. Thus, the next chapters seek to look at the clinical usefulness of the psychoid concept, to contemplate how it is applied in the practices of certain contemporary Jungians, and more especially how it may inform our everyday clinical work.

To do this, an empirical technique has been employed, not merely to investigate how contemporary Jungians envisage and understand the psychoid concept but to interrogate the concept and evaluate its clinical significance and application. To comprehend the results of this empirical study, it is necessary first to take a step back and review the methodology used. This chapter and the next will therefore cover the methodology underpinning the empirical study, together with a specific example by way of illustration, before moving on in further chapters to consider and discuss the results generated by such study.

Methodology

As mentioned in the introduction to this book, the overall methodology shaping the present research project is indebted to a form of research conceived by Dreher (2000), who proposed the systematic clarification of analytic concepts by tracing their origin and history, and also their current use. With respect to the latter, she suggested constructing a present-day picture of the clinical actualisation of a concept by means of an empirical research technique, such as expert interviews with practising clinicians.

Thus, the origins and evolution of the psychoid concept were addressed historically, according to Dreher, from a variety of different angles in Part I of this book. Part II will now contemplate the application of Jung's psychoid concept in the clinical setting, firstly by examining generally a clinical approach to embodiment in the countertransference, and next by employing the results specifically to interrogate the psychoid concept.

Dreher gives as an example of such empirical work the Trauma Project conducted by a research team of psychoanalysts[2] (of whom Dreher was one) at the Sigmund Freud Institute in Frankfurt in 1980s into the concept of *psychic trauma*. This example informs the present project, and will therefore be discussed by way of background.

Trauma Project

The Trauma Project originated in the early 1980s under the instigation of Joseph Sandler, and was conducted by a team of six psychoanalysts meeting twice weekly and working in cooperation with him. It was designed as a research project, whose aim was the examination of the scope of the analytic concept *psychic trauma*. This concept was selected for its historical significance, and for the fact that it had multiple clinical meanings attached to it (Dreher, 2000, p. 127). At the time, Sandler's reflections[3] on conceptual change attributed flexible dimensions of meaning to psychoanalytic concepts, with conceptual expansion taking place in the context of clinical experience. He envisaged practitioners developing subjective meaning spaces for concepts on a case-by-case basis, at first implicitly in the sense that this would be outside their conscious awareness.[4] Differentiation of the dimensions of these subjective meaning spaces to render them explicit would then enable psychoanalytic concepts to be delineated more completely and with greater precision in all their complexity. Such conceptual extensions could thus be absorbed into acknowledged theoretical understandings, and deviations highlighted for consideration.

In this context, a three-phase research model was designed, including:

(a) A general literature analysis;
(b) Interviews of psychoanalysts by psychoanalysts;
(c) Discussion and evaluation in the project group.

In phase I, the research team elaborated the public meanings for the concept, by reviewing the concept of trauma in different theoretical models, including Freud's original account, the notion of trauma in infant development, the impact of trauma on psychic structure, the link between external events and unconscious fantasy, and cases of extreme traumatisation in war. The result was a complex and confused picture.

The data collection of phase II took the form of ten semi-structured interviews by members of the research team, in which interviewees were asked, without specifying any delimitation of the term trauma, to give a spontaneous presentation of three terminated trauma cases. Each interview gradually progressed from a case-oriented discussion to a concept-oriented one, by creating a dialogue with the interviewee around the history and dynamics associated with the specific reported trauma, and seeking their reflections on the conceptualisations that they voiced, thereby encouraging developing theorisation.

Transcripts of the interviews were produced, and were then evaluated in regular group meetings in phase III, with the aid of theoretical understandings already reached from the literature analysis. In these discussions, the group first identified those statements that were part of the officially recognised versions of the trauma concept, and then they focussed on conceptual extensions that were not explicit but could be deduced. In this way, they worked towards identifying the implicit assumptions and conceptualisations of each interviewed analyst, and to establish how the subjective meaning space for each analyst structured the concept of trauma.

As Dreher (2000, p. 141) observes, interviews of psychoanalysts by psychoanalysts "allowed researchers to track down 'half-formed notions and beliefs' (implicit conceptualisation processes) relating to the trauma concept, and to encourage the reporting analyst to voice more explicit reflections":

> [W]hile practising analysts let their clinical behaviour be guided by their implicit assumptions, their use of concepts only becomes manifest to them . . . in all its relevant aspects once it is put into words.
> . . . In the interviews themselves, explicit statements and hidden implicit assumptions were, of course, closely connected.
> (Ibid., pp. 141–142)

Similarly to the uncovering of unconscious material in the psychoanalytic process, the researchers found that implicit material was brought to light by the research process, and a more differentiated view of the concept could be determined. Dreher (ibid., p. 166) noted that, through the teamwork, the group was enabled to achieve a systematic and comprehensive clarification of the trauma concept.

Her account of the Trauma Project highlights the way in which implicit assumptions guide the clinical behaviour of the analyst, until these are made consciously explicit, and highlights too how different dimensions of meaning may be associated subjectively with any particular concept.

For trauma, for example, the dimensions of meaning crystallised into characteristics attributed under the following headings: the traumatic situation, whether event or fantasy; the consequences of trauma including intrapsychic changes both immediate and long-term; the predisposition for trauma; and the treatment approach for trauma patients, as well as the interplay between these various categories. It was noted that, both in the literature and in the interviews, the term *trauma* tended to be used in an undifferentiated way without discriminating between these various meaning dimensions, and that the research project discriminated different aspects of the concept and increased the conceptual clarity significantly.

This lack of linguistic clarity indicated a significant need generally for conceptual clarification in psychoanalysis, and the Trauma Project was designed as a pilot study offering a methodological approach for doing such research. Dreher emphasised the importance of teamwork for this kind of project, since, as she points out, it avoids the possibility of personal bias distorting the results and affords opportunity for discourse to resolve difficulties.

Implicit theories

The above discussion demonstrates the gap between theory and practice, and the variety of different meanings attributable to only a single concept, and highlights a notion of implicit assumptions or theories of the analytic clinician.

Quite a number of people have addressed this area in one way or another, although mainly the psychoanalysts.

Sandler writes:

> With increasing clinical experience the analyst, as he grows more competent, will preconsciously (descriptively speaking, unconsciously) construct a whole variety of theoretical segments which relate directly to his clinical work. They are the products of unconscious thinking, are very much partial theories, models or schemata, which have the quality of being available in reserve, so to speak, to be called upon whenever necessary. That they may contradict one another is no problem. They coexist happily as long as they are unconscious.
>
> (1983, p. 38)

Fonagy (1982), writing before Sandler and referring to a personal communication from him proposing a study of private, preconscious theories, offers an alternative viewpoint. Fonagy does not use the term "implicit theory", but his description suggests that he is addressing a generally similar arena:

> It is possible that by using metaphoric language, theorists are able to incorporate into their developing ideas intuitions about the mechanisms

of their own psychological functioning derived from preconscious sources.

(1982, p. 135)

Fonagy suggests that such metaphors may have value in directing the integration of psychoanalytic hypotheses and empirical research. Fonagy, through his discussion of "metaphor", suggests that what constitutes a private theory reflects an *as yet unknown* theoretical function, for which there is insufficient information concerning the underlying psychological process.

In a later paper on the role of implicit knowledge, Fonagy (2006) offers the view that psychoanalysts do not understand how or why their treatment works but that theories orient clinicians and support understanding. Implicit theories may be seen as metaphoric approximations at a subjective level for both analyst and patient of certain types of deeply unconscious internal experience of the analytic relationship, he says, observing that "science uses metaphor in the absence of detailed knowledge of the underlying process" (2006, p. 82).

He refers to a container of knowledge, designated *the implicit psychoanalytic knowledge base*, gained through and deepened by intensive psychoanalytic work when two human minds try to fit together ideas and meanings, in that "proximity to another mind afforded by psychoanalytic treatment will inevitably deepen an implicit, non-conscious, procedural, action-focused understanding of mental function" (ibid., p. 84).

It is to be noted that the accounts of Sandler and Fonagy are not co-extensive, since Sandler specifically relates such implicit arena to a whole spectrum of context-dependent meanings of psychoanalytic concepts, and thus to formal psychoanalytic theory, whereas Fonagy refers simply to preconscious knowledge concerning the psychological processes within ourselves, implying more of a clinical bias for the term.

On the Jungian side, Dieckmann wrote, "There are certain fundamental ideas that have crystallised as methodological essentials with which every analytical psychologist works. Each of us works with the unconscious and hence with dreams and fantasies. Each of us must create the necessary conditions for setting an analytic process in motion, and certain techniques are part of it" (1991, p. 7). He added, "every analyst is compelled to develop a technique in the course of training and from experiences with patients that corresponds to one's own individuality" (ibid., p. 13).

Clearly, any attempt to investigate a present-day clinical understanding of the psychoid concept must first consider how analysts conceptualise potentially relevant aspects of their clinical practice.

This is achieved here by an empirical investigation of a particular clinical event *that might reasonably be expected to be covered by the psychoid concept* but for which no delineating theory had been proffered. Clinicians' conceptualisations of the event were then compared with understandings of the psychoid concept achieved in the historical study of Part I of this book, to elaborate a new position.

Present research

In this research, Dreher's model was followed, but with some modifications to her schema to adapt it to the present area of study. By contrast with Dreher, this project is a piece of individual research, since it was not practical within the confines of a PhD to undertake the kind of group work described with reference to the Trauma Project. Nonetheless, it is believed that useful results can still be obtained, as discussed below.

Another departure was to incorporate an extra strand in the empirical study, by seeking to uncover ab initio implicit theories relating to a given category of clinical event, and only thereafter seeking to integrate practice with theory. In the Trauma Project, semi-structured interviews were employed to generate data, and interviewees were asked to present their own trauma cases and were guided from case discussion towards conceptual discussion. By guiding the interviewees thus, the focus was directed towards the concept, namely trauma, and the dynamics of all the different cases become subservient to the single concept.

As per Dreher, this project comprises an empirical study, based on a series of individual expert interviews, and a small group discussion, with practising clinicians. The present project differs, however, in that all the interviewees discuss the same example, without imposing any conceptual focus. Instead of elaborating the psychoid concept by focussing on it directly, as by structured or semi-structured interviews, the participating clinicians were invited here firstly to conceptualise a particular embodied clinical event from a single case. Secondly, their respective different conceptualisations, as derived by data analysis of the transcripts of the interviews, were evaluated to establish whether they were consistent with the psychoid formulations determined from the historical study.

The interviewees included both post-Jungians and post-Freudians, for the sake of comparison, and a few of the former unprompted drew links with the psychoid concept. These Jungians enabled the application of direct elaborations on the public dimensions of meaning already attributed to Jung's concept. The actual conceptualisations of these Jungians were also subjected to a comparison with the public theory to evaluate the consistency of their viewpoints with such theory, and to highlight any departures from the known position. The conceptualisations of other analysts from different affiliations were also compared likewise, to establish whether their views matched the public dimensions of meaning for the psychoid concept, albeit employing different terminology. In this way, the empirical study served to interrogate the psychoid concept to evaluate its validity and practical value.

1. Methodological instrument

To achieve this, it was necessary to develop a methodological instrument for the interviews. Such instrument included a single set of process notes, and a set of guidelines for discussion of these process notes, such that the interviews generated data and did not simply re-create a series of supervisions.

The guidelines were designed to respect the patient, the analytic work, and the interviewees, whilst at the same time both capturing the fluidity and subtlety of the analytic process and avoiding fragmenting the data, through breaking down complex information into sections and applying codes without holding and working with the whole in mind, as described by Hollway and Jefferson (2000, pp. 68–70).

Assistance over the design of the guidelines was obtained from the work of Canestri (2006) and the working party of the European Psychoanalytic Federation (EPF) on theoretical issues, and Tuckett (2008) and the EPF working party on comparative clinical methods. Both such working parties are predicated on a psychoanalytic, mainly Freudian, approach, but their findings can be more generally applied, as here.

a. Canestri

Acknowledging Dreher, Canestri (ibid., p. 23) views the creative activity of the analyst as essential to the work of transformation in the analytic process, and knowledge as having a personal component that is the result of the combined creative working of the unconscious, preconscious and conscious and that is metabolised in the preconscious.

Following extensive discussion with analysts from different psychoanalytical societies, the EPF working party on theoretical issues chaired by Canestri arrived at a notion of lived theory as the living process of conceptualisation taking place in a clinical session, conscious or unconscious (ibid., p. 29). Wishing to identify the origins of these conceptualisations, they conceived a generalised map of implicit theories found in analysts' clinical work, comprising a set of six vectors, as follows:

(a) A topographical vector, taking into account the location of the analyst's theoretical thinking in the conscious, the preconscious or the unconscious, and accordingly the associated dynamics.
(b) A conceptual vector, covering the influences of cultural, clinical and affiliational trends, and the analyst's technical assumptions as to process elements, such as theories of change, meaning and the transference, as well as approaches to interpretation, and the prioritisation of image or language.
(c) An action vector, pertaining to the analyst's actions towards his patient, including listening, formulating interpretations and delivering them.

(d) An object relations of knowledge vector, concerning the analyst's relationship with psychoanalytic concepts, and with his own internal objects relating to them.
(e) A coherence versus contradiction vector, addressing the way that the analyst balances coherence and contradiction within his own process, tolerates contradiction, and handles these in his interactions with his patient. The use of metaphor is noted to be important here.
(f) A developmental vector, concerning the analyst's understanding of developmental models and his attitudes to developmental stages/phases.

The working party identified this map as "a methodological instrument for analysing the private, implicit and preconscious theories of the analyst at work", for identifying the theories or models that the analyst is employing in his clinical practice (ibid., p. 42).

In the course of designing the methodological instrument for the present project, reflection on these generalised vectors suggested that they could be adapted to suit the specific example of an embodied countertransference in a clinical session. Further, it was felt that, thus adapted, they could furnish a framework for use in the present interviews for guiding the discussion of case material.

b. Tuckett

Further assistance was obtained from the work of the EPF working party on comparative clinical methods chaired by Tuckett (2008, 1), which set out to design a new method for "abstracting the models that lay, usually implicitly, behind the different ways of working" of different practitioners. They developed a two-step model, in which an individual clinician presented successive sessions from an analysis in a small group discussion with fellow psychoanalysts, and the group evaluated the clinical material by means of the following procedure:

Step 0 – the group engages in a free discussion of the material;
Step 1 – the group reviews each intervention of the analyst and places it in one of six categories according to the function of the intervention (ibid., pp. 136–137, Table 6.1);
Step 2 – the group attempts to determine the approach of the presenting analyst with reference to five discussion dimensions or axes (ibid., p. 165, Table 6.4).

Step 0 allows the group to familiarise themselves with one another and with the material. Step 1 was conceived as a structural aid to help the group to focus on the approach of the presenting analyst, rather than the case material, since the purpose was to consider the model of the analyst and is thus to be distinguished from supervision. And, Step 2 was designed as a more

Interrogation of the psychoid concept 99

conceptual instrument for abstracting the main elements or dimensions of analysis in the hands of a particular practitioner.

The group work in Steps 0 to 2 occupied a period of approximately thirteen hours over a weekend. The aim was to elicit the presenter's explanatory working model of analysis, embracing the complex mix of beliefs and feelings, both explicit and conscious and implicit and preconscious, that the presenter has about the analytic process, that is, what brings the patient to analysis, how analysis works to transform the patient's situation, what must be attended to in an analytic session, and what the analyst believes is the function of his or her interpretations. Tuckett's method, although directed at locating explanatory models for analysis generally, rather than specific concepts, nonetheless offered some useful pointers for this project.

Firstly, the two-step method bases itself around a discussion of case material, in order to study the models of the analyst. It differentiates itself from standard case discussion and the closely associated task of supervision, but starts from a similar foundation of process notes. This demonstrated that case material and process notes could be discussed in different ways, respectively supervisory or research-oriented, according to the desired outcome. Thus, process notes could be employed to form an instrument for research interviews.

Further, for the present interview approach, Step 2, designed for the discussion of the dimensions of analysis generally, could also usefully be adapted to a set of dimensions relating to a specific area within analysis, namely that of sensory experience within the transference. Such a simplified model would also be suited to research by an individual researcher. Additionally, Step 2, as a conceptual tool, envisages axes for discussion rather than a rigorously structured framework, and could usefully aid free association and conceptualisation, in a manner suited to the flow of the analytic process.

For this project, therefore, interview guidelines were designed by modifying the "vectors" of Canestri, based generally on the conceptual approach of Tuckett and adapted to suit this specific project, as shown in Figure 6.1 below.

Figure 6.1 Interview discussion vertices

c. Comment

The result is an interview approach which is neither structured nor even semi-structured. The interviewee is faced with a methodological instrument, namely a set of process notes, in which the clinical event of interest is highlighted, and a set of discussion vertices to guide them in their discussion of the clinical material.

The process notes assist the interviewee to enter a familiar frame of mind, a form of evenly suspended attention that normally attends on case discussion in supervision or group presentations of case material, and the discussion vertices guide the interviewee away from a supervisory attitude into a new arena, where they are describing their own way of thinking and working. Even if, in some cases, there may be a tendency to lapse into a supervisory attitude, in spite of an injunction to avoid this, firstly no real problem arises since such attitude also reveals the interviewee's own models, and secondly the interviewee may be guided back to the task at hand by the interviewer by referring them back to the discussion vertices.

This approach is in contrast to the basic model described by Dreher in relation to the Trauma Project, where the interviews of psychoanalysts by psychoanalysts were conducted on a semi-structured basis and where interviewees were asked to present their own trauma case material as a starting point and then to enter into a conceptual discussion specifically around the trauma concept on the basis of their own cases.

It was believed that this approach would provide a better vehicle for "free" conceptualisation than would be achieved by means of such semi-structured interviews, the reason being that it would bring the participants closer to the analytic process, with all its subtleties and ambiguities, than could be achieved by carefully framed open questions, which would inevitably lead to a more cognitive attitude.

It is true that there could still be limitations as to how close the participants can get to the analytic process, since they will have only one session to use as a springboard, rather than a series spaced over a period, and since the here and now requires also a history for detailed, nuanced, understanding. However, this may also be a plus, because they will be less tied to a particular clinical scenario and thereby more able freely to associate into their own ideas and practices.

In order to avoid confusion, in view of the variety of accounts for "implicit theories" in the published literature, as briefly mentioned above, the term "private theories" will be adopted, from now on, to cover the analyst's personal theories, whether consciously elaborated or not.

The private theories generated in this present project were expected to be partially consciously worked out and partially preconscious or unconscious. It was believed that they would emerge in the interview process through two minds working together to understand the process notes, and this proved to be the case.

2. Interviews

The interviews were all conducted under identical conditions. Each interview focussed on the same set of process notes from the same single session of an intensive analysis, including highlighted a vignette describing an event experienced by the analyst in which the body and mind of the analyst were in relation. More especially, the event featured an imagistic sensory phenomenon of a man offering a child a small carved object, which the child snatches. This event was experienced by the analyst as both image and sensory value, since there was a psychic idea of the analyst as man facing the patient as child, coupled with a perception of hardness associated with the object and a perception of satisfaction apparently coming from the direction of the child/patient.

Each interview was limited to one hour. The focus group was conducted under the same parameters, with the exception that the time allocated was an hour and a half. All of the interviews were recorded and produced as transcripts as primary empirical data.

In the interview process, the interviewees were asked to discuss the session *from their own perspective* and *not in a supervisory capacity*, guided by the vignette and by the discussion vertices for focussing the dialogue, whilst encouraging them also to associate away into their own examples. The interviewer said little, except occasionally to draw the interviewee back to the process notes and the discussion vertices or to interject a question seeking clarification. By this means, it was sought to elicit how the different analysts conceptualise the kind of event described in the vignette and thereby how they conceptualise embodiment in the countertransference.

It is to be noted that this is not single session research, nor is it case study research, but that the process notes and the discussion vertices are employed as a methodological instrument in an interview process.

The interviews all produced a quantity of data, since all but one of the interviewees once started had a great deal to say. After a few interviews thus, an attempt was made to rein in the process, by asking more direct questions to focus the outcome. However, it was then found that the interviews tended to collapse, the material was less rich, as well as being more consciously proscribed, and the conceptualisations were more concealed. Thereafter, accordingly, the original approach of going with the flow was resumed.

It quickly became clear that the individual interviewees were often just warming up towards the end of the allotted hour and mostly had much more to say on the designated topic. In an initial review of the early transcripts, it was also discovered that some of their observations needed clarification. Therefore, a second interview was requested as a follow-through. The second interview was based entirely on the transcript of the first interview, and not on the process notes, in order to focus down, and not further open up, the enquiry.

3. Interviewees

In order to obtain as wide a set of outcomes as possible, within the limitations of the project, an interviewee distribution was selected including senior clinicians from a range of training affiliations, theoretical backgrounds, geographical location and, in some instances, generally known personal bias, for twelve individual interviews, and one small group discussion with six discussants.

There were equal numbers of analytical psychologists and psychoanalysts, in each case, of whom ten were men and eight were women. In the individual interviews, the numbers were nine men and three women, with four of the men and two of the women being analytical psychologists and five of the men and one of the women being psychoanalysts. In the group, one man and two women were analytical psychologists and three women were psychoanalysts.

It might be argued that a more even balance of men and women could have been selected, for the sake of comparison. However, the general nature of the phenomena being investigated applies equally to both genders, and thus conceptualisations are more likely to be affected by theoretical bias and affiliation than by gender.

The analytical psychologists practised in a variety of geographical locations, including the United Kingdom, Australia, France and the United States, and were members of five different societies, two of which are based in London. The psychoanalysts were all members of the British Psychoanalytical Society (BPAS) in London, but from different groups and theoretical orientations within the BPAS.

The issue of affiliation needs some comment. With reference to the analytical psychologists, Samuels (1985b) has envisaged the following schools in Analytical Psychology: Classic, developmental and archetypal, depending on criteria of respective bias in:

(a) The three *theoretical* areas of definition of: archetypal; concept of self; and development of personality; and
(b) The three *clinical* areas of analysis of transference-countertransference; emphasis on symbolic experiences of the self; and examination of highly differentiated imagery.

All of these schools were represented in one degree or another in the interviewees. Only one individual interviewee and two members of the small group came from the Society of Analytical Psychology in London, with its generally acknowledged developmental or Kleinian bias, whilst the other Jungians came from groups in London and abroad with other approaches, whether respectively more classical, more archetypal or closer to the views of the post-Freudians. The three from abroad all came from different training organisations, and thus there was a varied and balanced theoretical distribution amongst the Jungians.

The psychoanalysts all came from the BPAS in London, which also has a significant Kleinian component, although in practice this accounts for only a proportion of the membership, since the majority of psychoanalysts trained at the BPAS identify themselves with one of three groupings namely contemporary Freudian, Independent and Kleinian. The interviewees were distributed accordingly, mainly but not solely describing themselves as aligned with the Independent and Kleinian groups. Therefore, the psychoanalysts also represented a varied theoretical distribution. However, all being from London did imply that there would be a predominance of ideas aligned with a European way of thinking, and not that of North and South America, and that there could be an absence of interviewees designating themselves as relationalists and field theorists, in accordance with such tradition. These points are further discussed in the chapters on the empirical results.

Amongst the interviewees, there were five medically qualified doctors, two of these being analytical psychologists and three of these being psychoanalysts. The group included no medically qualified members. An initial expectation was that the medically qualified practitioners might have more of a tendency to focus on symptoms and psycho-somatisation than their non-medically qualified counterparts, but this proved not to be the case.

Accordingly, the selected distribution of interviewees was expected to yield a sufficient range of differing viewpoints for the purposes of the project.

4. Data analysis

Having obtained the primary data, the transcripts of the interviews were analysed, in order to draw themes and patterns from the data, whereby to elicit the conceptualisations of the interviewees, and discover their theoretical and practical views concerning embodiment in the consulting room, and especially in the countertransference. An approach was chosen based primarily on the technique of grounded theory, as described by Charmaz (2006), whose model is developed out of the original grounded theory of Glaser and Strauss (1967) aimed at generating theory out of data by means of systematic qualitative analysis.

The technique of grounded theory is well-known in the social sciences as an instrument for data analysis, having the advantages that the approach is grounded in actual empirical data, allows the results to emerge from the data by means of the grounded theory process, employs iterative feedback steps for repeated verification and validation of the emerging concepts, is adaptive in the face of unforeseen setbacks, and advances as the process evolves, thereby allowing the process to be continuously improved as it progresses. In grounded theory, therefore, the data rather than the researcher leads the outcome, the results emerge out of the data, and the hermeneutic circle of continual feedback and repeated re-evaluation of the different stages means that continual refinement of the results assists the generation of uncontaminated results. This is very important in an individual project, to avoid the risk of personal bias attributed by Dreher to individual research projects.

Further, grounded theory is the form of data analysis generally chosen to elicit theory, as opposed to narrative, meaning or subjective experience, and hence is especially suited to the present empirical study, which seeks above all to locate the personal models, conceptualisations and theories of the interviewees, namely their private theories.

Succinctly, the elements lifted here from Charmaz's method include: subjecting the collected data, namely the interview transcripts, to line-by-line coding and focussed coding; making comparisons between coded interview transcripts of the same and different individuals, and feeding the results back into repeated coding steps; and, both during and after the coding process, writing memos which highlighted categories pointing towards conceptualisations of the interviewees relevant to the research theme. Further iterations were introduced at this stage, feeding results back into more refined coding steps and generating and clustering new and more detailed categories.

In addition, at first a short while following, but later immediately after, each encounter and during the subsequent process of data analysis, field notes were made, recording reactions arising from the interview and the analysis (the researcher's countertransference to the research). This is a step proposed by Hollway and Jefferson (2000, p. 45), who wrote, "our feelings in and around the interview are of value for understanding the dynamics of the research relationship. . . . [T]hey are important to how the data are produced".

The purpose of these field notes was partially to add an additional level of understanding and reflexivity to the data analysis, since the empirical approach naturally involved participant observation, but also more significantly to address the researcher's own transference onto the research project and onto the interviewees. This important reflexive practice is discussed in Hollway and Jefferson (ibid., p. 65), in terms of elaborating the initial data and avoiding distortion of the data analysis, and in Romanyshyn (2007), in terms of differentiation of the researcher from the research by making conscious the researcher's own complexes so that they do not contaminate the results. It will be appreciated that this step is of particular importance given Dreher's reservations about the risk of personal bias entering the results of individual research.

Where this project differs from Charmaz, therefore, was in the production of the field notes, recording the researcher's impressions, reactions and associations arising: out of the interviews; in relation to the interviewees; and out of the data analysis process. Effectively, the unconscious intersubjective interview dynamics in the interview relationship were thus acknowledged. These field notes have been used primarily to differentiate out the researcher's own material, and only occasionally also to elaborate understandings of an interviewee's emerging implicit theory.

The conceptualisations of each interviewee were thus extracted from the transcripts, and the results were then compared in order to classify the different viewpoints of the interviewees.

A general chart of the different conceptual characteristics obtained from the complete set of individual interviews was compiled, and is included in Appendix A. It must be appreciated, of course, that this general chart in no way captures the complexity of the individual or overall results. In addition, certain key themes occurring repeatedly, in one guise or another, across plural interviews were extracted and are discussed in Chapter 8. These demonstrate that it was possible: to elaborate the psychoid concept directly from the results obtained from the interviews of those Jungians who brought in this concept; to evaluate whether the views of all of the Jungians were consonant with the public definitions for the psychoid concept; and to establish whether any of the psychoanalysts produced conceptualisations contiguous with those of certain of the Jungians, albeit employing different theoretical models and terminology.

Discussion

The empirical study has addressed the very interesting area of the implicit or private theories of the clinician, and their relationship with theory. This has been much more fully researched by the psychoanalysts than by the Jungians, who have published a number of studies, addressing both the nature of implicit theories and various methods for researching them. There are, however, very few publications scrutinising *actual* implicit theories arising in specific areas of clinical practice or offering examples of individual implicit theories under the microscope.[5] This limits the available understandings of the nature of such theories, as well as the possibility for evaluating their pertinence to the psychoanalytic method, their influence on psychoanalytic efficacy, and any need for adjustment, individually or collectively, in the face of such situation.

One author addressing this area is Hamilton (1996), who conducted a study of analysts' interpretive practices, focussing on their preconscious models for various psychoanalytic concepts, most especially the transference. She interviewed sixty-five analysts in Los Angeles, New York, San Francisco and London, using semi-directed interviews, and analysed the results in an attempt to "systematize the beliefs and actions that are typical of practising American and British psychoanalysts today" (ibid., p. 2). Her aim was to obtain generalised theoretical profiles amongst groups of analysts linked by affiliation, rather than to track closely particular implicit theories in individual clinicians, although she noted as her project progressed that analysts are guided preconsciously by many dimensions and tend to practice much more loosely than some publicly claim (ibid., pp. 3–4).

The present project, by contrast, has sought to understand the actual private theories of a specific set of individuals, in relation to a quite specific type of clinical event, and then and only then to generalise from these individual private theories to one or more common model(s) for the type of event, independently of theoretical affiliation. Further, the project has, again by contrast, sought to employ such model(s) thus derived for interrogating a specific concept. The result is a much more detailed account of particular private theories, associated with a much more focussed area.

A few points need to be addressed. The project has necessarily been limited by a number of factors, not the least of which is that it is the work of a single researcher only, within the ambit of a PhD study, and this affects the methodology, the range of the investigation and the amount of qualitative data that can be collected and analysed.

Most of the earlier studies into psychoanalytic concepts,[6] and implicit or private theories, have been generalised researches conducted by groups of researchers, making verification by group consensus a possible validation instrument and increasing the potential depth and/or range of the investigation. Tuckett (2008), addressing the question of the analyst's explanatory models for analysis, falls into this category. Such verification has not been possible here, but it is believed that this need not be an issue in this, more focussed and less ambitious, investigation. An advantage of an individual study is that group dynamics do not have to be taken into account in the methodology and in the analysis of the data, although safeguards against individual bias do need to be introduced.

In the present conceptual research, these safeguards have been achieved by: firstly, undertaking comparisons repeatedly and continually scrutinising, reflecting on, and tightening, definitions; secondly, utilising an interview technique as a methodological instrument that seeks understanding by two minds working together at the limits of their knowledge to understand clinical events metaphorically, as proposed by Fonagy (2003, 2006); and, thirdly, employing grounded theory for the data analysis, a technique whereby the data leads the results to generate private theories for the clinicians concerned, which can later be compared with definitions obtained from the historical study.

Likewise, the sample size for the interviews has been limited, but by selecting a range of interviewees from different theoretical traditions and orientations, and making comparisons between them, using the methodological instrument designed for the project, a clear and reproducible, and therefore believed satisfactory, result has been obtained.

Next, basing the research on the use of one set of process notes only, in the interview process, might be criticised. Here, it is to be reiterated that this is not a single case study: the process notes are *not* the research data but are merely an interview tool, to assist the interviewees to associate freely around the research topic of embodiment in the consulting room, akin to the questions employed in semi-structured interviews. Further, to have expanded the interview process by including more than one set of process notes for different analytic sessions in the same case would have pinned the subject down, and would have rendered it harder for the interviewees to avoid a supervisory stance. And, to have included more than one case would have overloaded the interviews. Actually, where interviewees wanted to illustrate particular points not forthcoming from the process notes offered, they advanced their own clinical examples freely.[7]

The research has generated another interesting and unexpected outcome. There are those who express doubt about the merits of research into clinical work, on the ground that research tends to be a blunt cognitive instrument unsuited to grasping the nuances and subtleties of the analytic process. It is believed that the present approach to interviewing clinicians and also the chosen approach to data analysis have permitted the capture of the analytic nuances and subtleties, as may be further appreciated from Chapters 7 and 8. In other words, this study shows that it is possible to conduct research that is attuned to the analytic process.

Notes

1 It is acknowledged that the latter account has by no means been exhaustive.
2 In Part II of the book, the terms "psychoanalyst" and "Jungian analyst" are employed respectively to distinguish the different affiliations, post-Freudians and post-Jungians.
3 Later published as Sandler, J. (1983).
4 Throughout the present chapter, the term "implicit" is employed in a general sense to mean: not wholly consciously developed, being half-formed or even initially unconscious, and thus not elaborated.
5 Tuckett (2008), whilst acknowledging the existence of implicit theories, sets out to investigate rather the question of analysts' explanatory models for analysis, enquiring how does analysis work?
6 With the exception of Hamilton, mentioned above.
7 These are not cited in detail here for reasons of confidentiality.

Part II

Empirical contexts

Chapter 7

The empirical study
An example of a data analysis by grounded theory

Introduction

By way of illustration, this chapter gives an example of the empirical process described in the last chapter, covering two interviews with one clinician, S11(PA),[1] references to the researcher's field notes and transcripts of the two interviews and different stages of the data analysis of the transcripts by grounded theory. The aim is to show how certain themes or clusters of ideas emerged in the course of this process.

It is to be remembered that all of the interviews were based on the same set of process notes, and were recorded, then transcribed, and afterwards analysed using the same grounded theory techniques. Hence, the example given here is representative of the approach taken with all of the other interviews.

As with all the interviews, this one focussed specifically on a vignette in the process notes of an event experienced by the analyst combining mental fact and physical fact. The patient, a middle-aged woman, presented as dissociated from her feelings and her body. At the start of the session in question, she speaks, without affect, of a fear of sinking back into depression. The analyst has trouble engaging the patient until the occurrence of the event, when the analyst experiences a sensory image of an adult offering a small carved object to a child, who snatches it with satisfaction. After this, the patient engages much more directly.

S11(PA) was the eleventh analyst to be interviewed for the project, and accordingly the interview process was by now familiar to the interviewer. Data analysis of a number of the interview transcripts had already been commenced. Certain general topics, such as development and regression, were noted to be coming up frequently in the interviews, and some initial ideas as to different ways of conceiving the transference were beginning to crystallise out of the different interviews. Other such themes included the significance attributed respectively to emergence, symbolic capacity and a relational approach.

Understandings of the transference were a key theme, and two structural conceptualisations had begun to stand out clearly, namely a hierarchical or asymmetric model and a mutual or symmetric model. In the hierarchical condition, the patient was seen as communicating events to the analyst by means of projection or projective identification, thereby lodging parts of themselves within the psyche of the analyst. Accordingly, the situation is asymmetric. In the mutual condition, the self-other interaction may involve either mutual self-other immersion in a common unconscious field, namely participation mystique, or the situation of an imaginal area between self and other, constituting a shared third zone. Accordingly, the situation is symmetric.

These earlier interviews, and the results gleaned from them, formed a backdrop to the current interview, and meant in the data analysis of the present interviews that particular attention was paid to clues offering further evidence for themes already noted. The results from each new stage of the interviews were being applied in a re-evaluation of the earlier stages, and the overall data analysis was becoming increasingly refined.

Example

In a recent seminar, S11(PA) had presented some interesting case material about a somatising patient, and so she was felt to be able to offer relevant insights.

1. First interview

The interview commenced with an explanation of the task and the set of discussion vertices, and with S11(PA) reading the process notes in silent deep concentration. She then began discussing the session, and especially the vignette, guided by the discussion vertices, adding some associations from her own clinical experience.

Following the interview, field notes on the interview experience commented that two themes stood out, namely: words have an action component to them that informs S11(PA) about the unconscious dynamic in the patient and that gets into the session in a form of enactment; and, she compares psychoanalysis and early parent-infant experience as two arenas where sensory or physical images and metaphors may arise.

2. Immersion and initial extraction

In order to become familiar with her views, and ensure that the transcript was accurate, the recording was re-played, and the transcript corrected, repeatedly, before sending a copy to S11(PA) for her agreement, and before starting coding. She accepted the transcript without amendment.

An initial line-by-line coding, sticking closely to the language employed by S11(PA), served to pick out tentative themes. Emphases, obscurities and potential queries were noted in the margins as comments.

Memos made straight afterwards captured immediate thoughts on the emerging ideas, including understandings of sensory experience, models of the transference, and references to regression.

The following excerpt picks up these themes:[2]

Line coding	1st interview transcript
Seeing event as: the analyst having thoughts about the transference relationship, that are not getting through to the patient, and moving intuitively from words to somatic images	**S11(PA)**: So, I would see that as [...] the analyst has a set of thoughts about the transference relationship and situation in that session, which in a way aren't really getting through to the patient. I mean they are, but they're not.... She's a bit stuck in this [...] being all frantic and not being soothed. And the analyst intuitively moves from trying to express that in ideas, which the patient is not really doing much with, to a set of somatic images and
Feeling this is a more direct expression of the infantile basis of the situation	experiences, which express something much more direct about the kind of infantile basis or the infantile version of that situation. (11, p. 5)[3]

This extract raises the issue of a shift in the analyst's understanding and response to the session material from words to somatic images that are felt to be much more direct. Later, S11(PA) described such shift in terms of different levels of functioning.

The memos commented that S11(PA) employed the expression "experience" frequently, in a variety of contexts, indicating a close attunement to analysis as process. Another significant theme was the notion that the words of both patient and analyst are unconsciously actions rooted in bodily experience. S11(PA) related this with infancy, considering that baby dynamics are at the centre of all our communications at an unconscious level, manifesting in our selection of words, grammatical structure and sentence flow. Linked with this, the researcher observed that S11(PA) believes that regression is a necessary and central part of the analytic experience, for both patient *and* analyst, in order to get to the more primitive, base level of issues that need addressing.

S11(PA) implied a familiarity with sensory and somatic experience in sessions, both in the patient and in the analyst, ranging from symptoms, such as headaches, feeling sick, having restless legs, to experience in the form of "sensory" or "somatic" images. She specifically acknowledged that this latter *kind* of experience is known to her, giving an example from her own personal training analysis, associated by her with an early state of mind.

The memos then noted that, based on the action level of words, S11(PA) felt, at the start of the session, the patient was like a complaining child, pushing mother away, while the analyst was employing words in a soothing way. She saw the event in the vignette as a turning point shifting the session into a different gear, "something emerging" in the transference relationship, bringing the analyst and patient into engagement with one another at a primitive parent-child level. She observed that the precise countertransference experience of the analyst would be predicated on their own internal world of imagination, and thus only they could know its interpretation by reference to their own meaning space.

She referred a number of times to material "emerging", although she did not highlight emergence as a primary characteristic of psychoanalysis.[4] She described psychoanalysis as giving permission for self-disclosure, which opens the way for unconscious phantasy[5] to emerge, and be recognised.

In her model of the transference, a form of "resonating" takes place at adult verbal levels of functioning, and projective identification takes over at more primitive levels. By way of reference, Laplanche and Pontalis describe projective identification in terms of phantasied projection of split off parts of the subject's own self into the interior of the other, so as to control the other from within (1973, p. 356). S11(PA) made one reference to baby and mother being fused, which did not seem to fit this model, and the memos noted a need to explore this further.

Finally, the memos highlighted the comments of S11(PA) on the role of interpretation. She feels that mere mirroring is insufficient, that the patient needs to receive an element of the analyst's self, and see that the analyst has personally created something out of the patient's communications. Therefore, relationship is an important part of analysis.

3. Shaping and further extraction

Next, in a subsequent focused coding, related ideas began to be apparent. The focused coding steps were re-done repeatedly, on each occasion noting key themes and commenting on them in the memos.

The following cluster headings started to emerge as worthy of exploration in conjunction with the elaborations and connections associated with them: sensory images; words as actions, and their links with sensory images; levels of functioning, linking both with words as actions and with sensory images; regression, linking with levels of functioning; shifts in functioning and relating, or turning points; emergence; the transference field; and psychoanalysis as a joint experience.

The following examples pick up references to the transference field, levels of functioning and regression:

Focussed coding	1st interview transcript
	Excerpt 1
	S11 (PA): It's a two-way thing, isn't it, because it feels to me as if the patient is managing to get through. It's
Seeing the vignette event as two-way: the analyst gets through differently *and* the patient is felt on a more visceral level	not just that the analyst finds a way of getting through differently. But it's as if the patient, the impact of the patient is felt on a more visceral sort of level, whereas previously [...] it felt like a patient being a patient and the analyst being an analyst ... and a bit too much on the level of thoughts, and not quite real enough. And so the reality of the drowning state of the patient, where she's feeling, you know, "I'm getting worse; I'm sinking into depression again. Nothing is getting better. I'm
Noting levels of functioning: the drowning state of the patient is initially related to on an adult level, *then* a more primitive level is reached and the immediacy of the transference gets through	really disappointed and angry, and all this crap is going on that I have to deal with and nobody is helping". [...] [A]nd she throws it all at the analyst. And yet it's related to as though it's an adult communication. And I think what then comes through, in that more visceral level of listening, is the immediacy, the panic actually, and also anger and frustration and a clamouring quality of the transference. (I1, p. 7)
	Excerpt 2
	S11 (PA): I think that probably links to what I was saying about the different levels of communication, the adult self, the continuing adult self of the patient, assuming it's an adult patient, and then the baby self, and actually
Associating levels of functioning with resonance and projective identification	the same for the analyst. And that the thing of two people resonating and having things going on and associating and having an interaction between the two is more like the two adult selves. And I felt to some
Linking resonance with adult interaction	degree that at the beginning of the session there was a bit about feeling that the patient comes along and says, "blah-blah-blah". The analyst says, "Maybe it's this", and she thinks, "Maybe, but blah-blah-blah", some
Noting gradual joint regression opens up access to more basic levels of both, increasingly yielding projective identification	more, and then gradually there is a joint regression, if you like, during the session, where access is opened up to the more basic levels of both people.
	And then I think the more that happens, the more it's in the nature of projective identification, where one person quite directly, although in a way that I'm still not sure
Describing projective identification as one person directly interfering with the other's psyche	how it happens, but quite directly interferes with the other person's psyche.... And I think you see that most powerfully, or at least it has been most powerful in my experience, between an actual parent and a very new baby. [...] [T]he two are really much more fused than I think any two people normally are in any other context.
Linking with infant levels, and fusion	And so, I think that's an extreme form of locked-in projective identification from, on both sides. (I1, p. 14)

These two extracts demonstrate how S11(PA) conceives different levels of functioning in the transference relationship, starting from words and shifting to somatic images of a much more direct and visceral nature. She links this with regression to a more primitive or infantile state, and associates the regression with a move from an interaction based on resonance to one based on projective identification.

4. Uncovering confusions

The memos at this point noted that the first interview yielded some important questions, having a bearing on the private theory of S11(PA): One question is the origin in the thinking of S11(PA) of words as actions, since this informs her understanding of psychic structure and is a significant element in her explanation for the existence of somatic images. Another concerns the use by S11(PA) of the term "emergence", since she employed the term almost unknowingly, but this dynamic is seen as crucial by a number of the other interviewees in their understanding of the analytic process.

Also, S11(PA) referred variously to projective identification, instances of locked-in projective identification on both sides, and fusion, and these terms would benefit from clarification, in order to evaluate the form of the transference field envisaged by S11(PA).

5. Second interview

A second interview was therefore fixed. This interview addressed only the transcript of the first interview, and not the process notes, to review these points.

S11(PA) began by giving a full account of the origins of her ideas on words as actions, as discussed further below.

Then, her attention was drawn to her use of the expression "emergence" in the first interview. She acknowledged that she had not noticed, and proceeded to contemplate forms of emergence, including: a person emerging more clearly; internal aspects of the patient emerging; and issues emerging from the work, "like something being born", starting with somatic experience for the patient and/or the analyst. She observed how often a symptom that she had experienced had turned out to be key for the patient.

Next, referring to the transference field, it became apparent from a description of her own analytic work that S11(PA) envisages a shared experience not actually covered by the term "projective identification", as follows:

Focussed coding	2nd interview transcript
	Excerpt 1 **S11(PA):** [H]e conjured up so, not so much in words but in affect, such a fragile, falling apart feeling, and he was able to, he began to cry a lot. [...] I felt as though we both slid into, and we regressed, regressed in the sense of very open and close and emotional, so that when he got to the bit where he started telling me how he visited X[6] who's clearly near to death with cancer, and that they'd had a very, very important emotional conversation together about what they had meant to each other and so on, I felt as though I was right there with him almost in this deathbed scene, and his child-self [...] being sent away and not knowing anybody and going to a country with a different language. I mean that's a very, very hard experience as a fairly young boy. I felt as though he'd become that young boy again, and I'd become somehow part of him or very intertwined with his situation. (I2, p. 17)
Describing feeling that *both* regressed to a close, emotional place, where she felt part of the patient and intertwined with his situation	
	Excerpt 2 **S11(PA):** It was more of a merging of experience rather than that he was disowning anything or relocating it in me. I felt he completely still owned it all the way through. But that he did induce it in me, and then there was something that travelled the other way as well, which I think enabled, it felt like, both of us to emerge from that experience of really a near death, the emotional experience going with really, really losing something that you absolutely need. And that of course, there is a transference dimension to that too, and by the end of the session we were talking again about [...] the reality of losing X [...] more in an ordinary adult way. But I think I would, yes, I think projective identification in that case is not really ... I don't know what the right expression would be, exactly, for it. (I2, pp. 17–18)
Describing "merging": feeling the patient still owned his own experience but induced it in the analyst, and something travelled the other way enabling both to emerge from a profound experience of loss	
Contrasting with something disowned and split off into the analyst as projective identification, and not feeling this accounts	

In these two excerpts, S11(PA) is discussing her views on projective identification and brings a clinical example to work out what she is contemplating and to illustrate what she means. She ends up describing a much more merged and mutual situation than her initial use of the term "projective identification" would imply, and she acknowledges that the terminology is not really accurate.

6. Clusters

Having coded both interviews, and noted the various themes emerging, clusters of linked themes began to form:

a. Words as actions, sensory images, levels of functioning

It emerged that S11(PA) had a structural notion of the psyche, relying on levels of functioning along a number of axes, adult and infant, cognitive and primitive, more rational and more physical. Commencing from what she called "the embodiment of thinking", meaning that the roots of thinking and feeling lie in bodily experience, S11(PA) described words as having a level at which unconsciously they are actions, expressing bodily processes, like eating, vomiting or hitting. The choice of words, the smoothness or choppiness of their flow, the looping back or complexity of a communication, all give the lie to the kind of word actions taking place. In the second interview, she explained that this view derived partly from Isaacs (1948) on unconscious phantasy, and partly from work undertaken by Fonagy and Target (2007) on embodied cognition, linguistics and attachment. That work opened up for her an understanding of the idiosyncratic forms of interaction arising between two people in analysis, comprising phantasy-to-action expressed through words, metaphor and images.

Referring to the vignette event, S11(PA) spoke about sensory and somatic images as: a more direct expression at an unconscious level of words as actions; a primitive base level of mental experience without the overlay of cognitive wrappings and cortical trappings; an expression of a shape of sensory experience, a tactile or action experience; a primitive or base level of mental experience; and imagery based on bodily infantile phantasies from the earliest baby experiences of sucking, taking in, getting hold of, pushing off, feeling breathless, internal-external negotiation, and parental holding. She also associated physical symptoms in patient or analyst with infantile bodily phantasies.

With reference to the session in the process notes, the memos summarised the views of S11(PA):

> The session started with the patient like a grizzling child using words as though fussing about what was being offered, pushing mother away, feeling nothing was right; and with the analyst employing words that at an action level were soothing, reaching out, like an adult kneeling down to the level of a child. The patient's words were echoed by her posture on the couch, staring at the ceiling, giving the same message of refusal. The analyst then moved intuitively from words into a more somatic arena, expressing directly an infantile basis of the situation. *Both* analyst *and* patient then got through to one another, and the analyst's next words

could be seen at an action level as an act of giving, received as such by the patient.

(Memos)

Thus, S11(PA) felt the event represented a shift into a more primitive and accessible level, where, in Bion's terms, some alpha functioning gets applied to the beta elements. The interviewer noted, for reference, that Lopez-Corvo describes alpha function as the capacity to change sense impression and information, namely beta elements, into simple objects and representations, such as images or patterns, namely alpha elements (2003, p. 26). The question of shifts like this can go either way, according to S11(PA). Something experienced at a thought level may emerge in a physical metaphor, as here, or bodily experience may become more abstract verbal representation:

> Just as adult verbal communication unconsciously incorporates bodily experience and bodily intention and impulses, I think that the things that are actually experienced as bodily impulses and intentions also have implicit within them the other side, which is the more represented, cognitively represented thought.
>
> (S11(PA), I1, p. 5)

b. Regression, levels of functioning

In the first interview, this led to a discussion of the nature of the psychoanalytic process, in which S11(PA) sees regression, conceived as openness to more primitive levels of mental functioning, as central and necessary. This may take various forms, including increased contact with physical experience, an emergence of previously unconscious phantasy, and greater access to material from infantile experience. She indicated that regression in psychoanalysis is to be distinguished from actually going back to *being* like a child, since an aspect of the patient continues to function as an adult and the patient reverts to normal adult life at the end of a session. Rather, a unique state of separation arises between different levels of functioning, including reality and phantasy. As analyst, S11(PA) described herself as being attuned to the baby in the adult, even when the adult is speaking in a cerebral manner. Furthermore, she said, regression needs to occur in *both* patient *and* analyst for psychoanalysis to be effective (S11(PA), I1, p. 14).

c. Emergence, regression, turning points

Early memos recorded that for S11(PA), the regression of patient and analyst to more primitive levels of functioning gives rise to unconscious phantasy, in that "constellations of previously unconscious anxieties, wishes, physical states, and the need to express them, emerge" (S11(PA), I1, p. 10). She defined regression as an openness, both to unconscious phantasy in a way that allows the recognition and elaboration of the phantasy through the analytic process, and to more physical and/or infantile kinds of experience. By way of example, she thought the session employed in the interview began with the analyst being an analyst and the patient being a patient, so that the encounter does not initially feel very real. Then, there is a joint regression and a more vital level of listening is engaged, which enables the immediacy and clamouring quality of the transference to come through. She described this episode as a typical crisis in a session, a turning point, where something breaks through or emerges.

In the second interview, she contemplated the nature of emergence in analysis:

> [There are] issues emerging from work, and quite often I think it goes through that sequence, which involves some sort of sensory or physical experience, and commonly for the patient and sometimes for the analyst. And sometimes I've been cued into something, which I probably might not have made contact with otherwise, through a physical symptom of my own, which has alerted me to something about the patient, which then has turned out to be a key thing, either a physical issue that they've got or some phantasy that they have. . . . [T]here's that kind of emergence where something . . . It's almost like being born, something is introduced into the analysis as something that can be known and worked on . . . almost indirectly through some much more visceral kind of resonance.
>
> (S11(PA), I2, p. 11)

She gave two examples of this kind of "painful birth" from her own practice, where "something going on between" patient and analyst produced quite specific symptoms in her countertransference that were fundamental to the analysis, in the first instance migraine headaches and in the second asthma. In both cases, it eventually became apparent that these symptoms were very significant in the life history of the respective patients, since in each instance they led after a long period of work quite spontaneously to something that proved a turning point for the patient. Subsequently, the significance of these symptoms for the patient emerged.

d. Transference field, resonance, projective identification, fusion, merging, symmetry

In the prior seminar mentioned above, S11(PA) had spoken about a form of play arising in psychoanalysis where the analyst resonates with something played out by the patient, and in the first interview she spoke about the analyst *resonating* with the patient's action speech. Enquiring what she meant by "resonating", and how this linked with projective identification, she said, "I probably don't sufficiently distinguish between those two things, because I think there's a whole spectrum between the two. . . . I think, practically always, there's both going on" (S11(PA), I1, p. 14). She described two people resonating as interaction at the level of their adult selves. Then, the more there is regression, the more access is opened up to the more basic levels, and the more the interaction is in the nature projective identification (S11(PA), I1, p. 14).

S11(PA) mentioned that projective identification can be witnessed most powerfully between a parent and a very new baby: The two are really fused in an extreme form of locked-in projective identification on both sides. She described this state as the infusion of one person's psychic experience with contents of the other person's experience, in a way that forces the recipient to take it in and react to it in some way. The memos noted that he spoke in terms of projective identification as a dynamic whereby one party (the baby/patient) acts on and interferes with the psyche of the other (the parent/analyst), which implied a hierarchical and asymmetrical notion of the transference field. However, when S11(PA) went on to describe the parent and very new baby as *fused* and existing in an extreme form of locked-in projective identification *on both sides*, it seemed that in her mind the field was actually more of a symmetrical one, where the two parties are at least in some respects in a relatively undifferentiated state and where differentiation is the developmental task.

Reverting to this in the second interview, S11(PA) gave an example, from her own analytic practice, of a brief moment in a session with a patient, confronting the loss of the dying X and facing childhood memories of his parents' deaths, where she felt there was a merging of the experience of analyst and patient. The patient did not disown anything, but S11(PA) had a very real sense of being right beside him in the presence of death. She described herself as feeling fused into the patient's experience. Similarly, she felt that she was at this moment able to share her own strength with the patient, and this enabled them both to emerge from the experience.

S11(PA) displayed some confusion over the language to be employed for this account, saying "I think projective identification is not really. . . . I don't know what the right expression would be, exactly, for it" (S11(PA), I2, p. 18). She offered that these events are more of a shared experience than people tend to acknowledge. Consequently, the conclusion was reached that what she was describing was a transference field having levels, and that in the more primitive level what occurs is not projective identification or unconscious communication but an experience of a shared symmetrical field.

e. Psychoanalysis as a joint experience, interpretation, relationship

This discussion of the transference led to a consideration of the analyst's role as container. The memos recorded that "relationship" is key, in a very particular manner having two separate aspects, namely the content of the analyst's countertransference and the nature of the analyst's analytic response. Regarding the former, the memos noted that, for S11(PA), countertransference may be seen as a function both of the analytic relationship and of the analyst's own history. In regression, the affect state in the patient constellates something in the analyst, calling forth something personal out of the analyst's own imaginal world, so that the meaning can be divined only by the particular analyst by reference to their own self-analysis. Patient and analyst thus relate unconsciously, each out of their own experience.

The analytic response *may* simply comprise the insight thus achieved on the part of the analyst, even if not verbally communicated, since the patient may feel met. However, to achieve a shift in the patient's situation, S11(PA) feels that the process needs also to include action on the part of the analyst, in the form of an interpretation. A significant point is that S11(PA) sees the otherness of the analyst as vitally important. In her view, the primitive levels of both patient and analyst are processed in the analyst's mind as a joint experience. On attaining a meaningful form in the mind of the analyst, the analyst seeks to find a way to feed this back to the patient, such that the patient can recognise that it is centrally about what he/she has been struggling with, but is also about "us" and has become a combined relational experience with additional meaning:

> So, the otherness is really important in that, because the patient needs to recognize . . . what's communicated back eventually, or over a number of interventions, as centrally to do with him or his . . . and not all about the analyst, for example, but also not all, not only about him or her, but about us. . . . [F]or me that feels very important. That it is an experience of a relationship that, that's built up . . . the relationship is actually the central thing that's represented.
>
> (S11(PA), I1, p. 17)

7. The private theory of S11(PA)

From the above clusters, a profile for S11(PA) was constructed. In her private theory, psychoanalyst and patient both regress to more primitive levels of functioning, and, depending on the extent of the regression, thereby find themselves jointly in a symmetrical unconscious field, from which insight emerges. In this aspect of the transference, the dynamic is not unconscious communication in the form of projective identification, but rather a shared, mutual and synchronous experience, in which each party arrives at something from their own history and personality. The analyst out of their own self-analysis seeks to create something from this joint experience to offer to the patient as an interpretation.

In this understanding, S11(PA) sees psychoanalysis as a unique situation, in which different levels of body and mind, development and functioning, of the patient and also the analyst, become bound with one another through regression, and can enable the issues needing to be addressed to emerge. The body may play a key role in this, as the regression reaches primitive levels of functioning, in which material is released as symptoms and somatic images, and is thus experienced in a direct form. Body and mind are closely woven together in this view, being seamlessly linked by levels of functioning, stages of development, and the action level of words, to produce symptoms, sensory images and metaphor, and "shapes of sensory, tactile and action experience".

This leads to the conclusion that S11(PA) effectively has a monistic understanding of a unified bodymind, manifesting different aspects in different contextual environments.

Discussion

The most salient of the above findings, for the purposes of the present project, are a symmetrical transference field and a monistic bodymind. The manner in which these findings emerged will be traced briefly in the light of the account of implicit theories given in the previous chapter.

Consequently, it may be helpful here simply to re-cap the set of vectors envisaged by Canestri (2006), for reference:

(a) A topographical vector, referring to the origins of theoretical thinking, and associated dynamics.
(b) A conceptual vector, relating to influences and trends applied to process elements, such as theories of change, the transference and interpretation, and the prioritisation of image or language.
(c) An action vector, pertaining to the analyst's actions, including listening, formulating interpretations, and delivering them.
(d) An object relations of knowledge vector, concerning the analyst's relationship with psychoanalytic concepts.
(e) A coherence versus contradiction vector, directed at the way that the analyst balances coherence and contradiction within his own process, and handles these in his interactions with his patient. The use of metaphor is noted to be important here.
(f) A developmental vector, concerning the analyst's understanding of and attitudes towards developmental stages/phases.

1. Symmetrical transference field

In the first interview, S11(PA), speaking about the nature of the analytic process, gave a relatively theoretical account of regression to primitive levels of functioning, describing unconscious communication in terms of projective identification. She employed standard terminology, adding her own understanding of the meanings that she was attributing to the terms. She then referred to the session forming the interview instrument, and the joint regression in patient and analyst that, she said, allowed projective identification to take place and the analyst to apply some alpha function to the patient's beta elements. Thereafter, she shifted to a developmental comparison, and began referring to *fusion* and *locked-in projective identification on both sides* (S11(PA), I1, p. 14).

These inconsistencies prompted a query in the second interview. At this point, she spontaneously produced a clinical example of her own, and after recounting an unfolding clinical moment, reverted unprompted to her theoretical understanding in a new way. Now, she spoke about transient moments of merging and shared experience, and made the observation that the term "projective identification" did not cover such experience. In the subsequent data analysis of both interviews, this generated an understanding of a symmetrical field existing at certain primitive levels of functioning.

Here is evidence of a private theory in accordance with Canestri, having topographical aspects in terms of thinking at conscious levels, as discussed in the interview, preconscious levels, in terms of partially thought through ideas, and unconscious levels, accessed by reference to clinical material. A conceptual vector is demonstrated in terms of S11(PA)'s account of the transference field, referring to Kleinian ideas of projective identification and Bion's notion of alpha functioning. The reference by S11(PA) to her clinical material may be seen as recourse to metaphor to assist in clarifying something not as yet understood, and this brings in Canestri's coherence versus contradiction vector, and its reference to the function of metaphor in dealing with contradiction. It also brings in Fonagy's understanding of the role of two minds trying to fit together understandings of the analytic process, and arriving at metaphor as a way of integrating psychoanalytic hypotheses and empirical research.

2. Bodymind monism

In the first interview, S11(PA) spoke of words having an action level. She referred to the embodiment of thinking rooted in bodily experience, mainly in early infancy, and the way that this shapes language. She went on to describe primitive equivalents of words as actions, manifesting as sensory images and symptoms, these more direct versions of words as actions often being released in analysis.

Asked in the second interview about the origins of such understanding, S11(PA) gave a detailed account of the evolution of her views, starting from

Isaacs's paper on unconscious phantasy (1948). Next, she referred to published work on embodied cognition, and various training and research projects in which she had participated, involving evaluation of tape-recorded sessions, bringing together ideas from the fields of linguistics, attachment and cognition. Her account was full and coherent, and demonstrated views based in years of careful thinking.

Referring to Canestri, it was clear that by now the topographical vector was operating mainly in the conscious mode, supplemented in the conceptual vector by a range of well-formed technical assumptions, demonstrating S11(PA)'s established relationship with her own internal conceptual objects in the object relations of knowledge vector. Canestri's developmental vector also features in an elaborated fashion.

Conclusion

The above description shows how two interviews with S11(PA), and an accompanying data analysis, yield a private theory for S11(PA), which is partially conscious and partially unconscious, in accordance with the literature on implicit theories.

It takes the interviews of S11(PA) as a detailed example of the manner in which the other interviews in this project were also conducted and analysed, to yield a set of individual interview profiles that were then collated and compared to produce an overall empirical result for the project.

Notes

1 Each interviewee is designated PA, psychoanalyst, or AP, analytical psychologist (i.e. Jungian) to distinguish differing affiliations.
2 Hesitations and repetitions have been removed from these excerpts.
3 I1 and I2 herein refer, respectively, to first and second interviews with the interviewee.
4 By contrast with some interviewees, particularly amongst the Jungians.
5 On enquiry, S11(PA) indicated that she preferred the spelling "phantasy" to "fantasy".
6 A couple of short passages and identifying details of X are omitted for reasons of confidentiality.

Chapter 8

The results of the empirical study

Introduction

Although the interviewees[1] were all given the same process notes and the same set of discussion vertices, their responses varied widely, linguistically and conceptually. Some interviewees tracked the process notes closely from a clinical or theoretical standpoint, while others used them to free-associate into metaphorical accounts of theory and practice, only loosely based around the session. The different voices were all, without exception, distinctive and idiosyncratic.

This brings in a complication over terminology. Every analytic concept mentioned has its public, that is established, meanings, but, in their private theories, each interviewee was found to have their own personal definition for any term, and to be employing public theory in their own idiosyncratic, but possibly neither conscious nor accurate, fashion. Further, the interview process was designed to encourage free association, and so it was not practical to interrupt interviewees repeatedly for definitions. Accordingly, the meaning in the moment is prioritised here over conceptual precision applied to public theory.

The range of approaches can be appreciated from the observations on the session:

Session

The session took place just before the Christmas break in an intensive analysis. The patient, a woman in her mid-50s, came into treatment feeling cut off from herself, and from other people. Initially, she mentions a fear of going back into a black cloud of depression, and associates to a memory of homeless people making demands. Her words are delivered in a cut-off manner, without any affect. Interpretations about the break are dismissed. Eventually, after an interpretation about being pushed out and made homeless by the analyst, she says that what comes to mind is how busy she is, and produces an agitated account of everything pressing in. When the analyst interprets the way that busy-ness pushes out an aspect of herself that then feels made homeless, she quietens. At this point, the analyst has an experience of a sensory imagistic event ("the phenomena") involving giving a small carved wooden object to a child, who snatches it. The analyst makes an interpretation about childhood experiences of absence, now received by the patient. Towards the end of the session, the patient recounts a dream of a woman diving over a cliff, leaving the analyst anxious and floundering to find an interpretation.

Some interviewees (S3(AP), S5(AP), S12(AP), S8(PA), S10(PA), S11(PA)) began with the session opening, while others (S2(AP), S5(AP), S6(PA), S9(PA)) launched straight into a consideration of the phenomena. A few (S3(AP), S8(PA)) made direct links between the phenomena and the closing dream. The responses generally fell into two camps, namely those (S1(AP), S2(AP), S3(AP), S5(AP), S12(AP), S8(PA), S9(PA), S11(PA)) who felt the event marked a real moment of meaning, a turning point in the session, and those (S6(PA), S7(PA)) who acknowledged the event simply as one clinical fact amongst a number. All of the interviewees considered that the event constituted countertransference, save S10(PA), who thought that it comprised primarily the analyst's own material and was therefore to be ignored.

It is interesting to look at the beginning, middle and end of the session in terms of these different responses.

Beginning: Those who commenced here picked up on a quality of dissociation, observing that the analyst was tracking the patient's words, and the patient responding, but the interchange lacked life. S3(AP) commented that the analyst did not feel very embodied when she took up the patient's anger over the approaching break: the interpretation was probably correct, but not something the patient could use. S11(PA) said that it was like the analyst being an analyst and the patient being a patient. S8(PA) noticed how cut off the patient was from an analyst, who was attentive and available, saying he would be monitoring this splitting. These interviewees stressed a dynamic involving *two separate people* speaking to the conscious material and not managing to meet one another.

Middle: All but one interviewee felt that the session shifted gear, and an unconscious element took over, when the event occurred.

Some interviewees described this in terms of regression. S8(PA) described the patient's fear of "going back" as fear of regression to an earlier stage involving a powerful, visceral demand for someone to watch over her, as in the phenomena. He observed that patients in the more somatic range of experience bring a literal need for objects that reassure, linking this with a central confusion on the part of this patient as to what belongs where and with whom. S9(PA) noted a deep level of aloneness in the patient, and the need for regression to a more primitive state of mind, to get to a place where the aloneness could be reached through the analyst being present in silence beside the patient. And, S11(PA) contemplated regression as a move to more primitive levels of mental functioning, involving the emergence of unconscious phantasy and/or increased contact with physical experience. He noted that the phenomena indicated a shift, where:

> [T]he analyst intuitively moves from trying to express [the transference relationship] in ideas, which the patient is not really doing much with, to a set of somatic images and experiences, which express something much more direct about [. . .] the infantile version of that situation.
> (S11(PA), I1, p. 5)

Other interviewees referred to depth. For example, S1(AP) described the moment as a significant shift, bringing the analyst to something deeper or earlier, the approaching break having engendered in the patient psychoid memory at a level of early separations where body and mind are the same thing (S1(AP), I1, p. 10).[2]

S3(AP) also referred to Jung's psychoid:

> [W]here distinctions between people do not really exist. [. . .] [T]his thing that happened in your body and in your fantasy, that's the deepest level of communication from her to you, around the deepest issue requiring healing still. [. . .] [T]his is psychoid material in the body.
> (S3(AP), I1, pp. 12, 15)

For S2(AP), the phenomena emerged from "the complex system, which results from the meeting of the analyst and the analysand. . . . [I]f we talk about unconscious, I would say that it's the unconscious of the meeting" (S2(AP), I1, p. 3).

These interviewees envisaged the event as a shift to body-mind and/or self-other undifferentation.

The following described this an undifferentiated self-other state or participation mystique: S1(AP), S3(AP), S12(AP). S5(AP) referred to the unconscious connection[3] in Jung's symmetrical transference diagram (1946, p. 221). And, the following felt that the new shift was based on the generation of a third zone between analyst and patient: S2(AP), S9(PA). The next set of interviewees considered the interaction to be projection or projective identification: S6(PA), S8(PA), S11(PA). The remaining interviewees did not specify a mechanism, S4(AP) simply describing the analyst's countertransference as "the sense of being one has contemporaneously with the patient", and S7(PA) observing that he would resist definitions as being too concrete.

End: Various interviewees highlighted a flow from the phenomena to the patient's final dream, and some (S3(AP), S8(PA)) specifically moderated their view of the dream, on the ground that a turning point took place when the phenomena arose. S3(AP) felt that the phenomena constituted a transitional object signalling that the patient could now manage separation, and in consequence the final dream was prognostic of the disappearance of an old, outmoded complex. S8(PA), likewise, considered that the phenomena represented something for the patient to hold on to, indicating a clinically significant shift or turning point in the session, possibly in the treatment, from a dissociation, where the analyst feels cut off, towards a real capacity for primitive communication. He thought this enabled her actually to bring the final dream, but that such forward movement might also terrify her. Therefore, he felt that the dream was probably more about the patient's fear that the analyst might not catch her rather than any intimation of actual disaster. S9(PA), whilst not specifically linking the phenomena and the dream, nonetheless juxtaposed comments about the primitive state of the patient, leading in the phenomena to somatic states of mind, with observations about her teasingly withholding information that she is all right in relation to the dream.

These interviewees, therefore, implied that, by the end of the session, some self-other differentiation has taken place, enabling the patient to bring the dream as a disclosure of her own and to be less exercised about the potentially disastrous dive in the dream.

Aliter: By contrast, S6(PA) viewed the session in terms of splitting. He felt that the patient was resistant to interpretations about the break, and then the phenomena came in a direct way, representing a form of transitional object to provide comfort over the break; this was helpful in assisting the analyst to understand what was split off and to shape an interpretation that could be received. However, he saw the closing dream as representative of disaster, and hence as a worrying, disturbing attack on the abandoning object, indicating another split. The first split involved something comforting, the second something disastrous.

S10(PA) felt that the phenomena should have been ignored, being the analyst's material, and that the focus should have been the patient's conscious communications about "black cloud" and "being homeless".

General results

As the results began to crystallise from the overall data analysis, two key strands emerged, relating to the transference field. Some interviewees, primarily but not solely the Jungians, described the transference as an *undifferentiated* field, in which differentiation is the task. This may be described as a symmetric model, in that both the analyst and the patient contribute equally at an unconscious level. At the same time, the fact that the analyst has had a training analysis implies that he is better able to process and discriminate his own material at a more conscious level. Others of the interviewees, primarily the psychoanalysts, described a situation in which the focus is on the patient and their unconscious, the patient is seen as projecting onto or into the analyst, and the analyst, whilst seeking to discriminate out their own material before making interpretations, nonetheless is viewing the dynamic primarily as being generated by the patient. This hierarchical condition may be described as an asymmetric model.

Basically, these two strands materialised as three specific categories:

(a) Mutual self-other *immersion*, namely participation mystique (S2(AP), S3(AP), S12(AP));
(b) An imaginal zone *between* self and other, constituting a shared third (S5(AP), S7(PA), S9(PA));
(c) A hierarchical condition, wherein the patient *communicates* events *to* the analyst by means of projection or projective identification, thereby putting parts of themselves into the analyst (S6(PA), S10(PA)).

Categories (a) and (b) designate the *symmetric* field, to which analyst and patient contribute equally, and category (c) designates the unequal and *asymmetric* field, as further discussed below.[4]

A number of the interviewees (S1(AP), S2(AP), S7(PA), S8(PA), S11(PA), S12(AP)) managed to combine both models, with a greater or lesser degree of coherence, for example contemplating an asymmetric field at a personal level or at the beginning of analysis and a symmetric field at an archetypal level or as analysis progressed. A further possibility embraced moments of symmetry, based on regression, in an otherwise asymmetric field.

Common clusters of ideas in the interviews of those inclining to a symmetric field were: undifferentiation, participation mystique, emergence, moments of intensity and meaning or turning points, and embodied countertransference, leading on to Jung, psychoid, and synchronicity. In the interviews of those favouring an asymmetric field, the following clusters of ideas were prominent: projective identification, pushing material onto/into the analyst, Klein, Bion, container-contained, alpha/beta elements, proto-mental. Symbolic capacity in one form or another was addressed by virtually all of the interviewees.

1. Symmetric model

Most of the Jungian interviewees conceived a purely symmetric model for the transference field.

S3(AP) contemplated a total self-other undifferentiation, and distinguished two levels of clinical work, namely a process level associated with the ego and an analytic level associated with the unconscious:

> [I] draw on Jungian theory throughout: first by invoking an understanding of the psyche and of psychic interaction that's connected with [Jung's] psychological types, i.e. types of consciousness that either meet or don't meet when people interact, including analyst and analysand in their present realities, and then Jung's theory of the psychoid to explain

that level in which patient and therapist are just commonly human at the somatic level, which is always connecting us to each other. Probably, all of this turns into a very elaborated Jungian theory of attachments.

(S3(AP), I1, p. 12)

In the case of the psychoid level, he employed the term "participation mystique", acknowledging that Jung borrowed the term from Lévy-Bruhl to refer to a relationship in which the subject and the object are undifferentiated, implying joint *immersion* in the transference field. In the opinion of S3(AP), Jung employed the terms "participation mystique" and "psychoid" as coterminous, using participation mystique earlier on in his theoretical development, and psychoid later. For S3(AP), individuals are "amazingly connected" at this level, where "there is no real subject/object split, and there also is no body/psyche split" (S3(AP), I2, p. 6). According to S3(AP), analysis fosters the development of an individual psyche, that has the capacity to reflect and that gradually becomes more and more differentiated (ibid., 7).

S2(AP) was also clear about this. For him, the meeting of patient and analyst in the clinical session creates a new system, which he calls *the encounter*, that is neither one nor the other but both. He had his own metaphor of *the chimera* for this, a symbol having a mythical aspect, as creature combining bodily parts from lion, goat and serpent, and a biological aspect, as a single organism combining cells of two zygotes, being neither one nor the other. There is a lack of differentiation in the encounter, which may be conceived like Winnicott's mother-baby unit, that there is no mother without a baby and no baby without a mother, but only a mother-baby and a baby-mother, and the task of analysis like the task of life is differentiation. Accordingly, for S2(AP), the encounter constitutes a third area *between* the patient and the analyst. The analyst moves in and out of this undifferentiated zone, allowing himself to be possessed by the encounter and then bringing his consciousness to bear to differentiate his experience.

The next few interviewees also conveyed notions of a shared unconscious arena.

S12(AP) employed terms, such as participation mystique, Pleroma and psychoid, as well as imaginal third zone, and mirror-touch synaesthesia. His overall account emphasised primarily a shared imaginal zone or third area, a transference field *between* patient and analyst, where sensual images can be experienced, and he spoke of his own work in a manner clearly displaying a sense of two people with such a dynamic between them. He described different stages of analysis, an early stage when analyst and patient are struggling together, and a later stage when this transference field arises. For him, the phenomena in the session represented the heart of the analytical process, an indication that patient and analyst are now in harness together and that such transference field has instantiated, with the phenomena bubbling up (emerging) from the depths out of the blue. Often, this kind of experience reflects turning points in a session or in the analysis as a whole.

He also made a distinction with projective identification:

> I think [there] is a crucial difference between projective identification and participation mystique. So, projective identification is seen, certainly by some, as a means of getting rid of unwanted unconscious material from one person *into* another, so that they feel it. And that's, you can certainly look at it that way, but that's not my standpoint.
>
> (S12(AP), I2, p. 4)

He sees participation mystique as something that many patients need:

> [I]n the hope that we will listen under the words, below what is visible, and pick up something that probably goes back to a mother-infant experience in terms of togetherness. And particularly to do with early infancy and the way that the sensory system is, certainly for very small babies, it is all interlinked. [. . .] It's both archetypal and developmental, because it comes from such an early stage that it has to have big archetypal elements.
>
> (Ibid., p. 5)

S1(AP) referred to a meshing of experience between patient and analyst, in which the analyst is affected and infected at the level of the autonomic nervous system. He described it as something that is happening to the mind and body, not just of the analyst but *between* analyst and patient, that is, in a third zone, engendering in the analyst experiences that he terms *sensuous imagery*. S1(AP) considered the phenomena to be an example of this, arising out of infant experience of the patient "terribly reactivated" at a psychoid level of early separations and intimately shared in the psyche-soma of the analyst (S1(AP), I1, pp. 5, 9). Critical reflection is then required on the part of the analyst, by contemplating his own pathology and potential influence on the interaction, in order to differentiate himself from the patient.

A few of the psychoanalysts also envisaged a shared unconscious area *enveloping* or *between* analyst and patient, although they did not employ the same terminology.

The account of S11(PA) at first presented some ambiguity: The analytic process, according to S11(PA), involves the analyst resonating with a scenario of the patient that is being played out, where resonating may be seen as two people associating and having an interaction at the level of their adult selves. Gradually, a *joint* regression takes place, where access is opened up to the more basic levels of *both* people. Then, the interaction is more in the nature of projective identification, where one person's psychic experience is infused with that of the other in a way that forces the recipient to take in and react to the other's experience. Such projective identification can be witnessed most powerfully between a parent and a new baby. He described this state as the two being *fused* in an extreme form of locked-in projective identification on *both* sides. This mutuality combined with use of the term "projective identification" lent some confusion to the nature of the transference field being envisaged.

Asked for further elaboration, he gave an example from his own practice of a brief clinical moment, where he felt a merging of experience took place with a patient, who was confronting the loss of his dying companion and facing childhood memories of his parents' deaths. There was a very real sense of being right with the patient in the presence of death. He described himself as analyst feeling fused into the patient's experience, and as sharing with the patient his, the analyst's, strength, thus enabling both to emerge from the experience. S11(PA) displayed some confusion over the language to be employed for this account, saying "I think projective identification is not really. . . . I don't know what the right expression would be, exactly, for it" (S11(PA), I2, p. 18). S11(PA) thinks in terms of levels of the unconscious, and, therefore, the researcher concluded that his model envisaged levels in the transference field, including a primitive one in which the experience is not hierarchical but shared and symmetrical. S11(PA), therefore, may be considered to hold a model displaying asymmetry normally but symmetry at a deeply regressed, primitive level.

S9(PA) also implied that his model embraces a deeply unconscious area that is mutual. For him, patients in primitive states of mind are often in one-person states, where words do not reach them and the analyst does not exist. Referring to Freud, he observed that regression is then needed to get into the room with the patient as an alive object, regression of the analyst as much as the patient. Only then can the history of the patient, and understanding, emerge. He implied that transformation involves an emergent dynamic between patient and analyst:

> I think that when you come into an analytic consulting room, you have the potential for the emergence of things other than the usual repressed stuff. It's a potential space. So, I think that it's always there, potentially, whether it's used or not at any given time, or might take time to be used – the deeper the repression, the more vital the emergence of something else, and the more difficult to allow that to happen. No, emergence is a potential space.
>
> (S9(PA), I2, pp. 20–21)

Noting to him that he had not used expressions such as "projection" and "projective identification", he responded that this was astute, and discriminated between a hierarchical model of analysis, where the analyst is the expert, and a shared situation, where analyst and patient are engaged in something together and an emergent dynamism *between* them aids transformation:

> [T]here's nothing special about being an analyst because, if an analyst doesn't have a patient, they actually can't do analysis. It needs an analyst and an analysand to do analysis. [. . .] What we have is two different positions in analysis. You're in one, I'm in another, but each on their own is not about analysis. Each, one on the couch, one on the chair behind, together, the we-ness of that structure is that analysis can happen.
>
> (Ibid., pp. 16–17)

This account is remarkably similar to that of S2(AP) of Winnicott's mother-baby unit. Thus, it was concluded that S9(PA)'s description of the consulting room as a potential space involving two positions implies a symmetric field situated *between* analyst and patient.

S7(PA) referred to projection a few times, but then described analysis as a *shared* situation, a complex whole, in which the patient experiences everything associated with the analyst as linked to early objects, and fantasies are evoked and enacted by *both* patient *and* analyst. He resisted any notion of delineating the process, saying, "I am more interested in this ongoing relationship in interaction between two people" and emphasising that he looks for the meaning within the complex wholeness of the work (S7(PA), I2, p. 9). Asked how he arrives at interpretation, he responded:

> I'm smiling because it would sound very strange. It has to be dreamed. [. . .] I]t's about allowing experience to evolve to the level of thinking, but not to forget the experience, because experience is crucial, staying with experience, staying with ambiguity, staying with, not rushing into thinking.
>
> (Ibid., p. 7)

This account also entertains a symmetric model for the transference field.

Within these accounts, it became apparent that various clusters of ideas were prominent, including embodiment, symbolic capacity, and emergence, as discussed below.

a. Embodiment

Embodiment was generally found to be more important for the Jungians than the psychoanalysts. Some interviewees (S1(AP), S2(AP), S3(AP), S4(AP), S11(PA), S12(AP)) were familiar with embodied experience in the countertransference, and considered imagistic sensory phenomena to be common. These analysts tended to have relatively developed ideas about, and language for, such experience, some (S1(AP), S2(AP), S3(AP)) believing the sensory experience of the analyst to be central to the analytic process. Other interviewees (S6(PA), S8(PA), S9(PA), S10(PA)) were not familiar with sensory forms of image but could recollect having vague symptoms, for example, sleepiness. These interviewees tended to place less importance on sensory aspects of the analytic process, although some (S6(PA), S9(PA)) had well-developed models for understanding patients' psychosomatic symptoms. A few interviewees (S4(AP), S11(PA), S12(AP)) spoke of a taboo in the analytic community against mentioning embodiment in the countertransference.

For S1(AP), S2(AP), S3(AP), S4(AP), S12(AP), the analyst's sensory experience is crucial.

At the outset, S3(AP) framed the field of enquiry as "what is happening in the body", indicating that he considers the embodied response of the analyst the *most reliable* source of information about the analytic process (S3(AP), I1, p. 2). For him, the personal is in the body, and the body is needed in order to process the archetypes, since:

> This thing that happened in your body and in your fantasy, that's the deepest level of communication [from the patient] around the deepest issue requiring healing still. [. . .] [T]his is psychoid material in the body. This is the part of all of our organisms that's below the cerebral cortex. It's the level of the sympathetic nervous system.
>
> (Ibid., p. 15)

Three interviewees linked embodiment with imagery.

S1(AP) said that he had developed his own theory for an "embodied countertransference"[5] informing his understanding of the patient. He described this theory as an internal theoretical object, combining ideas from Jung, Bion, other psychoanalysts and especially from philosophers, such as Spinoza, Herder and the German Romantics. Noting that Jung described body and mind as two aspects of a unitary bodymind, he said, "it's interesting to always have in mind and in experience that they [body and mind] are not different" (S1(AP), I1, p. 13). Such dual-aspect monism is thus a lived experience, for which he had coined his own term, "sensuous imagery", meaning imagery that has an effect on all the senses, the body, the brain and the emotions, that conveys "the hardness of things, the colour of things, the emotional tone of things" (S1(AP), I2, pp. 3, 6). He related this to Jung's psychoid concept, described by him as intimacy at the level of the autonomic nervous system, activating an unconscious *meshing* of experience in *both* patient *and* analyst, generating in the analyst psyche-soma information that then requires critical reflection on his part, in order to discriminate out material that belongs to the patient (ibid., pp. 5, 9).

S2(AP) described clinical meaning as "emerging from the unconscious through the body", implying that the analyst lends his body to being shaped by "the encounter" created by the meeting of analyst and analysand (S2(AP), I1, p. 7). He clarified this, by reference to Winnicott, commenting that the developmental process of differentiation begins with the differentiation of the bodies of the baby and the mother. The analytic process is similar, and the analyst assists this by bringing consciousness to bear and enabling meaning to emerge in his own imagination through his body. S2(AP) emphasised that true imagination involves the whole body.

Whilst, for S1(AP) and S2(AP), sensory countertransference images yield symbolic understanding and meaning generally, S12(AP) described suffering sensory images that later turned out to correspond quite literally with physical memories of the patient, of a kind felt to be unthinkable. He referred to Jung's psychoid concept to explain this situation, and also mentioned research on mirror-touch synaesthesia conducted at University College London (UCL) by Banissey & Ward (2007a).[6]

Amongst the psychoanalysts, S11(PA) considered it normal for the analyst to experience the countertransference in a sensory fashion. Commencing from what he called "the embodiment of thinking", meaning that the roots of thinking and feeling lie in bodily experience, S11(PA) described words as having a level unconsciously at which they are actions, expressing a shape of a sensory or tactile experience, like eating, vomiting or hitting. Physical images and metaphors are more direct versions of words as actions, arising at a primitive base level of experience associated with regression. Symptoms arise at an even more primitive level. For S11(PA), therefore, body and mind are seamlessly linked by levels of functioning, implying that S11(PA) has a monistic understanding.

S9(PA) associated an analyst's sensory experience with primitive states of mind and regression in the patient. Elsewhere, in his published work,[7] he mentions an interpenetrating psychotic muddle, and the need for the analyst to bear the auditory, visual and tactile hallucinations that occur in such states.

In summary, the Jungian interviewees generally approach embodied countertransference as essential to analytic work, and two of the psychoanalysts (S9(PA), S11(PA)) were clearly familiar with embodied countertransference. These interviewees all consider body and mind to be inextricably bound together, S2(AP) and S3(AP) both referring to deeply unconscious levels where body and mind are undifferentiated, and S1(AP), based on the ideas of Spinoza and Jung, quite specifically referring to a dual-aspect monism.

In contrast, most psychoanalysts gave less credence to embodiment. Specifically, S6(PA) described himself occasionally having vague symptoms, but being more focussed on psychosomatic patients. S10(PA) indicated that analytic listening involves getting into a particular state of mind, corresponding to Bion's "abandoning memory, desire and understanding", Freud's "evenly suspended attention", and Heimann's "freely mobile sensibility". Accordingly, he seeks to avoid being drawn into events, including his own internal images and sensory experiences, which would disturb such state of mind. He observed that it would be different if he felt that sensory experience was due to the patient, and gave an example where he could not shake off the idea that intense stabbing headaches were caused by elements that are:

> [P]rojected, either into the patient's own body or into their analyst's body, pretty directly, sometimes by resonance of voice, or what Meltzer used to say temperature of voice, or a mysterious way that we don't yet understand. [. . .] But whatever it is that's projected, it's not, as Bion would say, it is not suited for articulation, symbolic thought, communication. It's suited only for expulsion. [. . .] So these phenomena, proto-mental, I would take to be beta elements.
> (S10(PA), I1, pp. 15–16)

Thus, virtually all the interviewees acknowledged the existence of sensory countertransference phenomena in varying guises.

b. Symbolic capacity

Almost all of the interviewees were interested in symbolic capacity. In some instances, the significance of symbolisation was implicit, being evident rather in their personal use of symbolic language than stated as a clinical aim (S1(AP), S2(AP), S3(AP), S4(AP), S9(PA), S12(AP)). For example, S1(AP) employed the term "sensuous imagery" to describe imagistic experience having a sensual component, associated by him with the psychoid unconscious, that informs his understanding of the patient and hence his interpretations. Likewise, S2(AP) mentioned Jung's reference to true imagination, in relation to interpreting, dreams and active imagination, as informing *both* his own emerging understanding of his patients *and* their developing sense of self (S2(AP), I2, p. 4).

S5(AP) offered a more developed view of symbolising function, which he discussed in relation to patients who bring apparently symbolic dreams and yet have no conscious capacity for formulating symbolic meaning: the symbolic meaning is at a higher level than their conscious attitude can accommodate. He proposed the idea that symbolic meaning requires the addition of consciousness, on the ground that it is the "unconscious that's organising all the information, and therefore what comes into consciousness has already got a lot of organisation and symbolic potential in it, but it needs to have this extra thing that consciousness does, to bring it alive" (S5(AP), I1, p. 8). This suggests that the analyst may at times need to provide consciousness and a symbolising function for the patient.

By contrast, S6(PA), S7(PA), S8(PA), S10(PA) and S11(PA) all referred quite specifically to the development of the patient's symbolic capacity as a clinical aim.

S11(PA) contemplates assisting the patient to shift from a more symptomatic concrete level to a more symbolic level, and S8(PA) described himself as interested in a patient's ability to represent things in their mind, seeing "part of the therapeutic process being facilitating some movement from something that's less metabolised, less digested, less conscious, less formed, into something that becomes more conceivable, more elaborated" (S8(PA), I2, p. 4).

S6(PA) described an analytic model, which seeks to help patients elaborate their symptoms symbolically. He considers symptoms to be split off paranoid-schizoid objects displaced into the body, seeing them as primitive symbols approaching the symbolic equation of Hanna Segal. They are often associated with early developmental difficulties over symbol formation, and may be difficult to convert in the direction of symbolisation, but working through generally begins to be possible when affect or representations arise. S10(PA) is interested theoretically and clinically in a *lack of* symbolisation, but he also described seeking hidden parts of the patient and trying to help them to make a shift towards the depressive position, to enable symbolic work and thinking to take place (S10(PA), I2, pp. 13–14).

c. Emergence

Another aspect of the process featuring prominently in some but not all of the interviews was emergence. The interviewees for whom emergence occupies a significant role were S2(AP), S3(AP), S5(AP), S9(PA) and S11(PA).

S2(AP) was the most articulate, stating that "he would like to use the word 'emergence'" to describe the phenomena (S2(AP), I1, p. 3):

> For me, the important [thing] is not the phenomena itself, it is how the phenomena is going to shape our thoughts. And to allow us to think what we would be unable to think without that. [. . .] It is an emergent process. [. . . T]hese phenomena are linked to the complex system, [. . .] which is the encounter. [. . .] [F]rom this system emerges something which would not have emerged in another system. [. . .] I would say that, in this moment, the important thing for the analysis is that you have been able to accept to lose your [. . .] boundaries, so that's this complex system, which is the transference, will then take the place of your ego, inside your psyche, inside your body first, and then your psyche. And will create inside you some shape or representation, using your consciousness for that. And then you recovered your boundaries, and you have been able to think something, to be conscious of a thinking, which has emerged from this experience inside you. [. . . There is also] the necessity of time for the analyst to lose his boundaries and the necessity of time for the patient to be able to hear something about an important insight. And what is very mysterious for me is that this

necessity of time is coming from the encounter, and no one decides, it emerges. And usually, when it emerges like this, [. . .] if the analyst is able to say something, usually the analysand is able to hear.

(S2(AP), I1, pp. 3–5)

He emphasised that this emergence can assist in reuniting a split in the analysand, observing that the area from which such emergence arises is "the psychoid" (S2(AP), I1, p. 10).

S3(AP) described emergence in terms of Jung's *Seven Sermons to the Dead*:

[M]ost Jungians tend to get more excited about what the *Sermons* call the Pleroma, because that is the ultimate, unknowable source from which archetypes emerge to foster psychological development. But, the *Sermons* also speak of the Creatura. [. . .] Creatura is the Latin word for creature, i.e. our creatureliness, the body. [. . .] You need the Creatura to process [the archetypes] so that what they have to offer can become your own.

(S3(AP), I1, pp. 8–9)

[Jung] presents these two ideas, the Pleroma, out of which all the archetypes are constantly emerging, and the Creatura, which is the needy, human embodied creature that has to experience things, with attachment needs and with interdependence. And he creates his psychology of a relation to emergent archetypes, which may have the capacity of building psychic structure, experienced by a Creatura who is still a creature, a human creature, very much living in what I would call the psychoid realm.

(S3(AP), I2, p. 16)

S11(PA) also discussed the process of emergence:

[Q]uite often I think it goes through that sequence, which involves some sensory or physical experience, commonly for the patient and sometimes for the analyst. And sometimes I've been cued into something, which I probably might not have made contact with otherwise, through a physical symptom of my own, which has alerted me to something about the patient, which then has turned out to be quite a key thing, either a physical issue that they've got or some phantasy that they have. So, there's that emergence where something. . . . It's almost like being born, something is introduced into the analysis as something that can be known and worked on, but almost indirectly through some much more visceral kind of resonance.

(S11(PA), I2, pp. 11–12)

The remaining interviewees made brief references. For example, S5(AP) described the session phenomena in terms of:

> [A] purposive unconscious, or perhaps as I might say an unconscious that is organised and organising, so that the material that comes out of the unconscious is not random and is not simply chaotic or instinctual but I think there is also a lot of work that goes on in the direction of meaning, and formulation, that goes on unconsciously before things emerge into consciousness.
>
> (S5(AP), I1, p. 4)

He indicated that he found "the emergence idea" helpful, because it means that organisation arises through process (S5(AP), I2, p. 7).

S12(AP) referred to unconscious imagery bubbling up out of the blue, saying that the phenomena might be described in various ways, including Jung's transcendent function, emergence and synchronicity: "They're just different ways of describing phenomena that come from [the psychoid realm] and that have their feet in it, that are rooted in it. And there is a dynamic, energetic movement, between mind, between body, between spirit and psychoid" (S12(AP), I1, p. 15).

S9(PA) did not employ any of the same terminology, but he implied that his model of unconscious interaction is emergent. Regression enables the history of the patient, and understanding, to emerge. Interpretations should also emerge and be made in the authentic moment for *both* patient *and* analyst. He described the analytic consulting room as a potential space, where there is "the potential for the emergence of things other than the usual repressed stuff" (S9, I2, p. 21).

Accordingly, these interviewees contemplate an organising function in the unconscious, actively shaping material to produce emergent understanding in the analyst that fosters interpretation.

d. Summary

The key common themes arising out of these interviews were:

(i) A model of the transference based on an undifferentiated self-other unconscious area, namely a symmetric field (S1(AP), S2(AP), S3(AP), S5(AP), S12(AP), S7(PA), S9(PA), S11(PA))

    a. Having a developmental aspect (S1(AP), S2(AP), S3(AP), S12(AP), S7(PA), S11(PA))

(ii) An embodied countertransference (S1(AP), S2(AP), S3(AP), S12(AP), S9(PA), S11(PA))

a. Implying an undifferentiated, monistic bodymind (S1(AP), S2(AP), S3(AP), S12(AP), S9(PA), S11(PA)
   b. Needed for healing a dissociation in the patient (S2(AP), S3(AP), S12(AP), S11(PA))

(iii) An organising function in the unconscious combined with an emergent dynamism (S2(AP), S3(AP), S5(AP), S12(AP), S9(PA)) as a source of meaning and understanding (S2(AP), S3(AP), S5(AP), S12(AP), S9(PA)).

A number of interviewees attributed these characteristics to a psychoid factor associated with an ultimately unknowable psychoid unconscious. Whilst only the Jungians actually employed the term "psychoid", nevertheless the above Jungians and psychoanalysts all recognise a deeply unconscious and undifferentiated arena relating to primitive, archaic or developmental states of mind, an arena that is seen as a source of embodied transferential experience and of an emergent dynamism yielding an authentic, living process that brings about transformation.

2. Asymmetric model

The psychoanalysts, with the exception of S7(PA) and S9(PA) discussed above, all described a model for unconscious interaction based primarily around projection and projective identification, implying that there are two people in the room in a hierarchical situation. Accordingly, the models of S6(PA), S8(PA), S10(PA), and to some extent S11(PA), may be considered asymmetric.

S6(PA) described the transference in terms of a primitive arena, filled with the patient's persecutory objects and anxious phantasies.[8] In his model, the patient deals with events, such as unmanageable affect and loss that cannot be mourned, either by projecting them into the analyst, in whom "a value" then appears, representing the split-off experience in the countertransference, or by displacing them into his own body, as a symptom, leaving the analyst stuck in a rather stark position as an observer, worrying about the symptom but feeling powerless to make sense of it. His descriptions of his own work suggested an idea of analysis functioning as a relationship, in which the transference serves to convey crucial information about the patient's split-offelements and in which the analyst works on this basis and his knowledge of the history of the patient to formulate and make interpretations in the appropriate moment, which may be quite a struggle. He spoke about these split-off elements coming into the relationship between patient and analyst, as if the relationship helps to bring about change, and therefore gave a strong sense of mutual work in a relational approach.

S8(PA) also referred to splitting, describing a developmental model of projected emotional states, with active processing by the analyst as container. S8(PA) indicated that, for him, analysis has a significant relational aspect and the actual life experience and history of the patient are important. The challenge is how to bring the history of the patient and the transference together in an authentic fashion. He seeks to track the projective processes in the session:

> [T]ransference is actually the way in which you are perceived by the patient, which fits with their earlier experiences and with other significant relationships. And in that way you're being cast into a particular kind of role. The pressure of that is very real.
>
> (S8(PA), I2, p. 8)

He described this as a model of self-other in the domain of projection and introjection, based on an early developmental approach to projected emotional states, and active processing by the analyst as container.

S8(PA) said that he sees change as occurring when the transference is most alive and immediate and direct and, when asked what he meant by alive, he said:

> [I]t has something to do with affect and emotional connectedness. [. . . B]ringing it into the here and now and working with the transference makes it a much more emotionally laden experience. And I think that the emotionally laden experience actually means that you are more able to effect therapeutic change.
>
> (Ibid., p. 11)

These interviewees conveyed a very alive sense of their work combining working in the here and now with knowledge of the history of the patient, and bringing in a relational approach at the same time. The ways in which they described the transference were consistent with an asymmetric model but they also gave a sense of being alongside their patients in a relational way.

As mentioned earlier, S11(PA) conceives the transference field mostly as an asymmetrical situation. He also sees the otherness of the analyst and the role of relationship as vitally important. In his view, the primitive levels of both patient and analyst are to be processed in the analyst's mind as a joint experience, to be fed back to the patient such that the patient can recognise not only their personal issue but also the relationship of the analyst and patient. The relationship is the central thing being represented, not just the self of the patient.

There is a contrasting approach from S10(PA). S10(PA) works mainly in the here and now, observing that reconstruction of the patient's history does not play much part in his work. He acknowledged himself to be strongly influenced by Bion, describing his model of the transference as being based on an early stage of development involving a powerful degree of anxiety, for which the patient seeks a container, and thus as based on projective identification of early infantile material and container-contained. He observed that countertransference is the analyst's most useful instrument, and the issue is whether this can be grasped and brought to a focus, which as Freud said is painful for both patient and analyst.

> I think countertransference is very informative. It's the most useful tool that we have about what's being projected into us, but *only* if we have really allowed ourselves to be stirred up enough.
>
> (Ibid., p. 8)

a. Summary

Those interviewees favouring the asymmetric model all conveyed the importance of relationship in the analytic encounter, noting that the relational quality is crucial in achieving transformation. Additional common themes arising were:

(a) A model of the transference based on projection or projective identification by the patient, namely a hierarchical and asymmetric field (S1(AP), S6(PA), S7(PA), S8(PA), S10(PA), S11(PA))
(b) Embodiment, mainly symptoms, associated with primitive states of mind, seen as split-off elements projected into the body of the analyst or the patient (S6(PA), S8(PA), S10(PA), S11(PA))
(c) Accordingly, a dualistic view of the body and mind (S6(PA), S8(PA), S10(PA))

The asymmetric field was associated with the particular theoretical models of Klein and Bion, all implying duality.

3. Combined models

One of the psychoanalysts, S11(PA), managed to combine both symmetric and asymmetric models, referring generally to projective identification, then describing a situation where both parties are fused in an extreme form of locked-in projective identification on both sides (S11(PA), I1, p. 14). Based on an example from his practice, an emotional moment of meaning, where he had really felt part of the analysand and very entwined with their situation, he said, "It was as though we'd been together through some sort of fire or flood" (S11(PA), I2, p. 17). Musing, he felt that "projection" was the wrong word in this instance; "it was more of a merging experience" (ibid., p. 17).

Likewise, S7(PA) initially distinguished between communication *from* one party, the patient, *to* the other, the analyst, and a *shared* situation, in which both are affected. Subsequently, he employed the term "projective identification" but, when queried, observed that actually he considers the total situation is not clearly demarcated between patient and analyst.

Certain of the Jungians also need to be mentioned: S1(AP) seemed to manage to combine an asymmetric model with his primary symmetric model discussed above, using language, such as meshing, identifying, empathising, sympathising, to describe the way that the infantile stuff of *both* analyst *and* patient combine, linked with a psychoid level of experience, in which self and other are not separate; then employing Kleinian terms, such as splitting off, pushing out, evacuation. Asked about this paradox, he said:

> I do think in terms of evacuation, I certainly think in terms of splitting, I do. I do, I do, because evacuation, the idea of evacuating something, partly in communication, is surely, it's poetically at least, or conceptually, it is an incredibly psychoid idea, isn't it? Projective identification, I mean it's, good God, what is, so to speak, pure psychic and what is, happens almost somatically, which seems to me incredibly mixed up. [. . .] That's where my sort of monism comes in. [. . .] I don't think these two ways of looking at something transferentially, countertransferentially, those two different angles, are they that far apart?
>
> (S1(AP), I2, p. 12)

He qualified his comments with the caveat that for him it is all information irrespective of the mechanism. It thus appears that S1(AP) manages to combine both symmetric and asymmetric models simultaneously for unconscious interaction.

S2(AP), with a symmetric model, also referred to Bion's alpha and beta elements as a way of describing understanding coming through the body. When asked if he was making a link to Bion's proto-mental matrix, he responded, "but is that not simply beta elements"? (S2(AP), I2, p. 12). He did not overtly bring in the concept of projective identification, although this is an established aspect of beta functioning.

S12(AP), struggling to find language for the analytic process, offered a range of terms both technical and otherwise, including splitting off, projective identification, unconscious identity and participation mystique, as well as mirror-touch synaesthesia, a third area, a shared imaginal field between patient and analyst, a psychoid area linking with the unconscious of both patient and analyst, and the Pleroma. He also employed descriptions of a more symbolic nature, such as umbilical connection, the patient growing into the veins of the analyst, and a silence between two people, out of which something may emerge. Accordingly, his understanding embraced, both theoretically and symbolically, both types of field, firstly in participation mystique and the Pleroma and secondly in a shared imaginal space, as well as a hierarchical situation of projective identification. He contemplated that different ones of these variants might apply in different stages of an analysis.

Discussion

The methodological significance of these results is profound. The interviews yielded two very different conceptual models of the transference, symmetric and asymmetric, linked with very different approaches. Interviewees supporting the symmetric model mostly conceive analytic work to be directed towards a deeply unconscious, undifferentiated and unknowable area, from which emerge, in moments of intensity or meaning, both the issues needing to be addressed and the analytic response or interpretation. At least some of these interviewees felt that there was a numinous aspect to such area, which fosters the healing function. Those favouring the asymmetric model tended to locate analytic work in a more personal unconscious arena and to focus more closely on the tracking of projective processes for determining their analytic responses. These analysts conceive an evolving process, which is directed at overcoming deficit and in which understanding and transformation are seen as emerging gradually over time.

The symmetric model showed a high degree of correspondence with the characteristics of the psychoid concept, as conceived by Jung, and as developed by certain of the post-Jungians,[9] many of the Jungians (S1(AP), S2(AP), S3(AP), S4(AP), S12(AP)) starting primarily from an assumption of an equal and undifferentiated couple in a symmetric transference field. Significantly, one psychoanalyst, S9(PA), also described a symmetric model with a potential unconscious space *shared* between analyst and patient.

By contrast, although many of the psychoanalysts (S6(PA), S8(PA), S10(PA), S11(PA)) hold primarily hierarchical and asymmetric models for the transference field, where the focus is on the patient's material and the analyst is seen as the recipient and the one who processes, discriminates and knows, nevertheless the relational aspect, whether avowed or manifest but not discussed, was seen as significant. S6(PA), S8(PA), S11(PA), for example, embraced to varying degrees something shared and mutual at a relatively conscious level in their asymmetric models and hence suggested a more living and equal balance.

The exceptions to the classification entirely *either* by symmetry *or* by asymmetry, namely S1(AP), S2(AP), S10(PA), S11(PA), S12(AP), bear mention briefly. Both S1(AP) and S2(AP) managed to contemplate, alongside their symmetric models, hierarchical models from Klein and Bion. The former, describing the psychoid concept as situating experience symmetrically *between* the analyst and patient and happening to *both*, also brought in asymmetric notions of projective identification onto, and evacuation into, the analyst by the patient. The latter felt that Bion's notion of beta elements was compatible with his symmetric understanding, but without acknowledging the mechanism of projective identification attached to such elements. In both cases, therefore, notions of asymmetry were appropriated into the privileged symmetric model, at some expense of coherence.

S11(PA) and S12(AP), respectively, started out from entirely asymmetric and symmetric viewpoints, but then brought in contrasting examples. S11(PA) began by referring to projective identification as the mechanism normally taking place in the transference, then described an analytic situation of locked-in projective identification on both sides, and finally, working from an example from his own practice that felt more like fusion, came to the conclusion that projective identification could not account for this and instances of symmetry must be accommodated. Set in the context of his model of levels of functioning arising in analysis,[10] the conclusion may be drawn that projective identification accounts for less deeply unconscious, and mutual identity for more deeply unconscious, processes. S12(AP), by contrast, produced an account of a deeply unconscious and symmetric transference field, but offered the view that early stages of analysis might not have reached this depth and might thus be based more on projective identification and an asymmetric position. Both of these two interviewees thus appeared to have coherent accounts, envisaging a similar, symmetric model for the transference field when working with deeply unconscious processes or primitive states of mind.

Finally, S10(PA), although firmly declaring an asymmetric model based on projective identification, nonetheless spontaneously brought in Bion's proto-mental concept, acknowledging that at that deeply unconscious level elements are communicated in some "mysterious way that we don't yet understand" (S10(PA), I1, p. 15).

Conclusion

This study yielded some very interesting and surprising results. The idea of different kinds of transference field, respectively symmetric and asymmetric, emerged quite naturally from the grounded theory process, without any direction during the interview process on the part of the researcher. And, comparison of the two models allowed for increasing precision of the definitions of each.

Surprisingly, it was found that a number of the psychoanalysts, albeit employing entirely different language from the Jungians, were amongst the interviewees having symmetric models, and this is especially significant. Whilst it might be expected that the Jungians would produce psychoid-congruent results, such views amongst the psychoanalysts would not be foreseen and therefore constitute Popperian evidence in support of Jung's concept.

Notes

1 In this chapter, all interviewees are designated "he", to avoid distraction from the results.
2 I1 = 1st interview; I2= 2nd interview.

3 Described by Jung in certain phases of analysis as participation mystique (1946, para. 376).
4 "Symmetric" and "asymmetric" are expressions adopted by the researcher, not employed by the interviewees.
5 Acknowledged as a reference to terminology coined by Andrew Samuels, to refer to physical, sensual, embodied expression in the analyst of a patient's emotional experience in their inner world of a significant other.
6 This research describes how synaesthetic touch, in the form of tactile sensations that are phenomenologically akin to actual touch, arises in response to the witnessing of physical touch.
7 Included in the bibliography but here omitted for anonymity.
8 In each case, the psychoanalytic interviewees were queried as to whether they would employ the expression "phantasy" or "fantasy". Some (e.g. S6(PA)) indicated they were talking about unconscious phantasy, some (e.g. S11(PA)) employed both expressions depending on whether they were speaking about conscious or unconscious material, and some (e.g. S7(PA)) felt that theory was too delimiting and so chose not to specify.
9 This is discussed further in the next chapter.
10 Discussed in Chapter 7.

Chapter 9

Conclusion

Drawing together the results

Introduction

The last few chapters have focussed on the methodology, implementation and certain results of an empirical study into embodied experience in the analytic consulting room, with reference especially to Jung's psychoid concept. This chapter will now set these results against the historical development of the psychoid concept and its characterisation in Jungian thinking.

The historical study of the psychoid concept traced its origins and its evolution, through a variety of different lenses. For clarification and refinement of Jung's ideas, a comparative and contextual approach was taken, including observations on: the differences in the early thinking of Jung and Freud; the influence of various historical and philosophical schools of thought on Jung's developing conceptualisation of his psychoid concept; and the common origins and diverging evolution of Jung's psychoid concept and Bion's proto-mental concept. The empirical study also took a comparative approach, in the collection of data from analytical psychologists and psychoanalysts alike, and in a data analysis that generated two opposed models for the transference field, namely a symmetric model and an asymmetric model.

In order to draw all of these threads to a conclusion, a distillation of the historical psychoid concept will be proposed, and the empirical results, divided according to the symmetric and asymmetric transference models, will be compared with this. The purpose of the present chapter is thus firstly to enquire what conclusions may be drawn from a comparison of the formal theory and the combined private theories of a group of clinicians, and thereafter to propose a contemporary and clinically applicable view of the psychoid concept.

The chapter thus encompasses a number of different strands:

(a) Firstly, an interweaving of ideas from the different historical approaches will bring these to a focus, yielding a characterisation of the psychoid concept according to public or formal theory.

(b) Next, an empirical understanding of the theory will be generated through the lens of various specific references to the psychoid concept derived from the interview process. Such empirical understanding, hinted at in the results chapter, will be further expounded here. An initial comparison of the formal public theory and these private theories will be made.
(c) Finally, the private theories of the various clinicians concerning understandings of the relation of body and mind in the clinical situation will be evaluated for their impact on a contemporaneous understanding of the psychoid concept.

This will provide a platform for a discussion of the relevance and applications of the psychoid concept in the present day, accompanied by certain caveats concerning the limitations of this research and suggestions for possible future avenues for research.

The psychoid concept – a historical understanding

Historically, the work of Jung and, later, the Berlin Group makes various links between the psychoid concept and the transference field.

It is to be noted that Jung was first alerted to the question of a transference onto the physician by Freud's early reference to such event in *The Psychology of Hysteria* (1893). The transference was seen at the time as an obstruction, and Jung discussed this with reference to various clinical examples in his correspondence with Freud (McGuire, 1991). He did not initially develop his own theory of the transference. However, he made the scientific discovery early on in his own experimental work in the Word Association Tests (WATs) that family constellations exist, according to which different members of the same family display similar patterns or formations in their complexes. Although this suggested some form of correspondence between individuals in a close relationship, Jung did not then remark on the mechanism (1909b).

Later, his work on *The Red Book* led him to contemplate the dynamics between self and other in the process of individuation, or becoming oneself, according to which individuation is achieved through a dialectic between undifferentiation, defined as regression to unconscious states of unification of self and other and/or body and mind, and differentiation, defined as progression to conscious states of increasing distinction of self from other and/or mind from body. This dialectic may be seen as a series of such regressions and progressions, each cycle increasingly separating the individual out from the collective and enabling further integration of his/her personal psychological function and individual corporeity.

Jung's hermeneutic understanding, conceived out of his visions and especially out of his *Septem Sermones*, and his need to dissolve his identification with the various figures appearing in his visions by means of his active imaginations, brought him to this notion of individuation as a form of developing selfhood. His conceptualisations of this understanding were applied clinically, for example in the case of the young woman with hysteria and nervous asthma, whose libido was fastened on a young Italian man (1917a). Jung noted that a transference onto himself as physician developed *from* a projection of *personal* material to do with the young Italian *into* an upwelling and projection of *mythological themes*. This led him to an idea of a transference process conceived in terms of a dialectical relationship between self and other, developing from personal to universal or collective themes, in the attempt to integrate the personal-infantile material and overcome the neurosis.

His observations from his own clinical practice, and those of his contemporaries, lent credence to a view of individuation in the clinical process, through a negotiation between the ego of the patient and imaginal material, developed both through active imagination and through the transference, as discussed in Chapter 3. Ultimately, Jung arrived at his model of the transference depicted in his fourfold diagram (1946, para. 422), shown below in Figure 9.1, which has not been superseded in the Jungian literature, even in the present.

Here, the vertical arrows represent an intrapsychic link between conscious and unconscious, in each of analyst and patient. The horizontal arrows represent an interpsychic link in both directions between patient and analyst, respectively at conscious and unconscious levels. The diagonal arrows represent interpsychic links from the conscious of one to the unconscious of the other. In each instance, the arrows represent a two-way flow. As Jung (1946, para. 414) indicates, the different possibilities cannot always be kept apart, because they are invariably mixed up, and, especially in the initial stages of analysis, an unconscious identity[1] arises. The model is entirely symmetrical.

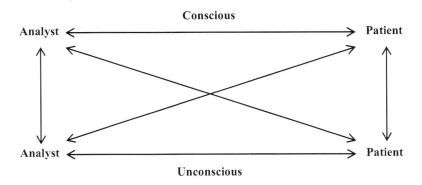

Figure 9.1 Jung's fourfold transference diagram

The evolution of Jung's views on the transference thus passed through a number of stages, starting from the idea, based on Freud, of the transference as a hindrance to clinical work, to an understanding of a transference of a personal nature offering insight into the patient's dilemmas, to a conceptualisation of an archetypal transference of a symmetrical character having a significant role to play in the symbolic unfolding of the individuation process.

A similar evolution arises in the development of Jung's ideas concerning the psychoid concept. His early conceptualisation of the psychoid concept has its hermeneutic roots in his *Red Book* work, including his *Septem Sermones*, from which he came to a view of the psychoid unconscious as a deeply unknowable arena, thereby limiting what can be said about it. He envisaged this unconscious as an area of undifferentiation, where psyche and soma are two aspects of the same basic element, and hence monistic, and self and other are in a participation mystique, from which the individual separates and differentiates himself in the process of individuation. This view became increasingly refined by his progressive understanding of his process of active imagination, including its relationship with the transcendent function, and his observations in his clinical work, out of which he began to envisage a purposive, structuring and organising principle, giving rise to psycho-physical patterns having emergent properties, by which the psyche is differentiated out of the body-mind matrix and self is differentiated from other, and new individual positions come to be realised.

Grounded in his Gnostic experience, and his interest in neo-vitalism, he saw the imaginal aspect as vital in the instantiation of meaning, leading to the symbolic resolution of the opposites in the transcendent function. His comparative studies of philosophy, mythology, and later alchemy, provided support for his thinking, and helped him to see that this same organising principle further served symbolically to link instinct and spirit by means of instinctual images and archetypal images.

The post-Jungians, most especially the Berlin Group as described by Dieckmann (1974, 1976, 1980), noted empirically the manifestation of a symmetric transference, serving to synchronise the associations of analysand and analyst in terms of physiological and psychic facts. They linked this transference with the psychoid concept.

Thus, Jung's parallel conceptualisations of his psychoid concept and of the transference come together in the work of the Berlin Group, and generate an understanding of a clinical analytic process, shifting between personal and archetypal transferences, the latter of which is characterised by symmetry as between the patient and the analyst, and serves as a platform for resolving the personal issues in new and unforeseen ways on the path towards personal growth.

As Dieckmann (1991, p. 7) writes, "there are certain fundamental ideas that have crystallised as methodological essentials with which every analytical psychologist works. Each of us must create the necessary conditions for setting an analytic process in motion, and certain techniques are part of it". Once instantiated, the unfolding analytic process then "cloth[es] the archetype per se in a specific imago capable of giving a symbolic direction and meaning to drives and instinctual energies", in the service of individuation (ibid., p. 8).

The psychoid concept – an empirical understanding

Interestingly, in the light of the above, the empirical study, entirely independently, generated two models for the unconscious interaction between patient and analyst, one of which was a symmetric model for the transference field aligned with Jung's ideas on the psychoid concept.

Certain of the interviewees (S1(AP), S2(AP), S3(AP), S12(AP)), who supported this model, also offered, unprompted, various ideas on the formal and public theory on the psychoid concept, and it is interesting to compare their views. These Jungians considered Jung's psychoid concept as the theoretical underpinning for their model of unconscious self-other interaction and/or the body-mind relationship, as will be discussed below. S3(AP) also worked in the historical development of Jung's ideas. S4(AP) and S5(AP) mentioned the psychoid concept only briefly, S4(AP) simply to acknowledge it as relevant. S5(AP) noted that the psychoid concept applied to ways of thinking in and with the body, but indicated that he himself found phenomenology more helpful for this.

S2(AP) defined Jung's psychoid concept as "the field of complexity that we are completely unable to be conscious of, just because *all* consciousness is an emergence from this field" (S2(AP), I1, 8). He sees the psychoid as Jung's way of writing firstly about the complex system of life, in the body, between bodies, and in nature itself, and next about a process organising differentiation in an undifferentiated field of energy (S2(AP), I2, 7). Associating the psychoid with analysis, he said, the job of the analyst is *just to be* and to allow whatever is going on inside himself to happen and emerge. The analyst has to observe and be guided by such emergence, and the analytic process will take shape accordingly.

Turning next to S12(AP), he spoke of a psychoid area linking the unconscious of both patient and analyst, generating images that come out of the blue, bubbling up from the depths (S12(AP), I1, p. 12). He attributed qualities of the Pleroma to the psychoid, as if the area is filled with a dark energy that we do not understand, a difficult territory between body, mind and something divine (ibid., pp. 12–13). He offered a metaphor:

> The god Indra made this wonderful net that extends in every single direction as far as eternity. And at every single intersection, where threads cross, there is a jewel, and if anything changes in any one of the jewels, it's reflected in all the jewels. So, it's a lovely ancient Hindu myth about interconnectedness.
>
> (S12(AP), I2, p. 6)

S3(AP) offered a similar metaphor, describing the psychoid as a basic underlying matrix of embedded human attachment and referring to a childhood fantasy of his bedspread extending out to join with the bedspreads of every other individual in the world and create a single overarching canopy connecting him with everyone else. As an adult, he saw this as an expression of a need to re-connect with an initial state of human interdependence residing in the psychoid level, in order to promote simple human attachment and healing (S3(AP), I2, p. 5).

According to S3(AP), "the individual psyche is a developmental achievement. I think probably the first thing was the human group" (ibid., p. 3):

> [B]efore we have a psyche, we have to have a matrix out of which a psyche emerges. Moreover, psyche can never forget its embeddedness in that original psychoid level, because it does so at its peril. In other words, we can only be individual consciousnesses so much, attachment matters to us. We are surprised by joy and embarrassed by tears all the time, because our connection to each other is being felt in all these ways. [. . . T]hese processes that link us all are far more fundamental to the human condition than the psyche that is able to reflect on them, which is built out of certain dramatic disappointments at that psychoid level that have become certain necessary evolutionary complexes, unconscious anxieties about survival. [. . .] What Jung is] really saying is psyche emerges out of something that is en route to being the psyche but it isn't exactly psyche yet. That something is the psychoid.
>
> (Ibid., pp. 5–6)

In analysis, the first order of business is thus to undo dissociation from the psychoid level, the second order of business being to develop a psyche.

In the view of S3(AP), *The Red Book* was Jung's attempt to overcome precisely this dissociation, having estranged himself not least through getting involved with Freud and the psychoanalytic movement.

Through recording his experiences of his unconscious in his Black Books, and then through entering into a sensate imaginative dialogue with such experience and developing his technique of active imagination, he came to the *Seven Sermons to the Dead*, in which he presents:

> [T]he Pleroma, out of which all the archetypes are constantly emerging, and the Creatura, which is the needy human embodied creature that has to experience things with attachment needs and with interdependence. And he creates his psychology of a relation to emergent archetypes, which may have the capacity of building psychic structure, experienced by a Creatura who is still a creature, a human creature, very much living in what I would call the psychoid realm. So both these elements of the psychoid give us a kind of the dynamics of the psychoid: The embodied creature with needs for attachment, and these amazing symbolic

archetypes that give us the opportunity to engage with them en route to building psychic structure.

(Ibid., p. 9)

For S3(AP), therefore, the Pleroma is the ultimate unknowable source of the archetypes, and the Creatura provides the embodied experience that is needed to process them and make what they have to offer our own. Both of these elements constitute the psychoid realm.

To S3(AP), the contribution of Jungian analysis is its understanding of how valuable it is for individuals to dip back into that level of experience in the moment when the psychoid is at its earliest emergent state of becoming psyche.

> [P]atients need to live at the threshold between psychoid and psyche. They have to have a kind of borderline state for the longest time in which we're partly relating to them in a very interdependent way en route to their building individual psychic structure, which will one day take them away from us. And take them away from us profoundly connected to that realm, and perhaps never forgetting it.

(Ibid., p. 10)

S1(AP) offered another approach. For him, the significance of the psychoid concept lies in its linking of the body-mind relationship and the transference field:

> I've tried to bring the idea of the psychoid as something that's happening to mind and body, not just to me but between us and trying to see it as relational, interpersonal. And I'm interested in where one would locate the psychoid under such circumstances. Is it between us? Are we both sitting on it, so to speak? Or is it a state we create around us? And this is a question of how imaginal it is, or how actual it is.

(S1(AP), I1, p. 12)

In his view, the concept encompasses a developmental standpoint, in that early mistakes are alive in the patient and psyche-soma information from this early experience informs the body-mind of the analyst at a level where body and mind are the same thing.

S1(AP) defines psychoid fantasy as sensuous imagery affecting the mind and body of *each* individual in the session. He described Jung's psychoid concept as a materialist concept, and referred to Santayana's materialism:

> I find that tremendously healthy, as I also find the idea of how matter stops us from being free imaginal beings, to a certain extent. We're constrained by matter. He calls this animal faith. We've got to have faith in

matter, which is Santayana. And I find this, like faith in body, faith in the fact that we're physical beings sitting together in the analytic room, conditioned by our gender, by our sex, by our physical illnesses, by our age, by our genes, I find that terribly liberating, the fact that we're constrained by this. I find it liberating to know that I'm predetermined, which is why the psychoid is so important to me.

(S1, I1, pp. 14–15)

When it was pointed out that he had not anywhere used the word "spiritual", he countered that "it must be a part of the psychoid whole" but is almost too difficult to talk about (S1(AP), I2, p. 11). For S1(AP), therefore, this indescribable area sets limits on what can actually be said about Jung's psychoid concept.

These interviewees offered highly developed private theories about Jung's psychoid concept. S2(AP), S3(AP) and S12(AP) gave accounts that were almost entirely in terms of Jungian ideas and language, supplemented in all cases by personal metaphorical examples. In all these cases, although embodied experience was a central theme, nonetheless the spiritual dimension of the concept was not neglected and was clearly felt to be significant. S1(AP)'s private theory was also closely based on Jung's psychoid concept, although much elaborated with ideas from philosophy and clinical experience.

The interest here is that the private theories, coming out of the empirical study and specifically referring to the psychoid concept, mostly elaborated on the public theory in symbolic ways entirely consistent with Jung's hermeneutic work in his *Red Book* study and with his subsequent theoretical conceptualisations, whilst yet still employing highly symbolic language and examples from the interviewees' own personal experience. S1(AP) in contrast had combined the public theory to a great extent with ideas from philosophy and made it personal in his private theory in a very down-to-earth clinical fashion.

The transference field – an empirical understanding

The private theories of both psychoanalysts and Jungian analysts were reviewed and individually compared in the previous chapter. It is to be emphasised that the intention was not specifically to compare the Jungians as a group with the psychoanalysts as a group, but rather that the empirical study proceeded from the assumption that there is merit in drawing interviewees from both traditions, on the grounds that, firstly, this ensures that the results are not contaminated by affiliational influence, and, secondly, it acknowledges the fact that any conceptualisations by the psychoanalysts in accord with Jung's psychoid concept, albeit employing alternative language, would carry greater evidential weight than such conceptualisations by the Jungians. In fact, confirmation of the concept through the psychoanalytic channel would count as Popperian evidence for the validity of the concept.

The empirical results yielded, for all of the Jungians and two of the psychoanalysts, a symmetric transference model, including, at least during certain phases or moments of analysis, a shared common area of unconsciousness. This model envisaged states of undifferentiation between self and other, for five of the Jungians and two of the psychoanalysts. Further, four of the Jungians and two of the psychoanalysts incorporated notions of embodiment in the countertransference in this model. For the Jungians, such embodiment is needed for healing dissociation in the patient. For four of the Jungians and one of the psychoanalysts, the symmetric transference is also associated with an organising function in the unconscious combined with an emergent dynamism, seen as a source of meaning and imaginal material.

The Jungians applied the term "psychoid" to these models, attributing a deeply unknowable unconscious factor to the dynamic. Naturally enough, the psychoanalysts did not employ the same terminology, even though their conceptualisations were congruent in most respects, except for the deeply unknowable aspect, on which most of them were silent.

Even a brief comparison of these two outcomes shows immediately that the empirical results match the historical ones to a very significant extent.

A very important aspect of this match is that not only the Jungians but two of the psychoanalysts offered private theories effectively according in certain key respects with the psychoid concept, specifically the manifestation of a symmetric transference, in which an organising function and an emergent dynamism yield symbolic material holding significant meaning for the analysis and for the patient.

These empirical results are completely free of bias, in that none of the interviewees was led to discuss any particular theory; they were simply asked to talk about a set of process notes and embodied clinical experience and to offer their own associations and conceptualisations. The Jungians spoke, unprompted, about psychoid processes, in each instance from their own individual perspective, while the psychoanalysts offered their private theories on embodiment and the transference, in their own terminology.

Significantly, it was clear that the psychoid concept is considered to be relevant to present-day Jungians, and clinically useful. It is familiar, absorbed into their private theories, and guides their thinking in their clinical work. Specifically, S2(AP), S3(AP) and S12(AP) had all incorporated the concept in a very developed and considered fashion in their understandings of the analytic process, and of the ways in which the analyst arrives at understanding through their countertransference and change emerges in the analytic process.

In other words, the psychoid concept was a prominent element of the theoretical thinking of the Jungian interviewees. And this, in spite of the fact that Jung himself did not lay especial emphasis on it in his published works, so that Jungian practitioners might not be expected to recognise its full significance.

More importantly, however, even though there was a substantially lower probability of the psychoanalysts supporting such a concept, because it is not part of their official language and they have no real counterpart in their theoretical structure, nonetheless two of them espoused private theories concordant with key aspects of the psychoid concept. This is particularly noteworthy, because it provides an unexpected confirmation of the validity of the psychoid concept, in the tradition of the philosophy of science as proposed by Popper.

An interesting further finding is the manner in which various clinicians had applied the notion of the symmetric transference, and hence the application of the psychoid concept, to their notions of different stages of the analytic process and/or different moments within a session.

The private theory of S11(PA) embraced a symmetric transference model applicable to certain clinical moments, arising occasionally in emotionally intense periods during specific sessions only. By contrast, the private theory of S12(AP) incorporated a symmetric transference model as the norm, but only after an initial transitional period of analysis when an asymmetric model would be expected. Thus, the work would shift from an asymmetric model to a symmetric model as it deepened. This is something that emerged from the data analysis, but was not consciously manifest in the interview comments of these interviewees. It makes for interest in thinking about the fluidity of individual sessions, and an analysis as a whole.

Accordingly, the empirical work supported a view that Jung's psychoid concept may appropriately be applied to clinical work, at the very least in certain clinical circumstances.

Discussion

In the historical account in Part I of this book, the vitalist origins of Jung's psychoid concept in his *Red Book* work, his active imagination, and its product in his *Seven Sermons*, generated a view of the psychoid unconscious as a deeply unknowable area of undifferentiation, where psyche and soma are monistic, and self and other are in a participation mystique. Through personal processing in active imagination and/or analysis, the individual differentiates himself out of such state by means of a separation of, and negotiation between, the opposites, in the course of individuation. Such differentiation is assisted through the action of psychoid processes, which offer a pattern-creating, structuring and organising principle, symbolically linking instinct and spirit by means of instinctual images and archetypal images. Such principle engenders an emergent dynamism, lifting the psyche out of the body-mind matrix and out of the self-other participation, so that new individual positions come to be realised. It also imparts a vitalising function having meaning-making aspects. Psychoid processes, therefore, have a purposive aim in driving towards individuation and spirituality. Jung's imaginal experimentation, and interrogation through his active imagination, followed by his later and ongoing theoretical conceptualisations led him to this view.

In the empirical study, it was evident that Jung's symmetric model underpins the private theories of all of the Jungians interviewed for the present research.

Both S2(AP) and S3(AP) make direct use of this concept in their clinical work.

S2(AP) described the dynamism of emergence arising out of the psychoid unconscious, manifesting in the transference successively through the embodiment, mind and word of the analyst. He observed that in his understanding this emergence tends towards increasing symbolisation on behalf of the patient in the service of healing dissociation, and he described the overall process in a manner implying that Jung's ideas may offer a methodology for the analytic attitude.

Interestingly, S3(AP) had incorporated elements from Jung's active imagination and the *Seven Sermons* into his own clinical understanding, with some modification to suit his own private theory.

For him, the Pleroma "is the ultimate, unknowable source from which archetypes emerge to foster psychological development"; and the Creatura is the personal in the body, "our creatureliness" where our "self is palpably felt by us in an ongoing experiential way" (S3(AP), I1, p. 9). Through such embodied experience, the archetypes are "discriminated, humanized, and incarnated by the patient". The Creatura is needed to process the archetypes, so that "what they have to offer can become your own" (ibid., pp. 9–10).

Accordingly, S3(AP) directly employs Jung's original hermeneutic, experiential work on the psychoid concept in his own lived theory and practice, alongside other aspects of Jung's theory, in a very original way.

As S3(AP) stated:

> [I] draw on Jungian theory throughout: first by invoking an understanding of the psyche and of psychic interaction that's connected with [Jung's] psychological types, i.e. types of consciousness that either meet or don't meet when people interact, including analyst and analysand in their present realities, and then Jung's theory of the psychoid to explain that level in which patient and therapist are just commonly human at the somatic level, which is always connecting us to each other. Probably, all of this turns into a very elaborated Jungian theory of attachments.
>
> (I1, p. 12)

It is to be noted, in these results, that both the historical research and the empirical research lay emphasis on the aspect of the psychoid unconscious that concerns an organising function and an emergent dynamic, in other words on its purposive or teleological direction in individuation. Less was offered in either strand concerning its relationship with pathology.

Historically, Jacobi (1959) discusses how dissociation may result from an overwhelming of the ego by archetypal material constellated through the psychoid unconscious, and Kalsched (1996) writes about dissociation and the psychoid unconscious.

In the empirical study, one of the Jungians, S1(AP), discussed his work with borderline patients, commenting on how his understanding of psychoid processes informs his views of the transference, which is very powerful with these patients, and how it assists him in addressing the difficulties of converting schizoid states into affective relationship by giving him a solid theoretical base. He appeared to envisage the transference in two alternative ways: on the one hand, he spoke in terms of psychoid space permeating the analytic dyad, creating an empathic/sympathetic connection at the level of the autonomic nervous system, so that the analyst is affected and infected by the patient's material; on the other hand, he described the patient pushing stuff into the analyst through splitting and evacuation. In his view, the idea of evacuating something, partly in communication, is poetically or conceptually a psychoid idea, because projective identification is a basic experience, in which the purely psychic and the somatic are incredibly mixed up, and his notion of a body-mind monism is thus applicable. As far as splitting is concerned, he observed how the process of splitting goes on in groups, it is what people do, to defend themselves, to play people off against each other, or parts of themselves. S1(AP) feels that these two ways of talking about what happens transferentially, these two different angles, are not so far apart or different.

S5(AP) also contemplated the organising unconscious in relation to more psychotic states, making a connection with the notion of archetypes, since, for Jung, the archetypes were the organisers. He mused that Jung had a view of the psychoid, which was related to the a priori, to something essentialist, and to forces that exist behind the scenes and are structuring things, that is, organising factors. In the view of S5(AP), the emergence idea or way of thinking is that things are self-organising, and organisation arises through process rather than there being organising factors or principles that are somehow shaping things. That leads to an idea of relative levels of organisation. Then, what does not get organised remains chaotic, as in psychosis, but you might contemplate that such material is not completely disorganised and has a tendency in the direction of organisation.

This tension between teleology and chaos would be an interesting area for discussion and further clarification. Nonetheless, the majority of the Jungian interviewees, namely four of the six, focussed on the beneficial, purposive aspects of the psychoid concept, including the healing effect of psychoid processes with respect to dissociation.

Hence, neither the historical study nor the empirical study addressed in detail a potential relationship between psychoid processes and psychotic functioning.

Whilst Jung's formulation of the psychoid concept permits of dissociation within its ambit, since he has written of dissociative states in relation to pathological conditions, such as hysteria and dementia praecox, and since Jacobi has noted dissociation resulting from archetypal effects swamping a weak or undeveloped ego, nonetheless, the bulk of Jung's writing on this concept are directed towards a teleological ordering function associated with the archetypes and an emergentist dynamism. Such dynamism is present from birth and manifests first in the constellation of instinctual images and later in the constellation of archetypal images, leading to individuation.

By contrast, the psychoanalysts, particularly in their discussion of Bion and his formulation of his proto-mental concept, focussed much more on psychotic mechanisms, including part-object modes of being and bizarre objects, designed to rid the psyche of accretions of stimuli and persecutory objects through splitting and projective identification. An important function of Bion's concept and its purposive intent is defensive. His early conceptualisations attribute this experience to group processes, manifesting in the individual, who is faced with the conflict of identifying himself with the current unconscious emotional state of the group or with the more sophisticated attitude of a wished-for work group in order to develop as an individual. His later accounts assume a group mentality in the individual alone.

The historical study noted that the two concepts have a common root in a deeply unconscious layer prior to the differentiation of mind from body.

Interestingly, both concepts may be considered to have a purposive drive applied to clinical practice, albeit of a completely different nature. That of the psychoid concept is teleological and directed at becoming more completely oneself in individuation. With its organising and emergentist dynamic, this drive is seen inherently as something that mobilises integration and growth for the patient and as an aid to clinical efficacy. By contrast, the purposive nature of the proto-mental concept is defensive, in the face of anxiety, in which unmanageable and as yet undifferentiated experience is split off and expelled and needs to be processed and made manageable by the analyst before it can be accepted by the patient. Accordingly, in the case of the psychoid concept, the focus is on fostering the emergence of meaningful symbolic material, while, in the case of the proto-mental concept, the emphasis is on analysing and/or interpreting the defensive nature of the dynamic, and on containing and metabolising experience for the patient.

It can be seen, however, that the two concepts are complementary, and that both offer important assistance in furthering the aims of analysis.

Conclusion

The primary interest of the present study is that it takes a look at Jung's psychoid concept in a variety of different contexts, both historical and empirical, and in so doing contemplates the concept hermeneutically, as a vitalist conceptualisation, comparatively with early psychoanalytic thinking and with Bion's ideas, and empirically. By reviewing the concept from different angles, it can be better appreciated theoretically and practically. Its ambit may be more fully appreciated, insofar as we can say anything about an area that is essentially unknowable, and possible clinical understandings and applications have been broached. The research supports and elaborates Jung's psychoid concept, and demonstrates that it is relevant and useful in clinical work today. It provides theoretical understanding of an area of clinical experience in the transference, where body and mind are in relation and where issues concerning early developmental deficits, such as trauma and separation, are prominent. It also offers a practical methodology for an analytic attitude.

The complementary nature of Jung's psychoid concept and Bion's protomental concept became apparent, both in the historical and in the empirical studies, and points also to the usefulness of referring to Bion's ideas for addressing lacunae in Jung's concept in the clinical treatment of dissociation, and the associated psychotic functioning and schizoid states.

It is, however, necessary to place the current findings in a specific context, since both the historical study and the empirical study have been set generally against a European tradition with respect to theories of the transference. It needs to be acknowledged that this influences the results, since not only different schools, Jungian and psychoanalytic, but also different regions, Europe and elsewhere, have followed different trajectories in their development of models for, and understandings of, both the transference field and analysis.

Other limitations of the study also need to be acknowledged, in that individual research has by its nature to be more modest in ambit than group research; in that I have chosen to focus more on the biological and monistic area of body, mind and spirit than on the later panpsychic aspect of Jung's ideas pertaining to synchronicity; and in that comparisons between Jungian and psychoanalytic ideas have been limited. Further, more extensive research into all of these areas would certainly be of interest.

One of the most interesting findings of the present work, however, is the fact that analysts' private theories are often significantly different from their public theories, to the extent that some analysts from different affiliations often seem nearer in clinical approach than various of their colleagues from similar affiliations. This would suggest that dialogue between training organisations and across theoretical affiliations would be a very fruitful subject to promote.

Note

1 He describes this as participation mystique (1946, paras. 376, 462).

Appendix A

Data analysis tables

	Vignette as transfer.	Symmetric field	Undiffn. self/other	Undiffn. of body/mind	Turning point	Moments of meaning
S1(AP)	Y	Y	Y	Y		
S2(AP)	Y	Y	Y	Y	Y	Y
S3(AP)	Y	Y	Y	Y	Y	Y
S4(AP)	Y	Im	Im	Im		
S5(AP)	Y	Y	Y	QY	Y	Y
S6(PA)	Y			QY		
S7(PA)	Y	Im		Im		
S8(PA)	Y	Im	QY		Y	Y
S9(PA)	Y	Y	Y	Im	Im	Y
S10(PA)	N			Y		
S11(PA)	Y	Y	Y	Im		Y
S12(AP)	Y	Y	Y	Y	Y	Y

	Vignette as deepening	Asymmetric field	Proj./Proj. Idn.	Prim. States of mind	Developt.	Regression
S1(AP)	Y	Y	Y	I	Y	Y
S2(AP)	Y		I		QY	
S3(AP)	Y		N		Y	
S4(AP)	Y				QY	
S5(AP)	Y		I		I	4
S6(PA)	Y	Im	Y	Y	Y	
S7(PA)	Y	QY	Y		Y	Y
S8(PA)	Y	Y	Y	Y	Y	Y
S9(PA)	Y			Y	QY	Y
S10(PA)	N	Y	Y		Y	N
S11(PA)	Y	Y	Y	Y	Y	Y
S12(AP)	Y	QY	QY		Y	

	Teleological/ organg. fn.	Emergence	Symbol. fn.	Embodiment in c-t central	Embodied c-t – image	Embodied c-t – symptm.
S1(AP)		2	Y	Y	Y	Y
S2(AP)	Y	Y		Y	Y	Y
S3(AP)	Y	Y		Y	Y	Y
S4(AP)			Y	Y	Y	Y
S5(AP)	Y	Y	Y	N	N	N
S6(PA)			Y	N	N	Y
S7(PA)			Y	N	Y	Y
S8(PA)			Y	N	Y	Y
S9(PA)	Im	Y	Y	N		Y
S10(PA)			Y	N	N	Y
S11(PA)				Y	Y	Y
S12(AP)	Y	Y	Y	Y	Y	Y

	Enactment	Disscn.	Splitting	Relation as central	Here & now	Gradual prog emerges
S1(AP)			4	Y		
S2(AP)		Y	Y	Im		
S3(AP)		Y		Y		
S4(AP)						
S5(AP)	I			Y		
S6(PA)			Y	Im		Y
S7(PA)	Y		Y	Y		
S8(PA)	Y	Y	Y	Y	QY	Y
S9(PA)	Y			Y		
S10(PA)	Y		Y		Y	
S11(PA)	Y			Y		Y
S12(AP)		Y		Im		

	Jung	Archetypal	Psychoid	Unknowable	Synchrony.	Undiffn.mind/ matter
S1(AP)	Y		Y	Y		
S2(AP)	Y		Y	Y	Y	Y
S3(AP)	Y	Y	Y	Y	Y	
S4(AP)	Y		Y	Y	Y	
S5(AP)	Y	QY	QY		QY	QY
S6(PA)						
S7(PA)	I					
S8(PA)						
S9(PA)						
S10(PA)	7			Y		
S11(PA)						
S12(AP)	Y	Y	Y	Y	Y	Y

(Continued)

(Continued)

	Klein/Bion	α and β fn	Proto-mental
S1(AP)	Y		I
S2(AP)	Y	Y	
S3(AP)			
S4(AP)			
S5(AP)			
S6(PA)	QY		
S7(PA)	2		
S8(PA)	Y	Y	
S9(PA)			
S10(PA)	Y	Y	Y
S11(PA)	Y	Y	
S12(AP)			

Index of abbreviations
Y   Yes, from personal belief/experience
N   No, from personal belief/experience
Im Generally implied but not clearly stated
Q   Interviewee qualifies and/or expresses reservations
Integer x   Number of times mentioned in interview, but not leading to a conclusion
Blank   Not addressed by interviewee and/or indeterminate from interview

Caveat
Most of the entries in the above chart are products of the data analysis, rather than specific statements by the Interviewees, and are therefore subject to interpretation
Where entries need qualification or explanation, this is included in the overall data analysis chapter

Bibliography

Addison, A. (2009) "Jung, Vitalism and 'The Psychoid': An Historical Reconstruction", *Journal of Analytical Psychology*, 54: 123–142.
Adler, G. (ed.) (1973) *C. G. Jung Letters: Volume 1 1906–1950*, London: Routledge & Kegan Paul.
Adler, G. (ed.) (1974) *Success and Failure in Analysis*, New York: G. P. Putnam's Sons.
Adler, G. (ed.) (1976) *C. G. Jung Letters: Volume 2 1951–1961*, London: Routledge & Kegan Paul.
Aisenstein, M. and Smadja, C. (2010) "Introduction to the Paper by Pierre Marty: The Narcissistic Difficulties Presented to the Analyst by the Psychosomatic Problem", *International Journal of Psychoanalysis*, 91: 343–346.
Alexander, F. (1950) *Psychosomatic Medicine: Its Principles and Application*, New York: W. W. Norton.
Anzieu, D. (1989) *The Skin Ego*, New Haven: Yale University Press.
Armstrong, D. (1980) "Madness and Coping", *Sociology of Health and Illness*, 2(3): 293–313.
Atmanspacher, H. (2014) "Psychophysical Correlations, Synchronicity and Meaning", *Journal of Analytical Psychology*, 59: 181–188.
Atmanspacher, H. & Fach, W. (2005) "Acategoriality as Mental Instability", *Journal of Mind and Behavior*, 26: 181–206.
Atmanspacher, H. and Fach, W. (2013) "A Structural-Phenomenological Typology of Mind-Matter Correlations", *Journal of Analytical Psychology*, 58: 219–244.
Aziz, R. (1990) *C. G. Jung's Psychology of Religion and Synchronicity*, Albany: State University of New York Press.
Aziz, R. (2007) *The Syndetic Paradigm: The Untrodden Path Beyond Freud and Jung*, Albany: State University of New York Press.
Bady, S. L. (1984) "Countertransference, Sensory Images, and the Therapeutic Cure", *Psychoanalytic Review*, 71: 529–540.
Banissey, M. J. and Ward, J. (2007a) *Mirror-Touch Synaesthesia: The Role of Shared Representation in Social Cognition*, London: University College London.
Banissey, M. J. and Ward, J. (2007b) "Mirror-Touch Synaesthesia Is Linked with Empathy", *Nature Neuroscience*, 10: 815–816.
Baranger, M. (1993) "The Mind of the Analyst: From Listening to Interpretation", *International Journal of Psychoanalysis*, 74: 15–24.
Baranger, M. and Baranger, W. (2008) "The Analytic Situation as a Dynamic Field", *International Journal of Psychoanalysis*, 89: 795–826.

Beebe, B. and Falzeder, E. (eds.) (2013) *The Question of Psychological Types: The Correspondence of C. G. Jung and Hans Schmid-Guisan 1915–1916*, Princeton: Princeton University Press.

Beebe, B. and Lachmann, F. (1988) "The Contribution of Mother-Infant Mutual Influence to the Origins of Self and Object Representations", *Psychoanalytic Psychology*, 5: 305–337.

Bergson, H. (1896 [1911]) *Matter and Memory*, London: George Allen & Unwin.

Bergson, H. (1907[1911]) *Creative Evolution*, London: Macmillan.

Bernfield, S. (1944) "Freud's Earliest Theories and the School of Helmholtz", *The Psychoanalytic Quarterly*, 13: 341–346.

Bick, E. (1964) "Notes on Infant Observation in Psychoanalytic Training", *International Journal of Psychoanalysis*, 45: 558–566.

Bick, E. (1968) "The Experience of the Skin in Early Object Relations", *International Journal of Psychoanalysis*, 49: 484–486.

Bion, W. R. (1940) "The War of Nerves", in *The Neuroses in War*, London: Macmillan.

Bion, W. R. (1948a, 1948b, 1949a, 1949b, 1950a, 1950b, 1951) "Experiences in Groups I, II, III, IV, V, VI and VII", *Respectively, Human Relations*, 1: 314–320 and 487–496, 2: 13–22 and 295–303, 3: 3–14 and 93–114, 4: 221–227.

Bion, W. R. (1950c) "The Imaginary Twin", in *Second Thoughts*, London: William Heinemann Medical Books Ltd.

Bion, W. R. (1952) "Group Dynamics: A Review", *International Journal of Psychoanalysis*, 33: 235–247.

Bion, W. R. (1954) "Notes on the Theory of Schizophrenia", *International Journal of Psychoanalysis*, 33: 235–247.

Bion, W. R. (1956) "Development of Schizophrenic Thought", *International Journal of Psychoanalysis*, 37: 344–346.

Bion, W. R. (1958) "On Hallucination", *International Journal of Psychoanalysis*, 39: 341–349.

Bion, W. R. (1961) *Experiences in Groups and Other Papers*, London: Routledge.

Bion, W. R. (1962) *Learning From Experience*, London: William Heinemann Medical Books Ltd.

Bion, W. R. (1963) *Elements of Psychoanalysis*, London: Karnac Books.

Bion, W. R. (1965) *Transformations*, London: William Heinemann Medical Books Ltd.

Bion, W. R. (1967) *Second Thoughts*, London: William Heinemann Medical Books Ltd.

Bion, W. R. (1976) "Interview With AG Banet Jr, Los Angeles, 1976", in *The Tavistock Seminars*, London: Karnac Books, 2005.

Bion, W. R. (1982) *The Long Weekend 1897–1919: Part of a Life*, Abingdon: Fleetwood.

Bion, W. R. (1985) *All My Sins Remembered: Another Part of a Life*, Abingdon: Fleetwood.

Bion, W. R. (1997) *War Memoirs 1917–1919*, London: Karnac Books.

Bion, W. R. and Rickman, J. (1943) "Intra-Group Tensions in Therapy", *The Lancet*, 2: 678–681.

Bleger, J. (2013) *Symbiosis and Ambiguity: A Psychoanalytic Study*, London: Routledge.

Bleuler, E. (1925) *Die Psychoide als Prinzip der Organischen Entwicklung*, Berlin: Julius Springer.

Bleuler, E. (1929) *Psyche and Psychoid*, Berlin: Julius Springer.
Bleuler, E. (1930) "Psyche and Psychoid", *Psychiatric Quarterly*, 4: 35–48.
Boechat, W. (2017) *The Red Book of C. G. Jung: A Journey Into Unknown Depths*, London: Karnac Books.
Bright, G. (1997) "Synchronicity as a Basis of Analytic Attitude", *Journal of Analytical Psychology*, 42: 613–635.
Bronstein, C. (2011) "On Psychosomatics: The Search for Meaning", *International Journal of Psychoanalysis*, 92: 173–195.
Brooke, R. (1991) *Jung and Phenomenology*, London: Routledge.
Buber, M. (1952) *Eclipse of God: Studies in the Relation Between Religion and Philosophy*, New York: Harper & Brothers.
Cadigan, J. L. (2007) *The Psychoid: Articulating a Psychophysical Reality*, Pacifica: Pacifica Graduate Institute.
Cambray, J. (2001) "Enactments and Amplification", *Journal of Analytical Psychology*, 46: 275–303.
Cambray, J. (2002) "Synchronicity and Emergence", *American Imago*, 59: 409–435.
Cambray, J. (2009) *Synchronicity: Nature & Psyche in an Interconnected Universe*, College Station: Texas A&M University Press.
Canestri, J. (2006) *Psychoanalysis: From Practice to Theory*, Chichester: John Wiley & Sons.
Casement, A. (2010) "Sonu Shamdasani Interviewed by Ann Casement", *Journal of Analytical Psychology*, 55: 35–49.
Charmaz, K. (2006) *Constructing Grounded Theory*, London: Sage Publications Ltd.
Chodorow, J. (1991) *Dance Therapy and Depth Psychology*, London: Routledge.
Chodorow, J. (1999) "Dance/Movement and Body Experience in Analysis", in *Authentic Movement: Essays By Mary Starks Whitehouse, Janet Adler and Joan Chodorow*, edited by Patrizia Pallaro, London: Jessica Kingsley.
Clark, G. (1996) "The Animating Body: Psychoid Substance as a Mutual Experience of Psychosomatic Disorder", *Journal of Analytical Psychology*, 41: 353–368.
Clark, G. (2006) "A Spinozan Lens Onto the Confusion of Borderline Relations", *Journal of Analytical Psychology*, 51: 67–86.
Colman, W. (2010) "The Analyst in Action: An Individual Account of What Jungians Do and Why they Do It", *International Journal of Psychoanalysis*, 91: 287–303.
Colman, W. (2011) "Synchronicity and the Meaning-Making Psyche", *Journal of Analytical Psychology*, 56: 451–585.
Connolly, A. (2015) "Bridging the Reductive and the Synthetic: Some Reflections on the Clinical Implications of Synchronicity", *Journal of Analytical Psychology*, 60: 159–178.
Costello, M. S. (2006) *Imagination, Illness and Injury: Jungian Psychology and the Somatic Dimensions of Perception*, Hove: Routledge.
Cranefield, P. (1966) "Freud and the School of Helmholtz", *Gesnerus*, 23: 35–39.
Crichton-Miller, H. (1920) "Physical Aetiology", in *Functional Disease: An Epitome of War Experience for the Practitioner*, Oxford: Oxford University Press.
Crichton-Miller, H. (1933) *Psychoanalysis and Its Derivatives*, London: Thornton Butterworth.
Cwik, A. J. (1991) "Active Imagination as Imaginal Play-Space", in *Liminality and Transitional Phenomena*, edited by Nathan Schwartz-Salant and Murray Stein, Wilmette: Chiron Publications.

Cwik, A. J. (2011) "Associative Dreaming: Reverie and Active Imagination", *Journal of Analytical Psychology*, 56: 14–36.
Damasio, A. (1994) *Descartes' Error: Emotion, Reason, and the Human Brain*, New York: Putnam Publishing.
Davidson, D. (1966) "Transference as a Form of Active Imagination", *Journal of Analytical Psychology*, 11: 135–146.
Davie, T. M. (1935) "Comments on a Case of 'Periventricular Epilepsy'", *British Medical Journal*, 3893: 293–297.
Deutsch, F. (1959) *On the Mysterious Leap From the Mind to the Body*, New York: International Universities Press.
Dicks, H. V. (1970) *Fifty Years of the Tavistock Clinic*, London: Tavistock.
Dieckmann, H. (1971) "Symbols of Active Imagination", *Journal of Analytical Psychology*, 16(2): 127–140.
Dieckmann, H. (1974) "The Constellation of the Countertransference in Relation to the Presentation of Archetypal Dreams", in *Success and Failure in Analysis: The Proceedings of the Fifth International Congress for Analytical Psychology*, New York: G. P. Putnam's Sons.
Dieckmann, H. (1976) "Transference and Countertransference: Results of a Berlin Research Group", *Journal of Analytical Psychology*, 21: 1.
Dieckmann, H. (ed.) (1980) *Ubertragung und Gegenubertragung*, Hildesheim: Gerstenberg Verlag.
Dieckmann, H. (1991) *Methods in Analytical Psychology: An Introduction*, Wilmette: Chiron Publications.
Dreher, A. U. (2000) *Foundations for Conceptual Research in Psychoanalysis*, London: Karnac Books.
Driesch, H. (1903) *Die "Seele" als Elementarer Naturfaktor*, Leipzig: Wilhelm Engelmann.
Driesch, H. (1905) *Der Vitalismus als Geschichte und als Lehre*, Leipzig: Johann Ambrosius Barth.
Driesch, H. (1907/1908) *The Science and Philosophy of the Organism*, London: Black.
Driesch, H. (1914) *The History and Theory of Vitalism*, London: Macmillan.
Driesch, H. (1929) *The Science and Philosophy of the Organism*, London: Black.
Driver, C. (2005) "An Under-Active or an Over-Active Internal World? An Exploration of Parallel Dynamics Within Psyche and Soma, and the Difficulty of Internal Regulation, in Patients With Chronic Fatigue Syndrome and Myalgic Encephalomyelitis", *Journal of Analytical Psychology*, 50: 155–173.
Dunbar, H. F. (1935) *Emotions and Bodily Changes: A Survey of Literature on Psychosomatic Interrelationships, 1910–1945*, New York: Columbia University Press.
Eshel, O. (2001) "Whose Sleep Is It Anyway? Or 'Night Moves'", *International Journal of Psychoanalysis*, 82: 545–562.
Falzeder, E. (2007) "The Story of an Ambivalent Relationship: Sigmund Freud and Eugen Bleuler", *Journal of Analytical Psychology*, 52: 343–368.
Ferenczi, S. (1955) *Final Contributions to the Problems and Methods of Psychoanalysis*, New York: Basic Books.
Ferrari, A. B. (2004) *From the Eclipse of the Body to the Dawn of Thought*, London: Free Association Books.

Field, N. (1989) "Listening With the Body: An Exploration in the Countertransference", *British Journal of Psychotherapy*, 5: 512–522.
Fonagy, P. (1982) "The Integration of Psychoanalysis and Experimental Science: A Review", *International Journal of Psychoanalysis*, 9: 125–145.
Fonagy, P. (2003) "Some Complexities in the Relationship of Psychoanalytic Theory to Technique", *The Psychoanalytic Quarterly*, 72: 13–47.
Fonagy, P. (2006) "The Failure of Practice to Inform Theory and the Role of Implicit Theory in Bridging the Transmission Gap", in *Psychoanalysis: From Practice to Theory*, Chichester: Whurr Publishers Ltd.
Fonagy, P. & Target, M. (2007) "The Rooting of the Mind in the Body: New Links between Attachment Theory and Psychoanalytic Thought", *Journal of the American Psychoanalytic Association*, 55(2): 411–456.
Fordham, M. (1955) "Active Imagination and Imaginative Activity", *Journal of Analytical Psychology*, 1: 207–208.
Fordham, M. (1957) "Reflections on the Archetypes and Synchronicity", in *New Developments in Analytical Psychology*, London: Routledge & Kegan-Paul.
Fordham, M. (1962) "An Interpretation of Jung's Thesis About Synchronicity", *British Journal of Medical Psychology*, 35: 205–210.
Fordham, M. (1977) "A Possible Root of Active I", *Journal of Analytical Psychology*, 22: 317–330.
Fordham, M. (1985) *Explorations Into the Self*, London: Karnac Books.
Fraiburg, S. (1969) "Libidinal Object Constancy and Mental Representation", *Psychoanalytic Study of the Child*, 24: 9–47.
Freud, S. (1895[1894]) "Obsessions and Phobias: Their Psychical Mechanism and Their Aetiology", in *The Standard Edition of the Complete Psychological Works of Sigmund Freud*, translated and edited by J. Strachey, vol. 3, London: The Hogarth Press.
Freud, S. (1900) "The Interpretation of Dreams", in *The Standard Edition of the Complete Psychological Works of Sigmund Freud*, translated and edited by J. Strachey, vol. 4, London: The Hogarth Press.
Freud, S. (1910) "The Psycho-Analytic View of Psychogenic Disturbance of Vision", in *The Standard Edition of the Complete Psychological Works of Sigmund Freud*, translated and edited by J. Strachey, vol. 11, London: The Hogarth Press.
Freud, S. (1915) "Instincts and Their Vicissitudes", in *The Standard Edition of the Complete Psychological Works of Sigmund Freud*, translated and edited by J. Strachey, vol. 14, London: The Hogarth Press.
Freud, S. (1923) "The Ego and the Id", in *The Standard Edition of the Complete Psychological Works of Sigmund Freud*, translated and edited by J. Strachey, vol. 19, London: The Hogarth Press.
Freud, S. (1925[1924]) "An Autobiographical Study", in *The Standard Edition of the Complete Psychological Works of Sigmund Freud*, translated and edited by J. Strachey, vol. 20, London: The Hogarth Press.
Freud, S. (1950[1895]) "Project for a Scientific Psychology", in *The Standard Edition of the Complete Psychological Works of Sigmund Freud*, translated and edited by J. Strachey, vol. 1, London: The Hogarth Press.
Freud, S. and Breuer, J. (1892–1895) "Studies on Hysteria", in *The Standard Edition of the Complete Psychological Works of Sigmund Freud*, translated and edited by J. Strachey, vol. 2, London: The Hogarth Press.

Friedman, H. S. and Mitchell, R. R. (1994) *Sandplay: Past Present and Future*, London: Routledge.
Gaddini, E. (1969) "On Imitation", in *A Psychoanalytic Theory of Infantile Experience*, London: The New Library of Psychoanalysis.
Geerken, I. M. (2010) "*La Vita Nuova*", *International Journal of Psychoanalysis*, 91: 469–483.
Giegerich, W. (2012) "A Serious Misunderstanding: Synchronicity and the Generation of Meaning", *Journal of Analytical Psychology*, 57: 500–511.
Gieser, S. (2005) *The Innermost Kernel: Depth Psychology and Quantum Physics, Wolfgang Pauli's Dialogue With C. G. Jung*, Berlin: Springer-Verlag.
Glaser, B. and Strauss, A. (1967) *The Discovery of Grounded Theory: Strategies for Qualitative Research*, Chicago: Aldine.
Goodheart, W. B. (1984) "C. G. Jung's First 'Patient': On the Seminal Emergence of Jung's Thought", *Journal of Analytical Psychology*, 29: 1–34.
Gordon, R. (1993) *Bridges, Metaphor for Psychic Processes*, London: Karnac Books.
Gray, R. M. (1996) *Archetypal Explorations*, London: Routledge.
Greene, A. (2001) "Conscious Mind: Conscious Body", *Journal of Analytical Psychology*, 46: 565–590.
Grossman (2006) "Some Perspectives on Relationships of Theory and Technique", in *Psychoanalysis: From Practice to Theory*, Chichester: Whurr Publishers Ltd.
Grotstein, J. S. (1997) "'Mens Sane' in Corpore Sano': The Mind and Body as an 'Odd Couple' and as an Oddly Coupled Unity", *Psychoanalytic Inquiry*, 17: 204–222.
Grotstein, J. S. (2007) *A Beam of Intense Darkness*, London: Karnac Books.
Gunter, P. A. Y. (1982) "Bergson and Jung", *Journal of the History of Ideas*, 43: 635–652.
Hadamard, J. (1945) *The Psychology of Invention in the Mathematical Field*, Princeton: Princeton University Press.
Hadfield, J. A. (1942a) "War Neurosis: A Year in a Neuropathic Hospital", *British Medical Journal*, 1(4234): 281–285 and 1(4235): 320–323.
Hadfield, J. A. (1942b) "War Neuroses", *British Medical Journal*, 1(4244): 592–593.
Hamilton, V. (1996) *The Analyst's Preconscious*, Hillsdale: The Analytic Press.
Hannah, B. (1997) *Jung: His Life and Work*, Wilmette: Chiron Publications.
Harrison, T. (2000) *Bion, Rickman, Foulkes and the Northfield Experiment*, London: Jessica Kingsley.
Haule, J. R. (2010) *Jung in the 21st Century Volume One: Evolution and Archetype*, Hove: Routledge.
Haule, J. R. (2011) *Jung in the 21st Century Volume Two: Synchronicity and Science*, Hove: Routledge.
Heimann, P. (1950) "On Countertransference", *International Journal of Psychoanalysis*, 31: 81–84.
Hillman, J. and Shamdasani, S. (2013) *Lament of the Dead: Psychology After Jung's Red Book*, London: W. W. Norton & Company.
Hinshelwood, R. D. (2002) "Countertransference", in *Key Papers on Countertransference*, edited by Robert Michels et al., London: Karnac Books.
Hinshelwood, R. D. (2013a) *Research on the Couch: Single Case Studies, Subjectivity and Psychoanalytic Knowledge*, London: Routledge.
Hinshelwood, R. D. (2013b) "The Tavistock Years", in *Bion's Sources*, Hove: Routledge.

Hinsie, L. and Campbell, R. (1960) *Psychiatric Dictionary*, 3rd ed., New York: Oxford University Press.
Hoeller, S. (1982) *The Gnostic Jung and the Seven Sermons to the Dead*, Wheaton: Quest.
Hogenson, G. B. (1994) *Jung's Struggle With Freud*, Wilmette: Chiron Publications.
Hogenson, G. B. (2001) "The Baldwin effect: A neglected influence on C. G. Jung's evolutionary thinking", *Journal of Analytical Psychology*, 46(4): 591–611.
Hogenson, G. B. (2005) "The Self, the Symbolic and Synchronicity: Virtual Realities and the Emergence of Psyche", *Journal of Analytical Psychology*, 50: 271–284.
Hollway, W. and Jefferson, T. (2000) *Doing Qualitative Research Differently*, London: Sage Publications Ltd.
Isaacs, S. (1948) "The Nature and Function of Phantasy", *International Journal of Psychoanalysis*, 29: 73–97.
Jacobi, J. (1959) *Complex Archetype Symbol in the Psychology of C. G. Jung*, Princeton: Princeton University Press.
Jacobi, J. (1964) "Symbols in an Individual Analysis", in *Man and His Symbols*, New York: Doubleday & Company, Inc.
Jacobi, J. (1967) *The Way of Individuation*, London: Hodder & Stoughton Ltd.
Jacobs, T. J. (1973) "Posture, Gesture, and Movement in the Analyst: Cues to Interpretation and Countertransference", *Journal of the American Psychoanalytic Association*, 21: 77–92.
Jacobs, T. J. (1993) "The Inner Experiences of the Analyst: Their Contribution to the Analytic Process", *International Journal of Psychoanalysis*, 74: 7–14.
Jacobs, T. J. (2001) "On Misreading and Misleading Patients: Some Reflections on Communications, Miscommunications and Countertransference Enactments", *International Journal of Psychoanalysis*, 82: 653–670.
Jaffé, A. (1979) *Jung, C. G.: Word and Image*, Princeton: Princeton University Press.
Jeromson, B. (2005/6) "*Systema Munditotius* and *Seven Sermons*: Symbolic Collaborators in Jung's Confrontation With the Dead", *Philemon Foundation Newsletter: Jung History*, 1(2): 7–10. Accessed 18 December 2014, http://philemonfoundation.org/wp-content/uploads/2015/01/phil.vol1_.iss2_.pdf
Jouvet, M. (1975) "The Function of Dreaming: A Neurophysiologist's Point of View", in *Handbook of Psychobiology*, edited by Michael S. Gazzanga and Colin Blakemore, New York: Academic Press.
Jung, C. G. (1896) "The Border Zones of Exact Science", in *The Zofingia Lectures*, London: Routledge.
Jung, C. G. (1897) "Some Thoughts on Psychology", in *The Zofingia Lectures*, London: Routledge.
Jung, C. G. (1902) "On the Psychology and Pathology of So-called Occult Phenomena", in *Collected Works, Volume 1, Psychiatric Studies*, 2nd ed., London: Routledge, 1970.
Jung, C. G. (1904–1907, 1910) "Studies in Word Association", in *Collected Works, Volume 2, Experimental Researches*, London: Routledge, 1973.
Jung, C. G. (1905) "Cryptomnesia", in *Collected Works, Volume 1, Psychiatric Studies*, 2nd ed., London: Routledge, 1970.
Jung, C. G. (1905/1906) "The Reaction Time Ratio in the Association Experiment", in *Collected Works, Volume 2, Experimental Researches*, London: Routledge, 1973.

Jung, C. G. (1907/1908) "Psychophysical Researches", in *Collected Works, Volume 2, Experimental Researches*, London: Routledge, 1973.

Jung, C. G. (1908) "The Freudian Theory of Hysteria", in *Collected Works, Volume 4, Freud and Psychoanalysis*, 2nd ed., London: Routledge, 1970.

Jung, C. G. (1909a) "The Analysis of Dreams", in *Collected Works, Volume 4, Freud and Psychoanalysis*, 2nd ed., London: Routledge, 1970.

Jung, C. G. (1909b) "The Family Constellation", in *Collected Works, Volume 2, Experimental Researches*, London: Routledge, 1973.

Jung, C. G. (1914) "The Theory of Psychoanalysis", *Psychoanalytic Review*, 1(4): 415–430.

Jung, C. G. (1916) *Collected Papers on Analytical Psychology*, London: Bailliere, Tindall and Cox.

Jung, C. G. (1916/1957) "The Transcendent Function", in *Collected Works, Volume 8, The Structure and Dynamics of the Psyche*, 2nd ed., London: Routledge, 1969.

Jung, C. G. (1917a) *Collected Papers on Analytical Psychology*, 2nd ed., London: Bailliere, Tindall and Cox.

Jung, C. G. (1917b) "The Conception of the Unconscious", in *Collected Papers on Analytical Psychology*, 2nd ed., London: Bailliere, Tindall and Cox.

Jung, C. G. (1919) "Instinct and the Unconscious", *British Journal of Psychology*, 10: 15–23.

Jung, C. G. (1923) *Psychological Types*, London: Kegan Paul, Trench, Trubner & Co., Ltd.

Jung, C. G. (1927/1931) "The Structure of the Psyche", in *Collected Works, Volume 8, The Structure and Dynamics of the Psyche*, 2nd ed., London: Routledge, 1969.

Jung, C. G. (1928/1931) "The Spiritual Problem of Modern Man", in *Collected Works, Volume 10, Civilization in Transition*, 2nd ed., London: Routledge, 1970.

Jung, C. G. (1928a) "On Psychic Energy", in *Collected Works, Volume 8, The Structure and Dynamics of the Psyche*, 2nd ed., London: Routledge, 1969.

Jung, C. G. (1928b) *Two Essays on Analytical Psychology*, London: Bailliere, Tindall and Cox.

Jung, C. G. (1928c) "The Relation Between the Ego and the Unconscious", in *Two Essays on Analytical Psychology*, London: Bailliere, Tindall and Cox.

Jung, C. G. (1934/1950) "A Study in the Process of Individuation", in *Collected Works, Volume 9i, The Archetypes of the Collective Unconscious*, 2nd ed., London: Routledge, 1968.

Jung, C. G. (1935) "The Tavistock Lectures", in *Collected Works, Volume 18, The Symbolic Life: Miscellaneous Writings*, London: Routledge, 1977.

Jung, C. G. (1936) "Psychological Factors Determining Human Behaviour", in *Collected Works, Volume 8, The Structure and Dynamics of the Psyche*, 2nd ed., London: Routledge, 1969.

Jung, C. G. (1938/1954) "Psychological Aspects of the Mother Archetype", in *Collected Works, Volume 9i, The Archetypes of the Collective Unconscious*, 2nd ed., London: Routledge, 1968.

Jung, C. G. (1940) *The Integration of the Personality*, London: Routledge & Kegan Paul.

Jung, C. G. (1945/1954) "The Philosophical Tree", in *Collected Works, Volume 13, Alchemical Studies*, London: Routledge, 1968.

Jung, C. G. (1946) "The Psychology of the Transference", in *Collected Works, Volume 16, The Practice of Psychotherapy*, London: Routledge, 1954.

Jung, C. G. (1947/1954) "On the Nature of the Psyche", in *Collected Works, Volume 8, The Structure and Dynamics of the Psyche*, 2nd ed., London: Routledge, 1969.

Jung, C. G. (1948) "Instinct and the Unconscious", in *Collected Works, Volume 8, The Structure and Dynamics of the Psyche*, 2nd ed., London: Routledge, 1969.

Jung, C. G. (1951) *Collected Works, Volume 9ii, Aion: Researches Into the Phenomenology of the Self*, 2nd ed., London: Routledge, 1968.

Jung, C. G. (1952) "Synchronicity: An Acausal Connecting Principle", in *Collected Works, Volume 8, The Structure and Dynamics of the Psyche*, 2nd ed., London: Routledge, 1969.

Jung, C. G. (1955/1956) *Collected Works, Volume 14, Mysterium Coniunctionis: An Inquiry Into the Separation and Synthesis of Psychic Opposites in Alchemy*, 2nd ed., London: Routledge, 1970.

Jung, C. G. (1956) *Collected Works, Volume 5, Symbols of Transformation*, 2nd ed., London: Routledge, 1974.

Jung, C. G. (1958) "A Psychological View of Conscience", in *Collected Works, Volume 10, Civilization in Transition*, 2nd ed., London: Routledge, 1970.

Jung, C. G. (1963) *Memories, Dreams, Reflections*, London: Routledge & Kegan Paul.

Jung, C. G. (1968) *Collected Works, Volume 9i, The Archetypes of the Collective Unconscious*, 2nd ed., London: Routledge, 1968.

Jung, C. G. (1973) *Collected Works, Volume 2, Experimental Researches*, London: Routledge & Kegan Paul, 1973.

Jung, C. G. (1977) "Comments on a Doctoral Thesis", in *C. G. Jung Speaking: Interviews and Encounters*, Princeton: Princeton University Press.

Jung, C. G. (1984) *Dream Analysis 1: Notes of the Seminar Given in 1928–30*, London: Routledge.

Jung, C. G. (1997) *Visions: Notes of the Seminar Given in 1930–1934 By C. G. Jung*, edited by Claire Douglas, London: Routledge.

Jung, C. G. (ed. Shamdasani, S.) (2009a) *The Red Book, Liber Novus*, New York: W. W. Norton.

Jung, C. G. (ed. Shamdasani, S.) (2009b) *The Red Book, Liber Novus: A Reader's Edition*, New York: W. W. Norton.

Jung, C. G. (2012) *Introduction to Jungian Psychology: Notes of the Seminar in Analytical Psychology Given in 1925*, Princeton: Princeton University Press.

Jung, C. G. and Riklin, F. (1904/1906) "The Association of Normal Subjects", in *Collected Works, Volume 2, Experimental Researches*, London: Routledge, 1973.

Kalsched, D. (1996) *The Inner World of Trauma*, London: Routledge.

Keller, A. (1914) *Eine Philosophie des Lebens (Henri Bergson)*, Jena: Eugen Diederichs Verlag.

Kerslake, C. (2007) *Deleuze and the Unconscious*, London: Continuum.

Klein, M. (1975a) *The Writings of Melanie Klein, Volume 1: Love, Guilt and Reparation and Other Works, 1921–1945*, London: The Hogarth Press.

Klein, M. (1975b) *The Writings of Melanie Klein, Volume 2: The Psychoanalysis of Children*, London: The Hogarth Press.

Knox, J. (2003) *Archetype, Attachment, Analysis: Jungian Psychology and the Emergent Mind*, Hove: Brunner-Routledge.

Kradin, R. (1997) "The Psychosomatic Symptom and the Self: A Siren's Song", *Journal of Analytical Psychology*, 42: 405–423.

Kradin, R. (2011) "Psychosomatic Disorders: The Canalisation of Mind Into Matter", *Journal of Analytical Psychology*, 56: 37–55.
Kradin, R. (2013) *Pathologies of the Mind/Body Interface: Exploring the Curious Domain of the Psychosomatic Disorders*, Hove: Routledge.
Lakatos, I. (1976) *Proofs and Refutations: The Logic of Mathematical Discovery*, Cambridge: Cambridge University Press.
Laplanche, J. & Pontalis, J. B. (1973) *The Language of Psycho-Analysis*, London: The Hogarth Press and the Institute of Psycho-Analysis.
Lindkvist, M. (1998) *Bring White Beads When Calling on the Healer*, New Orleans: Rivendell House Ltd.
Little, M. (1951) "Counter-transference and the Patient's Response to It", *International Journal of Psychoanalysis*, 32: 32–40.
Lombardi, R. (2002) "Primitive Mental States and the Body: A Personal View of Armando B. Ferrari's Concrete Original Object", *International Journal of Psychoanalysis*, 83: 363–382.
Lombardi, R. (2003) "Mental Models and Language Registers in the Psychoanalysis of Psychosis", *International Journal of Psychoanalysis*, 84: 843–864.
Lombardi, R. (2008) "The Body in the Analytic Session: Focussing on the Body-Mind Link", *International Journal of Psychoanalysis*, 89: 89–110.
Lopez-Corvo, R. E. (2003) *The Dictionary of the Work of W. R. Bion*, London: Karnac.
Main, R. (2004) *The Rupture of Time: Synchronicity and Jung's Critique of Modern Western Culture*, Hove: Brunner-Routledge.
Main, R. (2007) *Revelations of Chance: Synchronicity as Spiritual Experience*, Albany: State University of New York Press.
Martini, S. (2016) "Embodying Analysis: The Body and the Therapeutic Process", *Journal of Analytical Psychology*, 61: 5–23.
Martin-Vallas, F. (2006) "The Transferential Chimera: A Clinical Approach", *Journal of Analytical Psychology*, 51: 627–741.
Matte-Blanco, I. (1998) *Thinking, Feeling, and Being*, London: Routledge.
McDougall, J. (1989) *Theatres of the Body: A Psychoanalytical Approach to Psychosomatic Illness*, London: Free Association Books.
McDougall, W. (1908) *An Introduction to Social Psychology*, London: Methuen, 1948.
McDougall, W. (1920) *The Group Mind*, New York: G. P. Putnam's Sons.
McGuire, W. (ed.) (1991) *The Freud/Jung Letters*, London: Penguin Books.
McLaughlin, J. T. (1975) "The Sleepy Analyst: Some Observations on States of Consciousness in the Analyst at Work", *Journal of the American Psychoanalytic Association*, 23: 363–382.
Meier, C. A. (2001) *Atom and Archetype: The Pauli/Jung Letters 1932–1958*, London: Routledge.
Meltzer, D. (1964) "A Klein-Bion Model for Evaluating Psychosomatic States", in *Studies in Extended Metapsychology*, Perthshire: Cluny Press.
Meltzer, D. (1975) "Adhesive Identification", *Contemporary Psychoanalysis*, 11: 289–310.
Meltzer, D. (1986) *Studies in Extended Metapsychology*, London: Karnac Books.
Merchant, J. (2006) "The Developmental/Emergent Model of Archetype, Its Implications and Its Application to Shamanism", *Journal of Analytical Psychology*, 51: 125–144.
Merchant, J. (2012) *Shamans and Analysts: New Insights on the Wounded Healer*, Hove: Routledge.

Miller, E. (ed.) (1940) *The Neuroses in War*, London: Macmillan.
Minder, B. (1994) "Sabina Spielrein. Jung's Patient at the Burghölzli", in *Sabina Spielrein*, edited by Coline Covington and Barbara Wharton, Hove: Brunner-Routledge.
Mitrani, J. L. (1995) "Toward an Understanding of Unmentalised Experience", *The Psychoanalytic Quarterly*, 84: 68–112.
Money-Kyrle, R. (1956) "Normal Counter-Transference and Some of Its Deviations", *International Journal of Psychoanalysis*, 37: 360–366.
Moore, N. (1972) "Countertransference, Anxiety and Change", *Journal of Analytical Psychology*, 17: 51–65.
Moore, N. (1986) "Amplification, Transference Analysis and the Analyst's Inner Process", *Journal of Analytical Psychology*, 31: 113–133.
Nagy, M. (1991) *Philosophical Issues in the Psychology of C. G. Jung*, Albany: State University of New York Press.
Ogden, T. H. (1989) "On the Concept of an Autistic-Contiguous Position", *International Journal of Psychoanalysis*, 70: 127–140.
Ogden, T. H. (1994) "The Analytic Third: Working With Intersubjective Clinical Facts", *International Journal of Psychoanalysis*, 75: 3–19.
Ogden, T. H. (2003) "What's True and Whose Idea Was It?", *International Journal of Psychoanalysis*, 84: 593–606.
Papadopoulos, R. K. (1996) "Archetypal Family Therapy: Developing a Jungian Approach to Working With Families", in *Psyche and Family: Jungian Applications to Family Therapy*, edited by Laura Dodson and Terrill Gibson, Wilmette: Chiron Publications.
Papadopoulos, R. K. (2006) "Jung's Epistemology and Methodology", in *The Handbook of Jungian Psychology*, Hove: Routledge.
Petchkovsky, L. et al. (2013) "fMRI Responses to Jung's Word Association Test: Implications for Theory, Treatment and Research", *Journal of Analytical Psychology*, 58: 409–431.
Pick, I. B. (1985) "Working Through in the Countertransference", *International Journal of Psychoanalysis*, 66: 157–166.
Place, U. T. (1956) "Is Consciousness a Brain-Process?", *British Journal of Psychology*, 47: 42–51.
Plaut, A. (1956) "The Transference in Analytical Psychology", *British Journal of Medical Psychology*, 29: 15–19.
Polanyi, M. (1966) *The Tacit Dimension*, New York: Doubleday & Company, Inc.
Pollak, T. (2009) "The Body-Container: A New Perspective on the Body-Ego", *International Journal of Psychoanalysis*, 90: 487–506.
Popper, K. ([1934] 1959) *The Logic of Scientific Discovery*, London: Hutchinson.
Progoff, I. (1953) *Jung's Psychology and Its Social Meaning*, London: Routledge & Kegan Paul.
Progoff, I. (1959) *Depth Psychology and Modern Man*, New York: The Julian Press.
Proner, B. (2005) "Bodily States of Anxiety: The Movement From Somatic States to Thought", *Journal of Analytical Psychology*, 50: 311–332.
Quinodoz, D. (2003) "Words that Touch", *International Journal of Psychoanalysis*, 84: 1469–1486.
Quispel, G. (1992) "Jung and Gnosis", in *The Gnostic Jung*, Princeton: Princeton University Press.
Racker, H. (1953) "A Contribution to the Problem of Countertransference", *International Journal of Psychoanalysis*, 34: 313–324.

Racker, H. (1957) "The Meanings and Uses of Countertransference", *The Psychoanalytic Quarterly*, 26: 303–356.
Ramos, D. G. (2004) *The Psyche of the Body: A Jungian Approach to Psychosomatics*, Hove: Brunner-Routledge.
Rapaport, D. et al. (1945–1946) *Diagnostic Psychological Testing, Vols. I & II*, Chicago: The Year Book Publishers.
Redfearn, J. W. T. (1973) "The Nature of Archetypal Activity: The Integration of Spiritual and Bodily Experience", *Journal of Analytical Psychology*, 18: 127–145.
Redfearn, J. W. T. (1994) "Movements of the I in Relation to the Body Image", *Journal of Analytical Psychology*, 39: 311–330.
Redfearn, J. W. T. (2000) "Possible Psychosomatic Hazards to the Therapist: Patients as Self-Objects", *Journal of Analytical Psychology*, 45: 177–194.
Reich, W. (1927) "Die Psychoide als Prinzip der Organischen Entwicklung. By Professor E. Bleuler. (Springer, Berlin, 1925.)" *International Journal of Psychoanalysis*, 8: 105–107.
Reich, W. (1945) *Character Analysis: Principles and Technique for Psychoanalysis in Practice and in Training*, New York: Orgone Institute Press.
Renik, O. (1993) "Analytic Interaction: Conceptualising Technique in Light of the Analyst's Irreducible Subjectivity", *The Psychoanalytic Quarterly*, 62: 553–571.
Ribi, A. (2013) *The Search for Roots: C. G. Jung and the Tradition of Gnosis*, gnosis. org, Gnosis Archive Books.
Romanyshyn, R. D. (2007) *The Wounded Researcher*, New Orleans: Spring Journal Books.
Rosen, D. H. et al. (1991) "Empirical Study of Associations Between Symbols and Their Meanings: Evidence of Collective Unconscious (Archetypal) Memory", *Journal of Analytical Psychology*, 36: 211–228.
Rosenfeld, H. (2001) "The Relationship Between Psychosomatic Symptoms and Latent Psychotic States", in *Herbert Rosenfeld at Work: The Italian Seminars*, edited by Franc Masi, London: Karnac Books.
Rowland, S. (2005) *Jung as a Writer*, Hove: Routledge.
Samuels, A. (1985a) "Countertransference, the *Mundus Imaginalis* and a Research Project", *Journal of Analytical Psychology*, 30: 47–71.
Samuels, A. (1985b) *Jung and the Post-Jungians*, London: Routledge & Kegan Paul.
Samuels, A. (1989) *The Plural Psyche*, London: Routledge.
Sandler, J. (1976) "Countertransference and Role-Responsiveness", *International Review of Psychoanalysis*, 3: 43–47.
Sandler, J. (1983) "Reflections on Some Relations Between Psychoanalytic Concepts and Psychoanalytic Practice", *International Journal of Psychoanalysis*, 64: 35–45.
Sandler, J. (1993) "On Communication From Patient to Analyst: Not Everything Is Projective Identification", *International Journal of Psychoanalysis*, 74: 1097–1107.
Sandler, J. et al. (1997) *Freud's Models of the Mind: An Introduction*, London: Karnac Books.
Sassenfeld, A. (2008) "The Body in Jung's Work: Basic Elements to Lay the Foundation for a Theory of Technique", *The Journal of Jungian Theory and Practice*, 10: 1–13.
Schaverien, J. (1991) *The Revealing Image: Analytical Art Psychotherapy in Theory and Practice*, London: Routledge.
Schaverien, J. (2005) "Art, Dreams and Active Imagination: A Post-Jungian Approach to Transference and the Image", *Journal of Analytical Psychology*, 50: 127–153.
Schaverien, J. (2007) "Countertransference as Active Imagination: Imaginative Experiences of the Analyst", *Journal of Analytical Psychology*, 52: 413–431.

Schoenfeld, C. G. (1962) "Three Fallacious Attacks Upon Psychoanalysis as Science", *Psychoanalytic Review*, 49D: 35–47.
Schore, A. N. (1994) *Affect Regulation and the Origin of Self: The Neurobiology of Emotional Development*, Hillsdale: Lawrence Erlbaum Associates.
Schore, A. N. (2002) "Advances in Neuropsychoanalysis, Attachment Theory, and Trauma Research: Implications for Self Psychology", *Psychoanalytic Inquiry*, 22: 433–484.
Schwartz-Salant, N. (1989) *The Borderline Personality*, Wilmette: Chiron Publications.
Segal, R. A. (1992) *The Gnostic Jung*, Princeton: Princeton University Press.
Shamdasani, S. (2003) *Jung and the Making of Modern Psychology: The Dream of a Science*, Cambridge: Cambridge University Press.
Shamdasani, S. (2012) "After *Liber Novus*", *Journal of Analytical Psychology*, 57: 364–377.
Shapiro, S. A. (1996) "The Embodied Analyst in the Victorian Consulting Room", *Gender and Psychoanalysis*, 1: 297–322.
Shin, Y.-W. et al. (2005) "The Influences of Complexes on Implicit Learning", *Journal of Analytical Psychology*, 50: 175–190.
Sidoli, M. (1993) "When Meaning Gets Lost in the Body: Psychosomatic Disturbances as a Failure of the Transcendent Function", *Journal of Analytical Psychology*, 38: 175–190.
Sidoli, M. (2000) *When the Body Speaks: The Archetypes in the Body*, London: Routledge.
Smadja, C. (2011) "Psychoanalytic Psychosomatics", *International Journal of Psychoanalysis*, 92: 221–230.
Smart, J. J. C. (1959) "Sensations and Brain-Processes", *Philosophical Review*, 68: 141–156.
Solms, M. and Turnbull, O. H. (2011) "What Is Neuropsychoanalysis?", *Neuropsychoanalysis*, 13(2): 133–145.
Spiegelman, M. (1996) *Psychotherapy as a Mutual Process*, Scottsdale: New Falcon.
Stern, D. N. (1985) *The Interpersonal World of the Infant: A View From Psychoanalysis and Developmental Psychology*, New York: Basic Books.
Stevens, A. (1990) *Archetype: A Natural History of the Self*, London: Routledge.
Stevens, A. (1995) "Jungian Psychology, the Body and the Future", *Journal of Analytical Psychology*, 40: 353–364.
Stevens, A. (2006) "The Archetypes", in *The Handbook of Jungian Psychology*, edited by Renos Papadopoulos, London: Routledge.
Stone, M. (2006) "The Analyst's Body as Tuning Fork: Embodied Resonance in Countertransference", *Journal of Analytical Psychology*, 51: 109–124.
Sutherland, J. D. and Gill, H. S. (1970) *A Development of the Word Association Method*, London: Research Publication Services Ltd.
Swan, W. (2000) *C. G. Jung and Active Imagination: A Case Study of Tina Keller*, Berlin: VDM Verlag Dr. Müller.
Swan, W. (2008) "C. G. Jung's Psychotherapeutic Technique of Active Imagination in Historical Context", *Psychoanalysis and History*, 10: 185–204.
Swan, W. (2011) *The Memoir of Tina Keller-Jenny: A Lifelong Confrontation With the Psychology of C. G. Jung*, New Orleans: Spring Journal, Inc.
Symington, J. and Symington, N. (1996) *The Clinical Thinking of Wilfred Bion*, London: Routledge.
Teising, M. (2005) "Permeability and Demarcation in the Psychoanalytic Process: Functions of the Contact-Barrier", *International Journal of Psychoanalysis*, 86: 1627–1644.

Torres, N. (2008) *Disorders of Emotional Content and Their Somatic Correlates: The Protomental Nature of Addictions, Self-Harm and Non-Communicable Diseases*, Colchester: University of Essex.

Torres, N. (2013a) "Bion's Concept of the Proto-Mental and Modern Panpsychism", in *Bion's Sources*, Hove: Routledge.

Torres, N. (2013b) "Gregariousness and the Mind: Bion and Trotter, an Update", in *Bion's Sources*, Hove: Routledge.

Torres, N. (2013c) "Intuition and Ultimate Reality in Psychoanalysis: Bion's Implicit Use of Bergson and Whitehead's Notions", in *Bion's Sources*, Hove: Routledge.

Torres, N. and Hinshelwood, R. D. (2013) *Bion's Sources*, Hove: Routledge.

Trotter, W. (1916) *Instincts of the Herd in Peace & War*, London: Fisher Unwin.

Tuckett, D. (1993)"Some Thoughts on the Presentation and Discussion of the Clinical Material of Psychoanalysis", *International Journal of Psychoanalysis*, 74: 1175–1189.

Tuckett, D. (2005) "Does Anything Go? Towards a Framework for the More Transparent Assessment of Psychoanalytic Competence", *International Journal of Psychoanalysis*, 86: 31–49.

Tuckett, D. (2008) *Psychoanalysis Comparable & Incomparable: The Evolution of a Method to Describe and Compare Psychoanalytic Approaches*, London: Routledge.

Tuckett, D. (2011) "Inside and Outside the Window: Some Fundamental Elements in the Theory of Psychoanalytic Technique", *International Journal of Psychoanalysis*, 92: 1367–1390.

Tuckett, D. (2012) "Some Reflections on Psychoanalytic Technique: In Need of Core Concepts or an Archaic Ritual?", *Psychoanalytic Inquiry*, 32: 87–108.

Tustin, F. (1972) *Autism and Child Psychosis*, London: The Hogarth Press.

Tustin, F. (1986) *Autistic Barriers in Neurotic Patients*, London: Karnac Books.

Varvin, S. (2003) "Extreme Traumatisation: Strategies for Mental Survival", *International Forum of Psychoanalysis*, 12: 5–16.

Varvin, S. and Rosenbaum, B. (2007) "The Influence of Extreme Traumatisation on Body, Mind and Social Relations", *International Journal of Psychoanalysis*, 88: 1527–1542.

Vermote, R. (2003) "Two Sessions With Catherine", *International Journal of Psychoanalysis*, 84: 1415–1421 and 75: 3–19.

Von Franz, M. L. (1992) *Psyche and Matter*, Boston and London: Shambhala.

von Krafft-Ebing, R. (1879–80) *Lehrbuch der Psychiatre auf Klinischer Grundlage: für Practische Ärzte und Studirende*, Stuttgart: Enke.

von Krafft-Ebing, R. (1904) *Text-Book of Insanity Based on Clinical Observations*, Philadelphia: Davis.

Vonofakos, D. and Hinshelwood, B. (2012) "Wilfred Bion's Letters to John Rickman (1939–1951)", *Psychoanalysis and History*, 14: 53–94.

Whitehouse, M. S. (1979) "C. G. Jung and Dance Therapy: Two Major Principles", in *Eight Theoretical Approaches in Dance-Movement Therapy*, edited by Penny Lewis Bernstein, Dubuque: Kendall/Hunt.

Winnicott, D. W. (1949) "Mind and Its Relation to Psyche-Soma", in *Through Paediatrics to Psychoanalysis: Collected Papers*, London: Karnac Books.

Winnicott, D. W. (1966) "Psycho-Somatic Illness in Its Positive and Its Negative Aspects", *International Journal of Psychoanalysis*, 47: 510–516.

Zabriskie, B. (1995) "Jung and Pauli: A Subtle Asymmetry", *Journal of Analytical Psychology*, 40: 531–553.

Index

active imagination 11, 38–43, 48–52, 61–2, 71, 75, 78–81, 87–90, 136, 149–50, 152, 156–7; and *Red Book, The* 3, 10, 34, 36, 38–42, 44, 52, 62, 148, 151, 152, 154, 156; The Seven Sermons 42–6, 138, 152, 156–7; *Systema Munditotius* 43–4; Keller, T. 48; *see also* transcendent function

archetype 4, 6–7, 9, 27–32, 35–6, 42, 46, 48, 53, 56, 60, 69, 71–8, 80, 84, 134, 138, 151–3, 157–9; and archetypal image 10, 29, 32–3, 36, 44–51, 53, 60, 67, 71, 73–5, 77–8, 89–90, 151, 156, 159; instinctual image 10, 29, 32–5, 67, 151, 156, 159; primordial image 29, 44, 51, 56, 78; *see also* collective unconscious; development

asymmetric field 8–9, 11, 111, 120, 129, 140–147, 156; *see also* projection; projective identification; transference

Beckett, S. 51, 59, 68; *see also* The Tavistock Lectures

Bergson, H. 10, 52, 55–9, 62, 68; and *élan vital* 56, 58

Berlin Group, The 10, 75, 81, 85, 148, 151 and transference 10, 75, 81–6; *see also* Dieckmann, H.

Bion, W. R. 3, 9, 10, 52–5, 57–68, 77, 118, 123, 129, 134–6, 141–5, 147, 159–60; and basic assumption functionning 54, 64–7; *Experiences in Groups* 54, 63, 65; group work 54, 60, 62–7, 158; proto-mental concept 3, 9, 10, 52–4, 58–9, 62, 64–8, 78, 129, 143, 145, 147, 159; Rickman, J. 54, 63; world war I 9, 53–4, 57;

see also Bergson, H.; Hadfield, J.; Northfield experiment; The Tavistock Clinic; The Tavistock Lectures; War Neurosis; WOSBs

Bleuler, E. 3, 5, 10, 22, 24–8, 31, 35, 37, 69; and Burghölzli Clinic 3, 22–5, 37–8, 69; *die Psychoide* 3, 5, 24–5, 69; mneme 26; Semon, R. 26; *see also* psycho-physical parallelism; vitalism

body-mind relationship 1, 6, 9, 18, 24, 35, 50, 52, 57, 61, 70, 77, 85, 87, 89, 127, 151, 151, 153, 156, 158; and bodymind 6–7, 58, 70–1, 122–3, 134, 140; dualism 1; monism 2, 52, 57, 59, 62, 87, 123, 134–5, 143, 158; *see also* Descartes, R.; Spinoza, B.; synchronicity

Burghölzli Clinic 3, 22–3, 25, 35, 37–8, 69; *see also* Bleuler, E.; Jung, C. G.; Spielrein, S.

Canestri, J. 99–101, 122–4
Charmaz, K. 105–6; *see also* grounded theory
Clark, G. 7, 71, 75, 86–7
complexes 16, 23–4, 37–9, 48, 76, 88, 90, 106, 128, 148, 152; *see also* Word Association Test
collective unconscious 27, 36, 38, 43–6, 48, 52, 60, 62, 69, 84; and archetypes 27, 36, 44, 48, 52, 69; *participation mystique* 60, 83–4; psychoid unconscious 43, 46
Connolly, A. 7, 71, 86, 88
conversion 16; *see also* hysteria
creatura 43–4, 138, 152–3, 157; *see also* The Seven Sermons

Crichton-Miller, H. 54–5, 58; *see also* The Tavistock Clinic

data analysis 8, 11, 98, 105–6, 108–9, 110–11, 123, 128, 147, 156; *see also* grounded theory
dementia praecox 9, 37, 159
Descartes, R. 1–2; and Cartesian dualism 1, 36
development 6, 9, 17, 26–7, 30, 32–3, 35, 43, 45–6, 54, 64, 66–7, 71–2, 74–9, 87, 100, 104, 110, 120, 122–4, 130–1, 135, 137–41, 152–3, 157, 160; and archetypes 74–8, 131, 138, 157
Dieckmann, H. 7, 70, 81, 83–6, 97, 151
dissociation 9, 21–4, 46, 71, 75–7, 89, 128, 140, 152, 155, 157–9; and *cryptomnesia* 23; hysteria 21, 23–4; *somnambulism* 21–2, 76; psychoid processes 77, 89, 152, 158–9
Dreher, A. U. 3–5, 94–6, 98–9, 102, 106; and conceptual research 3, 5, 108
Driesch, H. 3, 5–6, 10, 17–19, 24–5, 27–8, 31, 33, 39, 50, 52, 55–6, 69, 72; and *das Psychoid* 3, 5, 18–19, 25, 52, 69; entelechy 18–19; sea urchin experiments 18, 35, 52, 69; teleology 6, 18, 24, 31–3, 35, 52, 69–70; *see also* vitalism

emergence 6, 9, 11–12, 29–30, 32–3, 35, 51, 53, 70, 72–5, 89–90, 110, 113, 115, 118–19, 126, 129, 132–3, 137–140, 151–54, 155–9; *see also* psychoid concept

Freud, S.: and Breuer, , J. 16; dreams 23, 60; Freud's method 22–3, 38, 54–5, 68; hysteria 17, 22–3, 55, 148; libido 15–17, 23–4; meeting with Jung 6, 15–17, 23–4, 35, 69; *Project for a Scientific Psychology* 16, 24; repression 21, 23; *Studies on Hysteria* 16, 22
Fonagy, P. 96–7, 108, 117, 123; and Target, M. 117

Gieser, S. 7, 71
Glaser, B. & Strauss, A. 105; *see also* grounded theory
Greene, A. 87–8

Gnosticism 42–3, 46, 51, 151; *see also* Quispel, G.; Ribi, A.
Gordon, R. 75, 78
Gray, R. M. 71, 73–4
grounded theory 4–5, 11, 105–8, 110, 145; and clustering 106, 110, 113, 117–21, 129, 133; coding 99, 106, 111–14, 116–17; field notes 11, 106, 110–11; transcripts 4, 11, 95, 98, 103, 105–7, 110–12, 114–16; *see also* Hollway, W. & Jefferson, T.

Hadfield, J. A. 53, 55–6
Haule, J. 31, 71
hermeneutics 10, 35–6, 38, 49–51, 148, 151, 157, 159; *see also The Red Book*
Hinshelwood, R. D. 54–5, 63
Hollway, W. & Jefferson, T. 99, 106
hysteria 16–17, 21–4, 37–8, 46, 55, 76, 148–49, 159; *see also* Burghölzli Clinic; Freud, S.; Jung, C. G.; Spielrein, S.

implicit theories 96–9; 102, 107, 109, 122, 124; and private theories 11, 102, 106–8, 115, 121, 123, 125, 147–8, 154–7, 160; *see also* Canestri, J.; Fonagy, P.; Sandler, J. ; Tuckett, D.
individuation 9–10, 12, 42–6, 48–51, 67, 72, 89, 148–51, 156–7, 159; and differentiation 10, 36, 43–5, 49–50, 53, 78, 88, 120, 128, 130, 135, 148, 151, 159; undifferentiation 10, 43–4, 49–50, 129, 148, 151, 155–6; *see also The Red Book*
interviews 4–5, 11, 94–96, 98–109, 110–12, 114–25, 129, 137, 139, 144–5, 148, 156–8; and interviewees 4, 8, 11–12, 95, 98–9, 103–9, 115, 124–137, 139–146, 151, 154–8; primary data 103, 105; transcript 4, 11, 95, 98, 103, 106–7, 110–12, 114–16; *see also* data analysis; methodology

Jacobi, J. 10, 49, 75–7, 90, 158–9
Jung, C. G.: and active imagination 11, 38–43, 48–51, 61–2, 75, 78–81, 88–90, 136, 149–50, 152, 156–7; Black Books 40, 152; Burghölzli Clinic 22–3, 25, 37–8; *Conception of the Unconscious, The* 44–7; *Cryptomnesia* 23; dissertation 21–2,

24; hysteria 21–4, 37–8, 46, 76, 149, 159; mandala 43–4; meeting with Freud 15–17, 23, 33, 69; *On the Nature of the Psyche* 5–6, 10, 15, 17, 27, 46, 69, 79; *Philosophical Tree, The* 46; *Red Book, The* 3, 10, 36, 38–42, 44, 148, 151, 152, 154, 156; *Relation between the Ego and the Unconscious, The* 44–5, 47–8; *Symbols of Transformation* 24, 38; *Synchronicity: an Acausal Connecting Principle* 6, 69; *Transcendent Function, The* 41; Word Association Tests 3, 10, 16, 23, 36–7, 59, 61, 148; *Zofingia Lectures, The* 20, 52; Zurich Psychological Club 56, 70; Zurich School 44; *see also* active imagination; archetype; collective unconscious; complexes; dissociation; individuation; participation mystique; psychoid concept; synchronicity; transcendent function

Kalsched, D. 75, 77, 158
Keller, T. 48
Klein, M. 54, 64–6, 129, 142, 144
Knox, J. 74–5
Krafft-Ebing, R. von 21, 36–7

libido 15–17, 23–4, 46–7, 55–6, 58, 78, 149

McDougall, W. 55–6, 58, 63; and hormic psychology 55–6, 58
Martini, S. 86, 88–9
Merchant, J. 7, 71, 74–5
methodology 5, 8, 11–12, 31, 89, 93, 108, 147, 160; *see also* Canestri, J.; Dreher, A. U.; Tuckett, D.
monism 2, 6–7, 50, 52, 57, 59, 62, 67, 70–1, 86–7, 89, 122–3, 133–5, 140, 143, 150, 156, 158, 160; *see also* Driesch, H.; Jung, C. G.; proto-mental concept; psychoid concept
Moore, N. 75, 79–80, 86

Northfield experiment 54, 63; *see also* Rickman J.

panpsychism 6–7, 57–9, 67, 70, 160; *see also* Bergson, H.; Bion, W. R.; Jung, C. G.; synchronicity
paranoid-schizoid position 65–6, 137

participation mystique 36, 45, 49–50, 60, 62, 72, 84–5, 89, 111, 129–31, 143, 146, 150, 156, 160; and Levy-Bruhl 45, 60, 72
Pauli, W. 6–7, 53, 68, 70
patterns of behavior 27, 29, 74
Plaut, A. 86–7
pleroma 43–4, 130, 138, 143, 151–3, 157; *see also The Seven Sermons*
Preiswerk, H. 21–2, 24; and Jung's dissertation 21, 24
primordial image 29, 44, 51, 56, 78; and Hymenoptera 56; leaf-cutting ant 28–9, 32–3; yucca moth 57
primitive states of mind 12, 62, 67, 132, 135, 142, 145
Progoff, I. 10, 71–4, 90; *see also* protoplasmic image
projection 8, 39, 47, 79, 83–4, 86, 111, 127–29, 133, 140, 142, 149; and projective identification 10–11, 65–6, 78, 111, 113–16, 119–21, 123, 127, 129, 131–2, 140–5, 158–9
Proner, B. 75, 77, 86
proto-mental 3, 9–10, 52–4, 58–9, 62, 64–8, 72, 78, 129, 136, 143, 145, 147, 159–60; and monism 50, 52, 59, 67; *see also* Bion, W. R.
protoplasm 72; and protoplasmic image 73
psychisation 27
psychoid: and archetype 4, 6–7, 28–31, 35–6, 46, 53, 69, 73, 76, 80, 84, 134, 138, 152–3, 157–9; body-mind relationship 6, 18, 24, 35, 50, 77, 85, 87, 89, 151, 153, 156, 158; collective unconscious 36, 43, 46, 62, 69; dissociation 46, 75–7, 89, 152, 155, 157–8; emergence 6, 12, 29–30, 35, 51, 53, 70, 73, 89, 138–140, 150–53, 155–9; individuation 12, 46, 50–51, 67, 89, 150, 156–7, 159; living meaning 51, 62–3, 68; meaning making 41, 157; monism 2, 6–7, 50, 52, 67, 70–1, 86–7, 89, 134, 140, 143, 150, 156, 158; organising function 31, 35, 42, 46, 51, 53, 67–8, 74, 84, 89, 150–1, 155–9; participation mystique 36, 49–50, 84–5, 89, 129–30, 143, 150, 156; pleroma 43, 130, 138, 143, 151–3, 157; psychic patterns 51, 76, 84, 89, 150; psychoid processes 3–4, 6, 10,

28–31, 33, 41, 44, 46, 50, 74, 77–8, 89, 155–8; psychoid unconscious 4, 24, 30, 35, 46, 49–50, 53, 56, 62, 73, 77–8, 80, 84, 86, 88–9, 136, 140, 150, 156–8; purposive dynamic 6, 20, 35, 50, 89, 150, 159; self-other relationship 129, 139–40, 151, 156; symmetric transference model 8, 11–12, 81, 85, 89, 129, 139, 143–5, 147, 150–1, 155–7; unknowable 3, 12, 35, 50, 52–3, 62–3, 67, 69–71, 74, 89–90, 138, 140, 144, 150, 153, 155–7, 160; vitalizing 156; *see also* Bleuler, E.; Driesch, H.;
psycho-physical parallelism 18, 25, 31, 57, 59, 61, 72
psychotic mechanisms 53–4, 65–8, 159–60

Quispel, G. 42

Red Book, The 3, 10, 34, 36, 38–42, 44, 52, 62, 148, 150, 152, 154, 156; and *Mysterium Encounter* 42–3, 45; Philemon 40; *The Seven Sermons* 42–6, 138, 152, 156–7; *Systema Munditotius* 43–4; *see also* pleroma, creatura, Gnosticism
Redfearn, J. W. T. 73, 75, 78, 87
regression 2, 12, 36, 45, 49, 67, 88, 110, 112–15, 118–23, 126, 129, 131–2, 135, 139, 148
repression 16, 21–3, 132
Ribi, A. 42–4, 46, 51
Rickman, J. 54, 63
Rowland, S. 3–4

Samuels, A. 10, 75, 81, 85–7, 89, 104, 146; and embodied countertransference 85–7, 89; *mundus imaginalis* 86, 90
Sandler, J. 16, 94, 96–7, 109
Schaverien, J. 75, 79–80; *see also* active imagination
sensory image 110, 113, 117, 122–3, 135
sensuous imagery 131, 134, 136, 153
Seven Sermons, The 42–6, 138, 152, 156–7; and Abraxas 42–3; creatura 43–4, 138, 152–3, 157; Gnosticism 42–3, 51, 150; pleroma 43–4, 130, 138, 143, 151–3, 157

Shamdasani, S. 38–40, 48, 56, 68
Sidoli, M. 75, 77, 87
Sinnott, E. 72; *see also* protoplasm
Smuts, J. C. 72
somnambulism 21–2, 24, 76
Spielrein, S. 22–3; *see also* Burghölzli Clinic
Spinoza, B. 2, 135; and monism 2, 135
Stevens, A. 7, 71, 74
Swan, W. 48, 79
symbolism and symbolic capacity 9, 110, 129, 133, 136–7; symbolic functioning 50–2, 79–80, 83, 88–9, 104, 135, 150–4, 156–7; symbolic representation 44–6, 49, 60, 67–8, 70, 72–3, 76–7, 80, 87, 130, 155; *Symbols of Transformation* 24, 38–9; *see also* active imagination; archetypes; transcendent function
symmetric field 8–9, 11–12, 50, 81, 85, 89, 111, 119–23, 127–129, 132–3, 139–7, 150–1, 155–7; *see also* archetype; transference
symptom 36, 55, 76–7, 79, 137; and hypnagogic symptom 44; somatic symptom 16, 23–4, 38, 68, 76–7, 80, 85, 87, 105, 112, 115, 117, 119, 122–3, 134–5, 137–8, 140, 142
synchronicity 5–8, 35, 53, 59, 61–2, 69–71, 93, 129, 139, 160; *see also* Pauli, W.; *unus mundus*

Tavistock Clinic, The 10, 53–5, 58–9, 64; and Crichton-Miller, H. 54–5, 58; Hadfield, J. 53; group work 54, 64; Nicol, M. 55; *see also* The Tavistock Lectures
Tavistock Lectures, The 10, 59, 77; and body-mind relation 59–61, 77; *participation mystique* 60, 62; synchronicity 59, 61; typology 59
teleology 2, 9, 16–18, 20, 22, 24, 31–3, 35, 52, 67–70, 157–9
Torres, N. 55, 57–9, 63, and Hinshelwood, R. D. 55, 63
transcendent function 41, 45, 49, 139, 158; *see also* active imagination
transference 8, 10–12, 46–51, 53, 71, 75, 79–89, 99, 101, 104–7, 110, 112–16, 119–23, 127–30, 132–7, 139–42, 144–5, 147–50, 153–8, 160; and archetypal transference

82–5, 87, 150; asymmetric field 8–9, 11, 111, 120, 129, 140–147, 156; countertransference 12, 75, 79–81, 84–9, 94, 100, 103–6, 113, 119, 121, 126–7, 129, 134–6, 139–40, 142–3, 155; embodied countertransference 85–7, 89, 100, 129, 135, 139; Jung's fourfold diagram 149; personal transference 82–5; *quaternio* 86; symmetric field 8–9, 11–12, 50, 81, 85, 89, 111, 119–23, 127–129, 132–3, 139–47, 150–1, 155–7; *see also* The Berlin Group; Samuels, A

trauma 16, 38, 68, 75, 90, 94–98, 102, 160; and Trauma Project 94–6, 98, 102; *see also* Kalsched, D.

Trauma Project 94–6, 98, 102; *see also* Sandler, J.

Trotter, W. 63, 68; and herd instinct 63

Tuckett, D. 99–101, 108–9

turning point 113, 118–19, 126–29, 131; and moment of meaning 129, 142, 144

typology 56

unus mundus 6–7, 43–46, 50, 70, 74, 80

vitalism 17–20, 22, 24–5, 35, 55–6, 62, 70, 85, 150

von Franz 84; *see also* transference

War Neurosis 53; and shell shock 53; Post-Traumatic Stress Disorder 63

wholeness 18, 20, 31, 35, 52, 69, 73, 78

Word Association Test (WAT) 3, 10, 16, 23, 36–7, 59, 61, 148; and family constellation 37, 50, 148; galvanometer readings 16, 37

War Office Selection Boards (WOSBs) 54

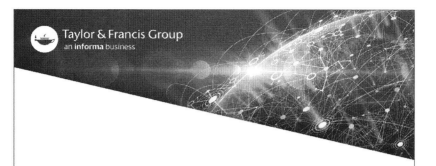